Fiscal Issues
in the Future of Federalism

CED Supplementary Paper No. 23

May 1968

COMMITTEE FOR ECONOMIC DEVELOPMENT

A CED Supplementary Paper

This Supplementary Paper is issued by the Committee for Improvement of Management in Government of the Committee for Economic Development in conformity with the CED Bylaws (Art. IX, Sec. 5) which authorize the publication of a manuscript as a Supplementary Paper if:

a) It is recommended for publication by the Project Director of a subcommittee because in his opinion, it "constitutes an important contribution to the understanding of a problem on which research has been initiated by the Committee for Improvement of Management in Government" and,

b) It is approved for publication by a majority of an Editorial Board on the ground that it presents "an analysis which is a significant contribution to the understanding of the problem in question."

This Supplementary Paper relates to the Statement on National Policy, *A Fiscal Program For A Balanced Federalism,* issued by the CED Research and Policy Committee in June 1967.

The members of the Editorial Board authorizing publication of this Supplementary Paper are:

Philip M. Klutznick **Sydney Stein, Jr.**	*Members of the Committee for Improvement of Management in Government of the Committee for Economic Development*
Jervis J. Babb	*Member of the Research and Policy Committee of the Committee for Economic Development*
Vincent A. Doyle **Frederick C. Mosher**	*Members of the Improvement of Management in Government Advisory Board of the Committee for Economic Development*
Alfred C. Neal	*President of the Committee for Economic Development*
Lawrence R. Kegan	*Project Director of the CED Subcommittee on Federal-State-Local Fiscal Relations*

It has also been read by the Improvement of Management in Government Advisory Board.

While publication of this Supplementary Paper is authorized by CED's Bylaws, except as noted above, its contents have not been approved, disapproved, or acted upon by the Committee for Economic Development, the Board of Trustees, the Research and Policy Committee, the Committee for Improvement of Management in Government, the Improvement of Management in Government Advisory Board, the Research Staff, the Improvement of Management in Government Staff, or any member of any board or committee, or any officer of the Committee for Economic Development.

4.

Contents

Foreword

The studies in this Supplementary Paper have been extracted from a larger group of papers prepared as background material for use by the Subcommittee on Federal-State-Local Fiscal Relations of the Research and Policy Committee of CED in preparing *A Fiscal Program For A Balanced Federalism*, a Statement on National Policy published in June 1967.

The essays include case studies of five metropolitan areas, a study of four relatively low-income states, and a staff analysis of the aggregate fiscal outlook for state and local governments. They are published in accordance with the provision of the CED bylaws concerning the publication of Supplementary Papers, as explained on page 3 of this volume.

Research by the subcommittee began early in 1965. It started with the consideration of a number of theoretical studies of the economics of fiscal federalism. These were prepared by such distinguished experts in this field as Joseph Pechman of The Brookings Institution, James Buchanan of the University of Virginia, and Harold Somers of the University of California. Since these papers covered ground already made familiar by their authors and other experts in the vast body of literature in this area, they are not included in this more specialized volume.

The theoretical papers were followed by the preparation of a number of studies designed to shed light on the fiscal problems, capacities, and needs of the lower levels of government, and to show how recent trends and emerging policy issues affect different state and local governments. Public finance theory generally has dealt with the federal government. Since many of the critical fiscal issues for the future of federalism involve metropolitan areas and their relationship to state and local governments, the subcommittee decided to focus on the intergovernmental fiscal problems now emerging in most metropolitan areas. Studies in this field, it was felt, would reveal what revenue problems would have to be faced if local public service requirements were to be met in the period ahead.

The commissioned papers were designed to show the common, as well as the diverse, fiscal issues among lower levels of government—those nearest to the general public. They were prepared by public finance experts already deeply involved in studying the problems of state and local governments.

The metropolitan areas to be studied were selected to show regional diversity and relatively distinct fiscal-political mixes. Among the range of characteristics considered in the selection process were population size, differences between daytime and nighttime population, independence of school districts, and the level of government responsible for welfare services. Part I contains the five studies of metropolitan areas which were selected on the basis of the range of the problems they present and the extent of success in dealing with them. These are on Indianapolis, by James Papke of Purdue University; Detroit, by Karl Gregory of Wayne State University; Boston, by Joseph Barresi, Executive Secretary of the Boston Municipal Research Bureau; Topeka, by Darwin W. Daicoff of the University of Kansas; and Louisville, by Roy W. Bahl, Post Doctoral Fellow in Urban Economics, Syracuse University.

Other studies on metropolitan areas which aided the subcommittee were undertaken by: Morris Beck of Rutgers University, Arthur Becker of the University of Wisconsin, A. James Heins of the University of Illinois, Dudley A. Johnson of the University of Washington, and Reuben A. Zubrow of the University of California.

To assist in its analysis of metropolitan areas, and especially of the central cities within them, the Bureau of the Census agreed to assemble for CED pertinent statistics for each of the metropolitan regions being studied, distinguishing between central cities and outlying counties for a number of expenditure, revenue, debt, and governmental aid categories for the years 1957, 1962, and 1964. The five metropolitan area studies make use of this important new census material.

Although these studies all include some assessment of

state fiscal problems, it was obvious that in some of the poorer states few metropolitan areas exist. Since these states have great fiscal problems, the subcommittee also undertook a study of the fiscal situations in four representative low-income states. In this examination the focus was on an analysis of the trends and issues relating to the present system of grants-in-aid and of the potential equalization effects of a new general assistance grant.

The four states selected for Part II of this Supplementary Paper were chosen because they provided a cross-section of problems and methods for dealing with them. Each of the four states had reasonably high standards of government administration, were without disproportionate political problems, and each was known to have done recent useful research on the condition of their finances. Maine, South Dakota, Georgia, and Mississippi, the states selected, provided a cross-section of low-income states by geography, average per capita incomes, and relative importance in the total picture of state-local finance. The study was prepared for CED by Richard Nathan of The Brookings Institution.

Part III of this Supplementary Paper is a "Statistical Study" prepared by Lawrence R. Kegan and George P. Roniger of the CED staff. The authors deal with the fiscal potential for over-all improvement of the scope and quality of public services in the coming decade with the revenue available (1) under existing conditions, and (2) with a strengthened revenue structure.

To aid in its work, the subcommittee also made use of other studies and the counsel of other experts. Murray L. Weidenbaum of Washington University provided projections of federal budget trends for the next decade. This work will be included in his forthcoming book, *Prospects for Reallocating Public Resources in the U.S.,* to be published by the American Enterprise Institute for Public Policy Research. Dick Netzer of New York University projected the trend of state and local finances for the next decade in a paper which has been published in Volume III on Federal-State-Local Fiscal Projections of the Joint Economic Committee reprint on *Revenue Sharing and Its Alternatives: What Future for Fiscal Federalism?* Use was also made of data in an extensive study by Selma Mushkin of George Washington University on the expenditure and revenue outlook of the 50 states in 1970. Finally, aid was received from Allen Manvel and Joseph Arbena of the Bureau of the Census; and from L. L. Ecker-Racz, John Shannon and Robert W. Rafuse of the Advisory Commission on Intergovernmental Relations.

Readers of these papers will find a striking contrast between the aggregate fiscal potential projected in the "Statistical Study" and the fiscal problems so evident in some of the individual case studies. The former concludes that state and local governments as a whole may find it easier in the coming period to finance substantial improvements in their traditional public services with the funds available to them, including the federal aid implicit in existing legislation. But the study does not predict that there will be no problems, even in the aggregate, for state and local governments. The "crisis of the city," for example, will undoubtedly require a substantial rate of improvement in scope and quality of public services. The fiscal outlook, then, will depend on how much improvement the people want, and on the real resources that can effectively be applied to public problems in the future.

The case studies provide evidence of the existence of the all-too-familiar ills of the central cities — concentrations of low-income persons, erosions of assessed property values, restrictions on taxing powers, under-representation at the state level, and excessive fragmentation of local governments and local government responsibilities. In contrast to the "Statistical Study," the case studies make it abundantly clear that individual state and local governments face a diversity of complex problems. Moreover, they indicate that there will continue to be problems of financing an adequate level of public services in certain individual states and in certain individual localities. This is particularly true if new specialized public programs — anti-poverty programs, for example — are to be acted upon, or if services traditionally provided on state and local levels are to be expanded or improved at substantially faster rates.

A further contrast appears in the discussion of the four poor states when compared with the studies of the central cities. The sense of urgency which appears to exist among central city officials does not seem to exist, or to exist in the same degree, among the officials of the poor states. Some federal categorical grants are under-matched in the poor states, particularly for welfare, and the conclusions of this study indicate that reductions in tax efforts from their own sources would, at least in part, be expected as a result of federal general grants given to these states.

The case studies conclude on notes which vary from distinctly optimistic to extremely cautious. They indicate that some areas are in the process of substantially improving their performance while others are more attached to a status quo; that local government fragmentation is an extreme problem in some areas and that its effects are being overcome in others; that local governments are greatly constrained in their ability to help themselves in some areas and that they have substantial room to maneuver in others. Disinterested states are a problem in some areas but not in others; greater home rule may be needed in some places; in others it may provide no solution.

The diversity of unsolved issues could be viewed as providing a most important lesson — that flexibility in response to problems is required and that state and local governments must be strengthened in order to permit more adequate responses to individual public conditions in specific areas of our nation. Thus, state and local governments will continue to have an important role to play in our federal system. And it appears proper to judge on the basis of these studies that many state and local governments are prepared to make serious attempts to improve their operations and fulfill their obligations.

Lawrence R. Kegan, *Project Director*

Subcommittee on
Federal-State-Local Fiscal Relations

I.

Metropolitan Case Studies

Indianapolis

Detroit

Boston

Louisville

Topeka

INDIANAPOLIS:

Sustaining the Momentum of Success

James A. Papke

Professor of Economics

Purdue University

The fiscal situation in Indianapolis and in the State of Indiana provides a measure of encouragement. The state has accepted increased responsibility toward its subdivisions and has undertaken major revenue reforms. In 1963 it enacted a personal and corporate income tax and a sales tax, which produced an immediate 50 per cent increase in general fund revenues. As a result, the state was able to increase its support of local government. Increased grants-in-aid, increased tax sharing, local supplements to the sales tax, and a strengthened property tax administration have also been achieved. But Indiana still suffers from an excessive number of "special authorities" that have sprung up to bypass a constitutional bonding limitation. As a result, every Indianapolis area resident is served by at least ten units of local government.

Problems associated with financing public services in major metropolitan areas have become a part of the national folklore. Satisfactory solutions, for the most part, have remained merely topics of good conversation. This paper is intended to provide an overview of the practices, policies, and problems of financing government in one metropolitan center — Metropolitan Indianapolis[1] — where a combination of recent state-local and public-private efforts has been employed with encouraging results.

A central theme runs through the discussion. It is that in Indiana the resolution of local finance problems generally and of metropolitan finance problems particularly is the responsibility of the state. To meet its fiscal obligations, the state has had to adopt new attitudes, techniques, and patterns of public finance and intergovernmental relations. The momentum of these recent changes will likely carry the state and its political subdivisions forward for a time. But the momentum will expire if new forces and actions are not introduced to sustain it.

Following a brief economic, demographic, and political profile of Metropolitan Indianapolis, the discussion explores these general questions:

1. How is the State of Indiana assisting in the financing of public services in Metropolitan Indianapolis?

[1] The terms "Metropolitan Indianapolis" and "Marion County" are used interchangeably in this study. They both refer to the Indianapolis, Indiana, Standard Metropolitan Statistical Area (SMSA) as defined in the *1962 Census of Governments* and *1960 Census of Population* The Indianapolis SMSA was redefined in 1963 to include, in addition to Marion County, the six adjacent counties of Hamilton, Hancock, Hendricks, Johnson, Morgan, and Shelby.

2. To what extent does the state participate in the promotion of metropolitan area solutions to metropolitan area fiscal problems?
3. How can Metropolitan Indianapolis' fiscal position be improved?
4. What are the major fiscal problems requiring the primary attention of state and local leaders?
5. What are likely to be the most promising policies to resolve these problems?

A Profile of Metropolitan Indianapolis

The economy of Metropolitan Indianapolis can be characterized as a scaled-down version of the United States economy. Manufacturing is the key sector, with trade, government, transportation, and finance playing important supporting roles. In 1964, the estimated total employment in the area was 338,000 workers, of which manufacturing accounted for 105,000. During the 15-year period from 1949 to 1964, employment in manufacturing increased 21 per cent and output, as measured by value added, recorded a gain in excess of 91 per cent. Producers of transportation equipment and electrical machinery were the most pronounced contributors to these gains.

Like the national economy, the structure of the Indianapolis Standard Metropolitan Statistical Area (SMSA) has undergone basic changes in response to changes in technological and locational factors. Thus, while manufacturing remains the dominant employment sector, the service-producing industries have become increasingly important in relation to the goods-producing industries. During the 1949-64 period the government sector showed the largest absolute and percentage employment gains (20,300 and 82 per cent, respectively), followed by finance, insurance, and real estate (73 per cent), and the service trades (49 per cent). Only agriculture experienced a decline.

The Indianapolis SMSA's geographic location is a strategic factor in any explanation of the development of its industry mix. It is within the overlapping boundaries of the

Northern Manufacturing Belt, extending roughly from the East Coast to the Mississippi River and bounded by the Ohio and Potomac Rivers, and the Midwest Corn Belt. This proximity to most of the major regional markets of the nation has contributed to a transformation of the area from one dominated by locally-owned enterprises to one where branch plants of national corporations predominate.

During the last decade, the population of the area increased at exactly the same rate as that of metropolitan areas as a whole — 26.4 per cent. Population now exceeds 750,000. Most of the growth occurred in the urban fringes. Similarly, the distribution of jobs by employee residence shows a marked trend toward locations in the outlying fringes. The percentage increase in resident employment over the last decade for the City of Indianapolis was 4 per cent and for the rest of the SMSA, 78 per cent. In short, the heaviest concentration of people with jobs is located in the urban fringe.

The racial composition of the population has also changed significantly in recent years. Between the last decennial censuses, the nonwhite population of the central city increased 54 per cent while the white population increased 4 per cent. In the rest of the SMSA, virtually all the population increase was in the white segment. Also, the movement of high-income population to the suburbs coupled with the concentration of low-income families in the central city has contributed to a relative loss in taxable property to the City of Indianapolis. It accounted for 77 per cent of the county total in 1950. Currently its share is 60 per cent.

Looking ahead, the growth prospects for the Indianapolis SMSA's economy appear bright. It is likely that it will continue to develop in its several different economic functions as a regional and urban center. Continued growth in population, employment, income, and output will, however, increase the need for more integrated and coordinated programing and planning in the development of appropriate public policies. While such actions are unlikely to be the dominant force in the area's future economic development, their absence can deter the expansion that is potentially possible. Examples of imminent problems include availability of water and patterns of industrial land use, decline of the central business district of Indianapolis, pressures of non-white immigration, and the implications of continued and rapid area dispersal on the efficiency and effectiveness of government services and the financial system for their support.

Local Governments

At the present time there are 62 local governmental units in the Indianapolis SMSA, including 23 municipalities, 11 school districts, and 18 special districts or authorities. The majority of the latter have been established by the Indiana legislature to operate on a metropolitan area-wide basis. A listing of the major metropolitan functional authorities is provided below.

Legislation in 1951 created the Health and Hospital Corporation of Marion County, a unified health and hospital agency, and provided it with separate taxing (of property) and bonding powers.

In 1953, the state established the machinery whereby one or more governmental units within a county could jointly set up a service corporation for the purpose of constructing, equipping, operating, and maintaining public buildings. This action was prompted more by the inflexibility of the restrictive constitutional debt limitation than by a desire to promote intergovernmental cooperation in metropolitan finance. The corporations are financed by the sale of revenue bonds not subject to the constitutional provisions relating to bonded indebtedness. The bonds are retired by annual "lease-rental" payments. The Indianapolis-Marion County Building Authority was created as a result of this legislation and recently completed a 26-store, $28 million City-County Building to house the various administrative agencies of both city and county governments.

The Indianapolis Airport Authority has provided airport facilities to the metropolitan area since 1961. It is another metropolitan-wide "unit of government" with semi-independent fiscal authority. It may incur indebtedness to be repaid by general property taxation, as well as issue revenue bonds to be retired from earnings or lease-rental payments.

The Metropolitan Thoroughfare Authority is a similar single function government with broad jurisdiction over the transportation facilities, including off-street parking, in Marion County. Its activities are financed from various revenue sources, including bonded indebtedness and a specific excise tax on commercial motor vehicles. The 1967 Indiana General Assembly substantially broadened the scope and authority of this body and changed its name to the Mass Transportation Authority of Marion County.

Two other functions are presently handled on a metropolitan-wide basis — flood control, and parks and recreation. The Marion County Board of Flood Control (1959) and the Department of Public Parks (1963) are providing services to all residents of the metropolitan community.

Legislation in 1955 established a single, metropolitan-wide planning agency in Marion County to supersede and replace 16 existing city, town, and county planning departments. The seven-member Metropolitan Plan Commission is directly involved in decisions affecting the development of Metropolitan Indianapolis, such as those concerned with zoning, building codes, and right-of-ways.

Several so-called "departments" within the governmental structure of the City of Indianapolis have also been given "extra-legal," independent fiscal powers by the state legislature in order to expand their services beyond the legal boundaries of the City of Indianapolis. Their bonding power, where applicable, is also outside the 2 per cent constitutional limit, and in certain instances they can levy a limited property tax. The single-purpose departments granted these special financing privileges include:

1. Department of Redevelopment, which is primarily engaged in slum clearance;

2. Department of Sanitation, which handles the construction, repair and maintenance of sewers, and the treatment of sewage;

3. Department of Off-Street Parking, which acquires and operates off-street parking facilities; and,

4. Department of Public Utilities, which is synonymous with Citizens Gas and Coke Utility, a wholly city-owned utility.

Metropolitan Indianapolis contains 11 separate and independent school systems. Combined they constitute the largest single governmental function, accounting for 54 per cent of all funds spent by all local governmental units in the area. Since 1959, school consolidation in Marion County has reduced the number of school corporations from 13 to 11. It is worth mentioning, however, that the parent Marion County School Reorganization Committee recommended adoption of a single metropolitan-wide school unit, but the forces operating to defeat the proposal prevailed. Major objections centered on the pupil "size" of the one-unit plan and on other so-called "disadvantages" of bigness (separation of parent and school board, dilution of the ability to influence or participate in decisions, etc.).

Of the 62 units of local government in Metropolitan Indianapolis, 47 have taxing authority. The number of governmental units which overlap or operate in any one of these taxing jurisdictions range from 10 to 16. Every property taxpayer regardless of his location within Metropolitan Indianapolis is supporting at least eight area-wide units of local government (Marion County, Health and Hospital Corporation, Flood Control Board, Airport Authority District, Fair Board, Building Authority, Thoroughfare Authority and Park District). Combined they currently account for approximately 20 per cent of the property tax levy.

State Policies and Metropolitan Finance

Local fiscal autonomy has long since ceased to be a realistic objective in Indiana. Instead, a broadly based and integrated state-local revenue structure is developing with emphasis on increased grants-in-aid and shared taxes.

State Tax Reform

The major state policy benefiting Metropolitan Indianapolis, as well as other local governmental units in Indiana, was the comprehensive overhaul of the state tax system in 1963. At that time, a full complement of tax devices was enacted: a personal and corporate net income tax and a retail sales tax.[2] The "tax package" produced an immediate 50 per cent increase in General Fund revenues, added substantially to the over-all responsiveness of taxes to increases in income, and improved significantly the equity of the distribution of state-local tax liabilities. Equally important, it served to dispel many conventional myths regarding the noxious repercussions—political and economic—of structural tax reform, thereby promoting the attitude that fiscal progress is attainable. Strengthening of the tax system and raising the level of taxation have made it possible for the state to increase its support of the services of local governments, especially for public education. To illustrate, in the period 1963 to 1967, total state aid for education will have doubled.

All earlier attempts to ease state-local fiscal difficulties by the adoption of "temporary" measures pointed to the need first for comprehensive state fiscal reform, and all subsequent developments have confirmed the course of legislative action taken. Once the state had "ordered its own house," it became less difficult to deal with the pressing demands of cities and other local units for financial assistance. For example, in the two legislative sessions following the enactment of the new tax program, virtually all the fiscal activity was concentrated on increasing the amounts of state-collected, locally-shared taxes accruing to cities and towns, on improving the administration of the local property tax, and on providing additional funds for local school support.

---

[2] For details of the reform program, see J. A. Papke, "Indiana Tax Policy: Revision, Reform, Reconstruction," *National Tax Journal,* Vol. XVII, No. 2, (June 1964).

Local Revenue Reform

The State Board of Tax Commissioners has final responsibility for administration of the local property tax, including supervision and review of local assessing and review and approval of local budgets, bond issues, and tax levies. The 1959 state legislature strengthened the administration of the local property tax by requiring a state-wide reassessment of all real property at regular eight-year intervals, by providing for the complete codification of the laws covering assessments, by authorizing the preparation of up-to-date manuals to guide assessors of personal property, and by requiring uniform assessments at one-third "true" (i.e., market) value.

When the first state-wide property reassessment program was completed, Metropolitan Indianapolis recorded a gain of $90 million of valuation; only a $2 million increment, however, was listed for the City of Indianapolis. The "core" of the central city (Center Township) experienced a net loss of almost $22 million in assessments, reflecting extensive land-use changes in the downtown area.

The 1965 legislature carried the local revenue reform movement forward by repealing outright the local personal property tax on household goods. It also approved the levying of a 3 per cent ("piggyback") retail sales tax on hotel and motel rentals for Metropolitan Indianapolis to be collected by the state on top of the state retail sales tax, with the proceeds to be returned to Metropolitan Indianapolis. The revenues are to be used initially to construct a major convention auditorium in the central city. The 1967 legislature approved sharing of the yield of the personal income and retail sales taxes with local units, with distributive shares based on the geographic (county) source of collections. Also, in the property tax area, the 1967 legislature adopted an optional annual averaging procedure for the valuation of business inventories—a major step in the direction of strengthening the application and administration of the local property tax.

Generally speaking, the State of Indiana has recognized the forces operating on the spending of governments in metropolitan areas. Only recently, however, could it afford to support this recognition with increased financial assistance. It has proceeded, albeit on a modest scale, toward providing greater taxing authority on an area-wide basis. At the same time, it is making substantial progress, within the framework of existing political institutions, to strengthen the administration of the local property tax. Perhaps equally significant with respect to the breadwinner of Indiana local governments, it has resisted continued and concerted efforts to impose an absolute ceiling on local property levies. Future success at combating these efforts very likely hinges on providing additional alternative sources of local tax revenue so as to de-emphasize further the relative importance of property taxation.

Reapportionment of the State Legislature

Representation in the Indiana General Assembly was realigned in the 1963 and 1965 sessions and in a subsequent special session. The most recent allocation of seats gives considerably more weight to urban cities and counties. For example, the seven largest county districts (out of a total of 92 counties), including Marion and all others located in Indiana SMSAs, now elect a majority of state senators. And the 9 largest county districts elect a majority of state representatives. The problems of the large urban areas are, therefore, likely to receive even more attention in legislative sessions than they have in the recent past.

Metropolitan Indianapolis elects its entire 23-member delegation to the Indiana General Assembly at large; there are no election districts within Marion County. The political implications of this feature are that virtually all the representatives and senators of Marion County are spokesmen for the central city.

The Past Is Prologue

Like most other major urban centers, the posture of Metropolitan Indianapolis is going to continue to change in line with the patterns established in the recent past. What are these patterns and what problems do they engender?

The resident and contact populations of Metropolitan Indianapolis are mobile. Two-thirds of the workers reside in the central city. A fifth live elsewhere in Marion County, and the remainder (14 per cent of the total) live outside the county.[3] The in- and out-central city commuting trend is increasing rapidly and portends rising transportation requirements.

The commuter-by-car phenomenon is largely an outgrowth of low population density. The average Marion County subdivision density of 5.5 persons per acre of 1.68 lots per acre is perhaps the lowest of any metropolitan area in the country. Low density development and high dispersion of population and employment opportunities have limited the potential for economic use of public transit and have added to the costs of providing other public services (sewers, roads, water systems, libraries, etc.) to suburban communities. The perpetuation of fragmented governments and the concentration of low-income, nonwhite families in the central city may, in part, be the result of these developments. The "core" of the central city, for example, contains 90 per cent of the entire metropolitan area's nonwhite population.

Expanding vehicular traffic has created critical transportation and land-use problems in Metropolitan Indianapolis, particularly in the central business district (CBD) of the central city. Some 60 per cent of the mile-square CBD is currently devoted to the movement and storage of automobiles. And 70 per cent of the CBD traffic is through-traffic. Moreover, at the completion of the interstate system, an estimated 5,000 low-income families will have been displaced in the City of Indianapolis alone.

The role of the federal government is of critical im-

---

[3] Commuting is a two-way street. According to 1960 census data, on a "normal" work day a total of 42,939 workers commuted to jobs in Marion County. Seventy-seven per cent of these were residents of the eight outlying counties. On the other side, 5,697 residents of Marion County were reported to be commuting to employment locations outside the county; the "net" daily commuter population was, therefore, approximately 37,000.

portance to the present and future development of the central city and Metropolitan Indianapolis, particularly in the areas of urban renewal and redevelopment, slum clearance, education, and poverty. For the two decades following World War II, however, the City of Indianapolis was on record as opposing most federal aid programs for city functions. Indeed it was the only Indiana community to request specific exclusion from participation in federal urban renewal programs. In place of federal assistance for these programs, the city established, with legislative approval, the "extra-legal" Department of Redevelopment to undertake the responsibility for slum clearance and rehabilitation of rundown residential and industrial properties.

It is clear now that the leadership of Indianapolis fully embraces the federal government's role in assisting urban centers to finance particular functions. The 1965 Indiana General Assembly, by request of the Indianapolis delegation, repealed the 1945 statute which excluded Indianapolis from urban renewal programs. In the short period since the close of the 1965 legislative session, the city administration and its congressional delegation have vigorously pursued programs which provide assistance from the federal government, including downtown redevelopment, renewal, urban planning, public housing, and re-education.

Metropolitan Indianapolis is still a major center for receiving southern (primarily nonwhite) migrants seeking new and expanding economic opportunities. Accommodation of this heavy in-migration and the consequent development of the necessary job skills for a growing labor force is probably the most important single social issue confronting the local economy. The great bulk of these people are concentrated in the older sections of the central city where obsolescence, high residential densities, congestion, inaccessibility, and low household income combine to generate vexing problems.

All the aforementioned growth problems have a significant bearing on the question of the effectiveness and efficiency of financing public services in Metropolitan Indianapolis. The property tax remains the backbone of local finance in Indiana. Currently, Indiana ranks last among the 50 states in the use of local nonproperty taxes. The serious imbalances between the demands for public services and property tax resources are already evident in Metropolitan Indianapolis and severe distortions exist in the distribution of tax responsibilities. They also highlight the importance of developing long-run arrangements for providing and financing governmental services on an area-wide basis.

Public and Private Policies: The Outlook

It is reasonable to expect that the pressures for increased expenditures by governments in Metropolitan Indianapolis will continue to mount. The experiences of the past suggest that there is insufficient elasticity in the existing local revenue structure to enable it to keep pace with these expenditure requirements. The resultant financial difficulties encountered by these local governments can be easily documented in terms of rising costs and increasing reliance, in absolute dollar amounts as well as relative to other sources, upon their major source of local tax revenue — real and personal property. They are also suggested in the growth of bonded indebtedness, within and without the constitutional borrowing limitation, and in the number of "extra-legal" governments being established.[4] Property tax rates applying currently to real and personal property in the City of Indianapolis, for example, include provision for the payment on the outstanding bonded indebtedness of nine separate governmental jurisdictions, five of which provide metropolitan area-wide services.

What public and private policies are being followed to relieve the financial difficulties of governments in Metropolitan Indianapolis?

(1) Increased state support for local schools is being provided from the relatively elastic supply of revenues accruing from the state's new tax structure. This is relieving

---

[4] Between 1957 and 1962, the number of special districts and authorities in Metropolitan Indianapolis rose from 5 to 14.

some of the pressures on the local property tax. At the same time, the formulas under the several state-collected, locally-shared taxes have been reshaped to reflect population concentration more adequately.

(2) To by-pass the constitutional bonding limitation, the number of special functional authorities continues to grow. If these authorities are designed to serve metropolitan area residents and are provided with area-wide taxing authority, this approach, while not ideal, is far preferable to each existing governmental unit seeking its own solution. Public education is undoubtedly Marion County's major service, and it should be re-examined with a view to establishing a single, metropolitan school district. It is not unlikely that the state will use its leverage under the distribution of general fund revenues to school districts to promote metropolitan area school district consolidation.

(3) Federal assistance, under existing arrangements and/or new programs, is playing an increasingly important part in the finances of Metropolitan Indianapolis. Because most of the programs for which federal aid is presently available coincide with outstanding problem areas, it will make little difference whether the assistance continues to be program oriented, or whether it is unconditional. There is ample evidence that new leadership is emerging in Metropolitan Indianapolis with a firm commitment to the use of federal financial assistance.

(4) Local supplements to the state personal income and/or retail sales taxes imposed on a county-wide basis are perhaps the most promising developments on the local finance horizon.[5] The precedent has already been established, and the extension of this device and financing by charging the user of individual public services (i.e., user-charges) appears imminent. A 1 per cent supplement to the state's personal income tax applied to all metropolitan area residents would likely yield between $17 million and $18 million annually. If it were extended to the income earned

---

[5] Legislation was introduced in 1967 for a local option, county-wide income tax for Marion County, but the session ended without a vote being taken on the measure.

in the metropolitan area by nonresidents, an additional $2 million would be realized. Alternatively or in addition, a supplement to the state's retail sales tax would yield approxi mately $15 million per year for a 1 per cent increase.

(5) The efforts to strengthen the application and administration of the local real and personal property tax through state supervision have been accelerated.

Outmoded constitutional borrowing restrictions constitute the greatest single obstacle to a rationalization of Indiana metropolitan finance. The possibility of securing an amendment to the present provision within the foreseeable future seems remote. The only consolation is that the restrictions have prompted on several occasions the shifting of service functions together with taxing privileges to metropolitan-wide authorities.

In sum, having put its own house in reasonably good financial order, the State of Indiana has proceeded to assist in the financing of local units to a great extent, primarily via direct state aid and shared taxes. And Metropolitan Indianapolis is sharing in this development. Top priority in new intergovernmental financial arrangements in Indiana goes to an extension of the county-wide tax, preferably as a supplement to the state personal income tax. With non-property taxing authority on an area-wide basis and intensive employment of user-charges, coupled with increasing state aid and full participation in present and future federal aid programs, there is every reason to expect that the governments in Metropolitan Indianapolis will approach the goal of fiscal adequacy, that is, a reasonable balance between public service demands and tax resources.

Metropolitan Indianapolis in recent years has been relatively successful in coping with the problems of the impact of economic growth. A joint public and private effort has begun to revitalize the economy of the area. The creation of the Greater Indianapolis Progress Committee, composed of top businessmen, leading citizens, and public officials, has been a constructive step in the direction of bringing new vitality to area leadership. And a concerted attempt is being made to assure continued comprehensive and integrated physical and economic planning and traffic engineering. The short-range consequences of these activities are encouraging. Whether the pay-off will continue for the long-range will depend as much on the positive forces already at work as on the willingness to accept the new mechanisms which are needed to sustain the present momentum.

DETROIT:

Crisis in the Central City

Karl D. Gregory
Assistant Professor
Wayne State University

on leave as
Executive Director
Federation for Self-Determination

Under a relatively alert city administration and with considerable federal assistance, Detroit has attempted to meet the problems of a central city hampered by overlapping and decentralized responsibilities and an eroded tax base. It is interesting to note the general warnings inherent in the paper's criticism of the State of Michigan: "…despite several previous noteworthy attempts to achieve over-all reform of the state's tax structures, each crisis has tended to run its course until something just had to be done. At that point — when continued inaction would have resulted in either severe reductions in already inadequate levels of public service or extensive deficit financing — some expedient legislation has been enacted, frequently involving one-time revenue gains, to tide the state over for a few years at most, until the next crisis."

The Detroit Standard Metropolitan Statistical Area (SMSA), like many others, contains fragmented and overlapping jurisdictions which result in diseconomies of scale, duplication of services, and disparities between public needs and resources. Such an inefficient and archaic local government structure can seriously affect political decision-making and reduce the efficient use of taxes and the quality of public services they provide.

In 1964, there were 246 governmental units in Wayne, Macomb, and Oakland counties — the three counties in Southeast Michigan which comprise the 2,000 square mile Detroit SMSA. Of these, there were 137 separate and independent local units of government: 58 cities, 25 villages, and 51 townships. The overlapping of local jurisdictions for any citizen is at least twofold (county and city or township) and is sometimes threefold (county, township, and village). There were, in addition, 109 special units of government, including 99 school districts and 10 special districts and authorities. Each of these special units has the authority for performing a single function.[1]

Of Michigan's total population, 48.1 per cent resided in the Detroit SMSA in 1960. This area had 3,762,000 persons. Wayne, the central county, had a population of 2,666,000 persons in 1960 and was more than twice as large as the other two counties combined. The smaller counties are, however, growing much more rapidly. The central city,

---

[1]For a more detailed description of governmental organization in the SMSA, see the Citizens' Research Council of Michigan, *Staff Papers on Governmental Organization for Metropolitan Southeast Michigan,* a study made under the auspices of the Metropolitan Fund, Inc. (Detroit, Michigan, 1965).

Detroit, accounted for almost 63 per cent of the population of Wayne County, and slightly more than 44 per cent of the SMSA.

Economic Trends

Michigan's salient economic characteristic, the great fluctuation in its output and employment, is due primarily to its manufacturing sector. Manufacturing provided over 41 per cent of wage and salary workers in nonagricultural establishments in 1965. The dominant element in manufacturing is durable goods, produced largely by the auto industry.

Reduction of employment in the automobile industry and in the share of military contracts awarded to Michigan firms was among the woes which, when superimposed on the recessions of 1958 and 1961, seriously affected Michigan's economy. The current recovery began in 1962 and has continued with five consecutive and excellent years of automobile production. However, by 1966 employment in the auto industry had not reached the levels of 1955. This was a result of technological changes and the decentralization of the auto industry in response to shifts in population, economies in transportation costs, and the desire to be located closer to markets. Accompanying the recession was a net out-migration from the state of about 400,000 persons between 1958 and 1962, reducing the labor force significantly. Since that time, however, the recovery and a diversification of the industrial mix have reversed the net out-migration.

The Detroit SMSA was characterized generally by similar trends and characteristics. It had almost 50 per cent of the state's wage and salary employment and over 52 per cent of the state's employment in manufacturing in 1965.

The Detroit SMSA is the fifth largest in the United States. Among 13 SMSAs with a population above 1,500,000 in 1960, it was fourth with regard to the value added in manufacturing in 1963, and second, below Newark, when adjusted on a per capita basis. This suggests the cyclical sensitivity of the Detroit SMSA, rather than the total level of economic activity, since other SMSAs exceeded Detroit in various nonmanufacturing activities.

Revenues and Expenditures

Direct general expenditures per capita of all governments in the Detroit SMSA amounted to $257 in 1962. They were exceeded by five of the most populous metropolitan areas and were followed closely by three others.[2] Detroit's expenditures per capita increased by 10 per cent in the following three years; in this respect, it ranked ninth among the 12 SMSAs (excluding the Boston SMSA for which no comparable data are available). The implicit price deflator for state and local governments, a proxy for the effect of rising prices, rose by 9 per cent in the same three-year period ending in 1965. Thus, the real purchasing power of Detroit's direct general expenditures per capita remained virtually unchanged.

It is helpful to divide the recent past into the recession years of 1957 to 1962 and the recovery period from 1962 to 1965. The patterns of the recession years take on added significance with the unusually prolonged recovery and sustained high levels of automobile production.

General revenues per capita for all local governments in the Detroit SMSA rose by 4 per cent annually, or 1 per cent less rapidly than direct general expenditures during the recession years. Partly as a consequence, debt per capita increased by 62 per cent in this five-year period.

The property tax was virtually the only source of tax revenues in 1962. Direct federal aid amounted to $3.3 per capita, or less than 2 per cent of total revenues. Apart from the property tax, the only major revenue sources were state aid produced $63 per capita or almost 27 per cent of total general revenue; charges produced about half as much as state aid.

---

[2]Problems arise in comparing the absolute levels of expenditures among SMSAs. Certain public services are performed at the state level in some states and at the local level in others. Caution must therefore be exercised.

Table 1   **Detroit SMSA: Receipts and Expenditures Per Capita and Per Cent Change, 1957-1962 and 1962-1965**

	Per Capita (in dollars)		Per Cent Change		
			Amount	Per Capita	
Item	1962	1965[a]	1957 to 1962	1957 to 1962	1962 to 1965
General revenue (net of interlocal)	236.9	282.2	30.4	21.3	19.1
Intergovernmental revenue	66.3	85.6	21.1	12.6	29.1
From state	63.0	77.9	17.9	9.6	23.6
From federal government	3.3	7.7	148.1	130.6	133.3
Taxes	137.2	153.8	33.5	24.1	12.1
Property	135.4	140.0	34.8	25.3	3.4
Other	1.8	13.8	− 22.1	− 27.6	N.C.
Charges and miscellaneous	33.4	42.7	38.5	28.8	27.8
Direct general expenditure	254.2	282.6	36.2	26.7	11.2
Current expenditure	198.9	227.5	41.5	31.6	14.4
Capital outlay	55.2	55.2	20.2	11.7	0.0
Direct general expenditure by major function:					
Education	110.6	128.3	34.3	24.8	16.0
Higher education	1.2	2.5	N.C.	N.C.	108.3
Local schools	109.4	125.8	N.C.	N.C.	15.0
Highways	16.6	17.4	1.7	− 5.5	4.8
Public welfare	11.8	8.7	105.7	91.4	− 26.3
Hospitals	16.7	20.4[b]	18.3	10.0	9.7[b]
Health	1.9		3.8	− 3.1	
Police protection	14.2	16.0	19.2	10.9	12.0
Fire protection	6.6	7.9	24.2	15.5	19.7
Sewerage	11.0	12.3	127.0	111.2	11.8
Sanitation other than sewerage	6.7	6.9	− 0.2	− 7.3	3.0
Parks and recreation	7.2	8.6	− 7.9	− 14.4	19.4
Natural resources	1.3	N.A.	N.C.	N.C.	N.A.
Financial administration and general control	9.7	10.6	22.2	13.7	9.3
Interest on general debt	9.4	11.4	102.4	88.1	21.3
All other general expenditures	30.5	34.2[c]	83.6	70.7	7.5[c]

N.C. — Not computed.
N.A. — Not available separately.
[a] Based on a sample of the smaller government jurisdictions and complete data for large jurisdictions.
[b] Health and hospitals are not shown separately in 1965.
[c] Includes natural resources in 1965 and in the change from 1962 to 1965.
SOURCE: A special tabulation by the Governments Division, Bureau of the Census. Also *Local Government Finances in Selected Metropolitan Areas in 1964-5* (Washington, D.C.: U.S. Government Printing Office, 1966), Table 4.

Property taxes provided most of the gain in revenue in the recession years. State aid, although expanded, accounted for a declining share of local budgets. Most of the 25 per cent increase in property tax collections resulted from higher tax rates. Many local jurisdictions found themselves increasingly unable to finance desired levels of expenditures without extra millage when voters would approve it. Assessed valuations had increased by about 8.4 per cent. The major reliance on this tax, with its inelastic base in many local government units — together with tax rate limitations — is a major problem in the Detroit SMSA.

Direct general expenditures per capita in constant dollars rose by 9 per cent in the five-year period, and consisted entirely of current expenditures. The increase in capital outlays in current dollars was outpaced by rising prices.

Almost 44 per cent of the SMSA's direct general expenditures in 1962 were for education — virtually all for local schools. In contrast to an increase of 22 per cent in enrollments, total expenditures for education, unadjusted for changes in population, increased by 15 per cent in dollars of constant purchasing power. Thus, merely maintaining educational services in some school districts is a major problem.

An 88 per cent rise in interest costs was brought about in part by increased debt and a decline in the credit ratings of some units of government. Lower levels of economic activity, together with a large number of marginal workers and low-income broken families, generated an increase of 91 per cent in outlays for public welfare. This was surpassed only by expenditures to expand sewerage services. Expenditure per capita in current dollars for highways, health, sanitation, and parks and recreation all declined, while most other expenditure classifications fell when measured in constant dollars.

From 1962 to 1965, state aid supplied a slightly increased share of local revenues, as the state's fiscal crisis subsided temporarily. Property taxes per capita in constant dollars declined 5 per cent, reflecting an almost constant level of assessed valuations, higher tax rates, and rising prices and population. Although direct federal aid more than doubled, it provided relatively small amounts of additional revenues, approximately $4.4 per capita in current dollars. With the pressure of demands for public services, borrowing continued, but at about one-third of the average annual rates prevailing in the recession years. Some units of government had reached their constitutionally determined or required debt limitations and other limitations set by state statutes.

With the constraints upon revenues, total direct general expenditures increased during the recovery period less rapidly annually than in the recession years. Current outlays per capita in constant dollars had increased 5 per cent in the three-year period, while capital outlays, on the same basis, declined 8 per cent.

Education and Other Services

Education commanded the largest proportion of the rise in total expenditures: $81 million or 19 per cent more than in 1962. Still, an 11.7 per cent increase in enrollments exceeded the 9.6 per cent advance in expenditures in constant dollars.

The recovery reduced substantially the number of persons on welfare and thereby released the local share of $3.1 per capita for other public services. A few improvements were made in police and fire protection, and junior colleges were expanded in some suburban jurisdictions. Some of the backlog of previously neglected parks and recreational services was corrected. The annual increases in "all other general expenditures" were reduced significantly from recession year levels. One reason for the decline was a deceleration of the pace in urban renewal partly in response to public clamor for "humanizing" the program and improving the relocation of the displaced.

These trends had varying impacts on the different components of the Detroit SMSA.

Contrasts: Central City and Suburbia[3]

From 1957 to 1962, total general revenues in the central city area rose 13.5 per cent in current dollars but declined when measured in constant dollars. In suburbia, general revenues rose by 49.7 per cent in current dollars, and by less than 1 per cent annually when adjusted for changes in both population and prices.

State aid for the central city area remained unchanged in current dollars during the recession years. In suburbia, it increased significantly but provided a declining share of total revenues. Direct federal aid rose very rapidly from a very small base, went largely to the central city area, but provided minor amounts—less than 2 per cent of total revenues in either area in 1962. With no alternative for significant expansion except their own sources of revenues, both areas increased average effective property tax rates. Added assessed valuations provided little relief. They advanced by less than 1 per cent a year in the central city area and by about twice as much in the balance of the SMSA.

Compared to the combined revenues allocated to the central city area, suburbia enjoyed greater revenues in 1962 in absolute amounts, but less on a per capita basis. Intergovernmental revenues, at about $66 per capita, were approximately equal in both areas. The property tax yield, $26

---

[3]The central city area, as defined here, comprises the City of Detroit, the Detroit School District which is coterminous with the City, and a proportion of the receipts and expenditures of two jurisdictions spanning a larger area and overlying the City. They are Wayne County and the Huron-Clinton Metropolitan Authority. The latter provides a regional system of parks. The receipts and expenditures of the overlying units were distributed between the central city area and suburbia in proportion to estimates of population in the relevant years and jurisdictions. (See also Table 2, footnote b.) This method of proration has the advantage of simplicity, although it appears to overstate the share of the outlays by the County and the Authority which benefited residents of the City. Suburbia, the balance of the SMSA, spans the governments in Macomb and Oakland counties, in addition to the expenditures and receipts of the two overlying governments not attributed to the central city area. Further, two cities and two associated school districts, Hamtramck and Highland Park, are enclaves located entirely within the boundaries of the City of Detroit. They are included arbitrarily with the balance of the SMSA.

The latest available data on an allocable, sub-SMSA basis, are for 1962.

Table 2

Central City Area and Suburbia: Receipts and Expenditures for 1962 and Per Cent Change from 1957 [a]

	1962 (in dollars)				Per Cent Change, 1957-1962			
	Amount (in millions)		Per Capita		Amount		Per Capita	
	CCA	Sub.	CCA	Sub.	CCA	Sub.	CCA	Sub.
General revenue (net of interlocal)	417.0	484.6	250.9	226.0	13.5	49.7	22.6	21.7
Intergovernmental	111.5	140.8	67.1	65.7	6.1	36.4	14.6	10.9
From state	103.3	136.3	62.2	63.6	0.1	36.3	8.2	10.8
From federal government	8.2	4.5	4.9	2.1	325.7	41.0	358.9	14.8
Taxes	252.4	269.8	151.9	125.8	15.4	56.5	24.7	27.2
Property	249.3	266.1	150.0	124.1	16.3	58.4	25.7	28.7
Other	3.1	3.7	1.9	1.7	−28.1	−15.2	−23.4	−30.9
Charges and miscellaneous	53.1	74.0	32.0	34.5	21.5	54.0	31.3	25.2
Direct general expenditure [b]	454.2	513.1	273.3	239.3	32.4	39.8	43.1	13.7
Current expenditure	353.5	403.5	212.7	188.2	24.6	60.7	34.6	30.6
Capital outlays	100.6	109.7	60.6	51.1	70.3	− 5.4	84.0	−23.1
Education	151.8	269.2	91.3	125.6	43.3	29.7	54.8	5.4
Current expenditure	128.1	221.4	77.1	103.2	31.9	70.8	42.5	38.8
Capital outlay	23.7	47.8	14.2	22.3	169.0	−38.7	190.6	−50.1
Highways	25.5	37.5	15.3	17.5	− 1.3	3.8	3.4	−15.6
Public welfare	34.1	10.7	20.5	5.0	129.5	54.8	147.9	25.9
Hospitals	29.2	34.3	17.6	16.0	5.4	32.0	13.9	7.3
Health	4.7	2.4	2.8	1.1	− 5.5	27.9	2.2	3.7
Police protection	33.9	20.2	20.4	9.4	7.5	45.8	16.1	18.6
Fire protection	12.8	12.4	7.7	5.8	8.5	45.9	17.3	18.6
Sewerage	23.6	18.1	14.2	8.4	122.5	133.3	140.5	89.9
Sanitation	17.7	7.6	10.6	3.6	− 4.8	12.4	2.9	− 8.5
Parks and recreation	16.8	10.6	10.1	4.9	−25.8	56.3	−21.1	27.1
Natural resources	1.5	3.5	0.9	1.6	55.0	472.4	68.5	368.6
Financial administration and general control	16.6	20.4	10.0	9.5	12.8	31.1	21.8	6.6
Interest on general debt	13.2	22.4	8.0	10.4	81.2	117.4	95.8	76.6
Housing and urban renewal	25.3	10.2	15.2	4.8	(c)	(c)	(c)	(c)
All other general expenditures	48.5	33.6	28.7	15.7	N.C.	N.C.	74.1[c]	94.6[c]

N.C. − Not computed.

[a] For a definition of the "central city area" and "suburbia" see text and footnote b, *infra*.

[b] Direct general expenditures for the central city area in 1962 are attributable to local units as follows: City of Detroit, which made outlays for all functions shown *supra*., except education, $231.1 million; the separate and coterminous School District of Detroit, which spent $153.0 million for education and interest on general debt exclusively; the overlapping County of Wayne, an allocation of $68.1 million for a wide variety of functions; and the overlapping Huron-Clinton Metropolitan Authority, an allocation of $1.8 for parks and recreation, exclusively.

per capita higher in the central city area than in suburbia, explains the entire difference in revenue per capita.

The statistics point to a higher tax effort in the central city area. Although assessed valuations per capita were comparable in both areas, residents of the central city area had lower average family incomes. Tax rates in the central city area in 1962 were $44 per $1,000 of state equalized assessed valuations in 1962, compared to $36 in Macomb County, almost $39 in Oakland County, and $43 in Wayne County (inclusive of the central city area, implying a lower average rate for out-county jurisdictions).[4] The central county of Wayne ranked second among the 83 counties in the state in this approximation of an average, effective, property tax rate. Such extra effort in the central city area may be overstated to the extent that suburban residents contributed to the central city property tax by buying products produced or sold in the central city at prices that were increased through the shifting of the tax by firms to their customers. Similarly, suburban demand for city products raised land values in Detroit. However, this spillover, or suburban contribution to central city taxes, was offset through purchases made by Detroiters at an increasing number of shopping centers located in suburbs just outside the central city area.

The 360,000 whites who left the City of Detroit between 1950 and 1960 were replaced by 183,000, primarily low-income, nonwhites. The net out-migration of whites conceals a similar substitution of low-income whites from the rural South and elsewhere — some of whom were unaccustomed to urban living — for urbanized, middle-income whites. This shift apparently took place largely between 1957 and 1960 and still continues with perhaps some acceleration as an aftermath of the riot of 1967. Such a substitution creates a greater need for public services but reduces the ability to pay for them. Many health and recreational services, for example, can be bought privately by those who can afford to pay for them. In a crowded slum, needless to say, private

---

[4] There were great variations in property tax rates among the over 200 government units in suburbia. Some of these units were and still are in a precarious financial state.

services are generally out of the question. Although the cost of providing public services in slum areas may be quite high, the cost of not providing them may be higher, as manifested by the behavior of alienated and hostile citizens.

Suburbia exceeded the central city area in 1962 in the percentage of school-age population, particularly in the age-group under ten. Further, the rate of growth in public school enrollments in the recession years was more than six times as high in the former as in the latter. On the other hand, the central city area had almost twice as many senior citizens, twice as many families with incomes in 1959 below $4,000, and three times as high a proportion of all families with children under 18 in broken homes.

A crude index of spillovers of expenditure benefits across government jurisdictions is the per cent of persons residing in one area who work in another and presumably consume its public services. About 34 per cent of the labor force residing in suburbia worked in the city, twice the percentage of workers residing in the central city who were employed in the suburbs. To the extent that such spillovers flow out of the central city, its expenditures overstate the benefits received by its residents, and the expenditures of the recipient or suburban jurisdictions understate the benefits that its residents enjoy.

Direct general expenditures rose in the central city area by $110 million in the five-year period, while suburban expenditures increased by $150 million. On the one hand, two-thirds of the increment in the central city area consisted of current expenditures, and one-third, capital outlays. Current items were held to minimum levels, salaries of government employees lagged, and capital outlays were deferred in 1962, except for urban renewal and self-sustaining sewerage facilities. The urban renewal program was accelerated; it accounted for half of the rise in capital outlays of the central city area. The cash drain on the city from this program was much below the amounts spent, since the federal government provided two-thirds of the net cost of clearance. Much of the remaining one-third was met by similar credits, such as those for new school buildings which were needed in any event because of overcrowded classrooms and obsolescent school buildings.

On the other hand, in the suburban areas, current expenditures rose more rapidly than total expenditures as capital outlays for schools fell by $32 million. Increased capital outlays for sewerage facilities, urban renewal, police and fire stations, and other public buildings made mandatory by large additions to population, only offset partially the decline for schools. Because of the larger number of governments characterized by different circumstances, it is difficult to generalize about wage levels for government employees and similar factors.

Approximately 44 per cent of the increase in current expenditures in the central city area was devoted to public schools, the enrollments of which had risen by 15,200 students. The rising annual deficits in the General Fund of the City of Detroit, totaling $34.6 million at the end of fiscal 1962, curtailed many other public services. Particularly hard hit were hospitals, health, sanitation, and parks and recreation.

Most functional expenditure categories expanded significantly in suburbia under the pressure of a 23 per cent increase in the total population. Several, however, declined on a per capita basis in constant dollars.

It is interesting to note that direct general expenditures per capita in the central city area in 1962 were $34 higher than in suburbia. This difference was occasioned by the prolonged recession, compounded by the social pathology of the inner core of the central city together with a statistical deficiency in the census data.[5] Most of the difference is accounted for by assistance to the poor (public welfare, $15.5), law enforcement (police, $11.1), and reductions in the growth of blight (housing and urban renewal, $10.4). Specialists in evaluating social welfare services bemoaned the low levels of transfer payments under federal, state, and local programs, and the ceilings on general assistance programs; law enforcement continued to be an important public

---

[5] The City of Detroit provides certain reimbursable services with regard to sewerage and sanitation for suburban communities. The data do not portray "domestic consumption" by netting against Detroit's expenditures these "exported" services.

issue, and the forces generating blight continued to operate, but perhaps at a slower pace. Comparable observations could be made concerning several pockets of poverty within suburbia, largely low-income, property-poor and often non-white enclaves.[6] Suburbia is far from a homogeneous area.

Trends in the recent past do not augur well for those who use public services in the central city area. From 1962 to 1965 aid from the state had barely been keeping up with rising prices. The City of Detroit has been most aggressive in applying for federal aid. Such aid, particularly for urban renewal and the anti-poverty program, has provided the margin of difference between further curtailments and a modicum of needed improvements in a few affected public services. The enactment of an income tax in the City of Detroit—effective in 1963 after years of annual deficits, despite large reductions in budget levels—brought in $41.3 million in 1964. This new tax corrected temporarily the initial imbalance between income and outgo, offset reductions in property tax collections, and permitted some increases in wages and salaries of government employees which had lagged behind those in the private sector.

All governments were severely constrained by the lack of expansiveness in the tax base they rely upon most. Since 1960-61 state equalized assessed valuations had fallen each year from $5.7 billion to below $5.0 billion in 1966-67. This has posed serious fiscal difficulties, particularly for the Detroit School District, although increased charges and licensing fees helped somewhat by providing small amounts of additional revenue.

As costs of public services advanced more rapidly than revenues, local governments in the central city area have in recent years postponed capital outlays when possible to maintain current expenditures for public services. Current expenditures in current dollars in the central city area rose by 2.9 per cent from 1962 to 1964, and by another 2.3

---

[6]About 95 per cent of the nonwhites in Michigan in 1960 resided in the Detroit SMSA. Of those in the SMSA, 86 per cent resided in the City of Detroit. Detroit ranks third among large cities in the proportion of its population which is nonwhite.

per cent in 1965. Capital outlays fell in current dollars by 21 per cent between 1962 and 1964, despite a reversal of earlier declines in population and a backlog of unmet needs. A subsequent increase in capital outlays in 1965 was almost totally accounted for by federally-supported urban renewal programs. It is significant that the expenditure category with the largest rate of increase from 1962 to 1964 was the cost of servicing debt. This stabilized in 1965 when many capital outlays were curtailed and as Detroit's income tax reduced the additions to its debt.

There is a stark lack of symmetry between the continued fiscal stress upon the local public sector and the long and vibrant recovery in the private sector which lowered the unemployment rate in the SMSA from 15.3 per cent in 1958 to 3.2 per cent in 1965. More insights into this fiscal stress and the prospects for the future may be gained through a review of each of the major governments in the central city area.

City of Detroit

Detroit's fiscal storms between 1959 and 1962 were subsequently weathered with an income tax, budgetary stringency under the direction of two able controllers, an alert Mayor and Common Council, and increasing utilization of federal aid. Budgetary curtailment has proceeded with little abatement since 1959. One may well doubt that there is much left to squeeze while maintaining the quality of existing public services.

The margin initially provided by the income tax has been absorbed. It is the one elastic, self-imposed source of revenue. But yielding less than 20 per cent of total revenues, its elasticity is offset by the rest of the revenue structure. Enacted in 1962 at a 1 per cent rate on the incomes of residents and the earnings of nonresidents in the City of Detroit, it was soon restricted and made less elastic by a state law. The state enacted a "Uniform City Income Tax" which limited local income taxes to a 1 per cent rate on residents and to a half of 1 per cent on nonresidents. Aside from not being able to rely more on this source of revenue in the future, Detroit lost $7 million per year by having to cut in half the rate on nonresidents, a rate which helped to recapture some of the spillover of benefits of Detroit's public services to nonresidents.

Improvements in property taxation may supply some limited hope for additional revenues. The foundations for this hope rest with the results of a recently completed reassessment of all properties, and with the completion of urban renewal projects which are expected to add to the tax base. Moreover, assessed valuations have been reduced in recent years by a complex of factors, some of which may not recur. Among them are the large scale demolition of taxable properties for public facilities, additional tax exemptions, the lowering of high and discriminatory assessments on business personality, and reduced demands for realty as businesses and households have moved to suburban locations. A partial offset has been supplied by complementary business and government financed renewal of the downtown area.

State aid to the city declined slightly from 1962 to 1964 and again in 1965. Significant additions to state aid await the state's putting its own fiscal house in order and a commitment at the state level for greater involvement with the problems of central cities and urban low-income communities.

At the very best, state legislation has not been of significant assistance in helping to solve Detroit's fiscal problems. In addition to the "Uniform City Income Tax," the state reduced by 25 per cent the valuation under the property tax of tools, dies, jigs, and fixtures. Under the same law, Detroit was to be reimbursed on a sliding scale for the revenue losses in the following three years, after which the full loss was Detroit's.

The preponderance of a rural influence in the state legislature ended with its reapportionment, the impact of which is now being felt. It is still too early to form reliable judgments as to whether the gain in influence has been toward urban areas generally or to suburban areas almost exclusively. In any case, the more rapid growth in population of suburban areas would appear to signal for the future

Table 3   **Central City Area: Receipts and Expenditures**
1964 and 1965 and Per Cent Change to 1964

Item	Amount (in million dollars) 1964	1965[a]	Per Cent Change 1957 to 1964	1962 to 1964
General revenue (net of interlocal)	471.8	481.3	28.4	13.1
Intergovernmental revenue	125.3	127.3	19.2	12.4
From state	114.8	113.0	11.2	11.1
From federal government	10.5	14.2	449.4	29.1
Taxes	285.0	285.9	30.3	12.9
Property	240.3	238.3	12.1	− 3.6
Income	41.3	44.0	(b)	(b)
Other taxes	3.4	3.7	−25.4	13.6
Charges and miscellaneous	61.5	68.1	40.6	15.7
Direct general expenditures	443.4[c]	455.7	29.3	− 2.4
Current expenditure	363.8	372.2	28.2	2.9
Capital outlay	79.6	83.5	34.7	−20.9
Direct general expenditure by function:				
Education (all for local schools)	150.9	151.5	42.4	− 0.6
Highways	31.0	31.1	20.0	21.7
Public welfare	28.1	26.6	89.0	−17.7
Hospitals	28.7	29.9	3.5	− 1.8
Health	5.0	5.3	0.1	5.9
Police protection	36.0	38.7	14.3	6.4
Fire protection	14.7	16.3	24.6	14.8
Sewerage	20.0	21.4	88.5	−15.3
Sanitation other than sewage	16.9	16.7	− 9.2	− 4.6
Parks and recreation	18.6	21.4	−19.0	10.7
Housing and urban renewal	8.5	13.2	95.5	−66.5
Financial administration	6.2	18.5	N.A.	20.4
General control	12.0		−18.7	4.5
Interest on debt	17.1	17.0	134.0	29.1
Correction	5.4	N.A.	23.6	−16.4
Natural resources	1.7	N.A.	73.2	11.8
Other and unallocable	42.6	48.1[d]	N.C.	N.C.

N.A.: Not available separately.

N.C.: Not computed.

[a] Data for 1965 are Census estimates for the City of Detroit in 1965 and 1964 data for all other governments attributed to the central city area. All of the changes from 1964 are therefore occasioned by the City of Detroit only. Insufficient information was available to update the data on other government units; the changes, however, from 1964 are believed to have been negligible in total.

[b] The City of Detroit enacted an income tax in 1962, effective fiscal 1963.

[c] Direct general expenditures for the central city area in 1964 include: $221.6 million by the City of Detroit, down $9.5 million from 1962; $153.1 million by the School District of Detroit, virtually unchanged from 1962; $66.5 million allocated to the center area for Wayne County, down $1.6 million from 1962; and $2.1 million allocated for the central area out of the outlays of the Huron-Clinton Metropolitan Authority, up $0.3 million from 1962.

[d] Includes natural resources and correction.

SOURCE: A special tabulation by the Governments Division of the U.S. Bureau of the Census and U.S. Bureau of the Census, *City Government Finances 1964-1965* (Washington, D.C.: U.S. Government Printing Office, 1966).

a relative decline in whatever influence the central city now has.

One of a few recent exceptions to the pattern of state-city relations historically is an act, passed in the legislature in 1966, which established a state agency to borrow in the private sector and to make funds available to nonprofit sponsors of low-cost housing. This is the state's first major move in helping to provide decent, safe, and sanitary housing for persons of low income. Such housing is a critical problem in Detroit. It has been in the absence of such assistance by the state in the past that the city has increasingly turned to the federal government.

Another exception is the recently passed law, which enabled a consolidation of state, county, and city welfare services. Prior to the implementation of this act in December 1966, there was much duplication, overlapping and confusion, and welfare clients were frequently shunted from one agency to another. Consolidation should make possible a more efficient operation.

Federal assistance, dashed by the budgetary impact of the war in Vietnam, appears to be the major hope of city officials, in the absence of more state assistance. This hope arises out of the proven ability of the city administration not only to qualify for such aid, but to influence the content of federal programs. Also enhancing the city's prospects would be action by the state either to increase grants-in-aid or to provide additional local tax authority, or both.[7] Detroit's almost exhausted power to borrow for some purposes could be enlarged. The state could also become more involved in large city problems, as it already has to some extent in housing.

As a depository for the poor, the aged, low-income migrants from rural areas, and handicapped minority groups,

---

[7]There is, however, some doubt that additional tax authority, applying to Detroit and not to neighboring jurisdictions, would be utilized to produce a net revenue gain. Detroit's tax effort is already high compared to adjacent jurisdictions. Subjecting such additional authority to a vote of the electorate for approval would further weaken its chances. Taxes to reach the transient population, say, a levy on charges for hotel rooms and higher local income taxes which reach commuters, are an exception.

Detroit's prospects for providing adequate public services in the future need great improvement. This would be true under the current revenue structure and existing levels of federal and state aid, even if the auto industry should continue to have sales at a high level. A substantial drop in auto sales could lead to much larger deficits than those of 1959 through 1962. A $50 million deficit has already been estimated for fiscal 1968-69.

Detroit School District

The major sources of revenue for the Detroit School District are state aid and the property tax. Many of the previous statements with regard to both state aid and the property tax for the City of Detroit are also pertinent for the School District. State aid declined slightly between 1962 and 1964. Since then it has risen significantly, offsetting lower property tax collections; school enrollments have also increased to almost 300,000 students in the fall of 1966. But despite small improvements, there remains a backlog of defects—overcrowded classrooms, poor performance by students on nationwide exams, salary levels that fail to retain and attract sufficient teachers, and high "dropout" rates. Indeed, some problems are getting worse.

Direct general expenditures for education per pupil enrolled were about the same in the central city and suburbia in 1962 — $519 and $524, respectively.[8] State aid to suburban schools amounted to $162 per pupil, as contrasted to $135 in the central city in 1962. This distribution reflects the operation of state school aid formulas, which involve many factors; but often given casual treatment are the special needs of a school district with a large number of students who begin kindergarten with a handicap and who fall progressively behind national and citywide averages on achievement tests. Approximately 57 per cent of the pupils in Detroit's public schools are nonwhite. An apparently increasing but still small number of Negro parents who can afford it and can gain ad-

---

[8]Detroit still spent approximately the same amount per pupil in 1966.

mission are sending their children to private and suburban schools, and white parents with children of school age are predominant among those who have been leaving the city for suburbia.[9]

Wayne County

Wayne County shares a 15 mill constitutional property tax limitation with the school and library districts. The county does not obtain, like other units of government, the state's centrally collected, locally shared revenues, except some gas and weight taxes for use in constructing and maintaining roads. Yet, it has the responsibility for a wide variety of functions. Moreover, of the 8.46 mill total property tax levy for the county in 1965-66, one mill for general operating purposes will expire in 1968-69, and another three-quarters of a mill for capital improvements will expire in 1969-70. Continuation of both of these extra millages will require approval by voters.

The direct general expenditures of the county in current dollars that were allocated to the central city area declined from $68.1 million in 1962 to $66.5 in 1964, while the deflator for state and local purchases rose by 5 per cent, and population, by 1 per cent.

Crisis is almost a perennial characteristic of Wayne County. The City of Detroit has been trying for years to collect a debt owed it by the county. But the problems of the county are not financial alone. Its structure for decision-making is unwieldy and uncertain.

One solution to Wayne County's problems is complete reorganization through home rule. Enabling legislation has been enacted by the state legislature recently. Committees have been established to study the problem and make recommendations for the initiation of a charter commission which would undertake efforts to obtain a new form and structure for this government.

---

[9] Some suburban school districts, often non-white enclaves, fare even worse than Detroit. The Inkster School District, with an assessed valuation of $5,200 per pupil, may have to close its school doors in early 1968, for available revenues will be insufficient to meet its payroll.

A strong and efficient county government would present opportunities for shifting to the county some functions now performed more expensively below the county level. With changes in state law, it could also permit the levying county-wide of new taxes to be shared with other governments within the county. How well these and other possibilities could be developed depends upon current efforts to completely re-structure county government.

Recommendations For Action

The Detroit metropolitan area extends functionally beyond the SMSA. It includes three additional counties for most purposes — Monroe, Washtenaw, and Genessee counties — and for some purposes, Livingston County. There were 404 governments in this six-county region in 1964. The problems occasioned by overlapping and fragmented governments, fiscal spillovers, diseconomies of scale, gaps between needs and resources, and a cumbersome array of public decision-making units can only be solved with some form of area-wide coordination.

Metropolitan Coordination

A significant step toward a solution is currently being made in response to a report by the Metropolitan Fund.[10] This report presented five recommendations:

(1) It would create a boundary commission to hear petitions for incorporations or annexations, with power to disapprove them if they disregard good planning and good economics. Approved petitions would be subject to a popular vote.

(2) It would limit the use of special districts to those performing functions that could hardly be performed by existing units, such as mass transportation.

---

[10] Metropolitan Fund, Inc., *Regional Organization,* Part I (Detroit, Michigan, May 1965).

(3) It calls for enabling legislation for county home rule, with a broad range of discretion to voters in reorganization and other matters, and for a charter commission on specified matters. This recommendation has already been enacted. It also suggests that enabling legislation should extend the taxing power of counties to include nonproperty taxes, increase the functions they can perform, countywide or otherwise, and protect cities performing the same functions. The Metropolitan Fund had the faith that conflicts between city and county could be resolved by mutual agreement or by the legislature.

(4) It encourages more extensive use of techniques for intergovernmental cooperation. Almost 2,000 specific agreements between governments in the six county region are identified in an incomplete survey. These cover voluntary agreements, transfer functions, joint service contracts, informal agreements on matters of joint interest, and others.

(5) It attempts to come to grips with the maladies underlying proposals for metropolitan-wide consolidation. It reviews the progress of previous efforts at metropolitan consolidation in Miami-Dade County and Nashville-Davidson County, and is against its application in Detroit. The report points out that these areas were not comparable to the Detroit area in that they each encompassed only one county. The consolidation of individual counties in the Detroit area is deemed unsatisfactory, because many functions extend across county lines and because all six counties are considered to be too large in area and population. Moreover, consolidation is considered politically not feasible. It would establish instead a voluntary metropolitan council of governments which would serve as a means of communication and a channel for voluntary cooperation for government officials. This approach has the advantage of starting with currently established organizations.

The Federal Highway Act of 1962 provides an example of the coordination and planning that higher levels of government can stimulate with grants-in-aid. Section 9 of this Act requires comprehensive planning, carried on cooperatively by states and local communities in urban areas exceeding 50,000 in population. The six-county Detroit metropolitan area responded with TALUS, a comprehensive and cooperative Transportation and Land Use Study to provide guidelines for future transportation programs. The study, proceeding currently, is funded by a multi-million dollar grant from the former Urban Renewal Administration of the Housing and Home Finance Agency. Focusing upon the future, through 1990, it should provide long-range information essential to rational and coordinated planning for transportation and land use.

Efficiency in Decision-Making

Efficiency is no doubt reduced by ambiguity in statements of the goals some programs are designed to achieve. Without clearly stated goals, it is difficult to select effectively among the alternative long- and short-run means for accomplishing them and to establish criteria to gauge achievement as the program proceeds. Further, participation by citizens can be made less meaningful. Budgets reveal little except payroll costs, equipment and supplies, and other items. Measures of performance, or the benefits citizens are receiving for their taxes, would be much more informative and would increase efficiency in decision-making.

Techniques now being used by some agencies at the federal level could have substantial application at the local level. Investments to improve these techniques for local application could have a high rate of return. These techniques are variously referred to as cost-benefit analysis; performance budgeting; Planning, Programming and Budget Systems (PPBS); and cost-effectiveness analysis. Mayor Cavanagh's January 1966 budget message stated that explorations were being made to apply some of them in Detroit. A grant recently received under Detroit's antipoverty program funds attempts to build into the program various evaluative methods. Detroit is also developing a social and a physical data bank that could permit many important analyses, once considered either impossible or too expensive.

The Outlook

Conjectures about the future of a Standard Metropolitan Statistical Area are subject to large margins of error. Nonetheless, the private sector of the SMSA has many of the requirements for continued growth up to the point at which a lagging public sector becomes an inhibiting factor. The confidence of private investors appears to be very favorable. The area has an unlimited supply of water, access to the St. Lawrence Seaway and all of the Great Lakes, and an extensive system of freeways tied in to transcontinental routes. It is a service and communications center with a vast hinterland. It is well endowed with technical and scientific know-how, strong financial institutions, and utilities capable of supplying extensive amounts of light, heat, power, and communications facilities. A strong public sector would further enhance the area's growth prospects.

The crystal ball is cloudier with regard to the future of the public sector. Certain qualified, but still heroic, statements can be made, however, based upon the assumption of a continuation of current tax structures and patterns of state and federal aid. Apart from cyclical movements, rising levels of economic activity will generate added local revenues, but not in proportion to the advance in income and output. From 1962 to 1965, total revenues of local governments in the SMSA rose by 22 per cent; Michigan's personal income increased by 23 per cent; and the personal income of the SMSA, it can safely be inferred, rose more rapidly than the state's. Almost all of the added revenues appear to have resulted from increases in tax rates and not from the tax base. About 22 per cent of the change in revenues was provided by Detroit's newly enacted income tax, the rates of which are at an absolute ceiling. More jurisdictions have property tax rates at or beyond tax rate limitations with what appears to be increased voter-discontent concerning extra millage. The 2.4 per cent increase in assessed valuations from 1962 to 1965 in current dollars portends little relief for the future. However, some reforms in property tax administration may help. Additional cities can levy income taxes at a low maximum rate, and some have since 1965. This, however, is a nonrecurring gain. Moreover, the advance in revenues from 1962 to 1965 amounted to a rise of only 9 per cent after adjustment for both rising prices and population and was divided disparately among the many jurisdictions in the area.

Some current problems in providing public services will be solved; some will get worse; and new, currently unanticipated, problems will develop. Without major public policy changes, traffic safety, water and air pollution, and mass transportation are likely to worsen. The forces of urban blight will outpace redevelopment. The trend towards a smaller number of governments, largely because of fewer school districts, will continue. Educational services will be improved in many jurisdictions, especially those with a declining growth of enrollments, and will deteriorate in some of the others.

The central city, without multi-billion dollar social redevelopment and conservation programs and major gains in the area of vastly improved educational opportunities for all, will either decline significantly relative to the remainder of the SMSA and/or become more of a limited service center for the region. In the latter event, the number of spillovers will increase, worsening the efficiency of the public decision-making process. A substantial number of the poor, tucked away as inconspicuously as their political weakness and numbers permit, will be seen and heard primarily when they react spontaneously to not participating fully in rising incomes and in decisions affecting their well-being.

The suburban jurisdictions immediately surrounding the cities of Detroit and Pontiac — except for the high-income, bedroom suburbs and jurisdictions that are well endowed with industrial property — will develop problems now identified with the inner-city area. In effect, as the central city core is physically redeveloped and as other land uses are substituted for residential low-income usage, the problems of the central city will shift outward. The remainder of the SMSA will suffer the large growth pains accompanying increasing density, although the pressure of rapidly growing school enrollments will be relaxed. The property-rich suburban jurisdictions will continue to fare relatively well.

Alternatives for the State

In the absence of metropolitan coordination involving area-wide taxing authority, the major pragmatic alternatives are additional federal and state assistance. Only the latter is within the purview of this case study.

State aid to local jurisdictions, particularly schools, rose significantly in fiscal 1966 and 1967 when the state temporarily had an accumulated surplus in its General Fund for General Purposes. Comparable increases in the near future to restore the proportion of total support of schools supplied by state aid to the ratio which prevailed in the early 1950's may be precluded by the tax package enacted during calendar 1967.

The state was confronted in fiscal 1967 with a deficit in excess of $100 million. The estimated shortfall of revenues required during fiscal 1968 to maintain continuing programs and meet expanded workloads and higher costs was estimated to exceed $300 million.[11] The newly enacted tax package, containing for the first time in Michigan both personal and corporate income taxes, will provide a net yield of about $240 million.

Larger revenues would have to be forthcoming for the state to become more involved in urban problems and to provide more than token relief to local governments through additional grants-in-aid or local credits against the state income tax for local income and property taxes. Alternatively, the state could permit local units of government to (a) utilize added local revenue sources, particularly excises, (b) rely more upon local income taxes by raising the ceiling on the maximum local tax rate, or (c) add a supplement to either the state income or sales tax. The "fiscal reform" package of 1967 did very little in any of these directions to strengthen the fiscal status of local governments.

There are no guidelines as to whether or not future reform will extend to the curtailment of arbitrary restrictions on local borrowing and property tax rates and the provision of

---

[11] The estimate for fiscal year 1967 is based upon statements of Governor Romney in recent public addresses. The estimates for fiscal year 1968 are the author's.

other local tax sources for these units of government. Many of the constraints on local units of government are imbedded in the Constitution. Thus, the complex process of amending it, which requires time, effective political action, and sustained efforts of education on the issues, would have to be undertaken. The more involved the process for securing change, the less optimistic one can be about the outlook.

Fiscal reform that is comprehensive and sufficiently pinpointed in its focus on fundamental state and local financial problems to permit more lasting solutions does not currently appear to be a likely item for effective action by state authorities. The responses to Michigan's financial crises of the past are foreboding. Despite several previous noteworthy attempts to achieve over-all reform of the state's tax structures, each crisis has tended to run its course until something just had to be done. At that point—when continued inaction would have resulted in either severe reductions in already inadequate levels of public services or extensive deficit financing—some expedient legislation was enacted, frequently involving one-time revenue gains, to tide the state over for a few years at most until the next crisis.[12] The civil disturbances which occurred in several central cities in Michigan during 1967 point up both the crises that exist in these centers now and the urgency of providing for public services designed to get at the root causes of these crises.

---

[12]Michigan's fiscal problems have been the subject of frequent study. Harvey E. Brazer, Robert L. Gilliat and Karl D. Gregory, "Survey of State and Local Finance in Michigan," Chapter 1 and other chapters in the *Michigan Tax Study Staff Papers*, Citizens' Advisory Committee to the Legislative Committee, House of Representatives (Lansing, 1958); Harvey E. Brazer, "Michigan's Fiscal Outlook," *Wayne Law Review*, Vol. II, No. 2, (Winter, 1965), and *Taxation in Michigan: An Appraisal* (Ann Arbor: Institute of Public Administration, University of Michigan, 1961).

BOSTON:

The Need for Regional Solutions

Joseph R. Barresi
Executive Secretary
Boston Municipal Research Bureau

■

Boston, an historic city set in a rich metropolitan area in one of the nation's richest states, has many problems that it probably cannot solve by itself. Among them: fragmentation of local governments, stringent limitations placed on local authorities by state authorities, and too little interest expressed by the Commonwealth of Massachusetts, and by surrounding communities, in the overwhelming problems of the city. State limitations on local taxing powers and inter-tax competition have forced Boston to raise an inordinate proportion of its funds from the property tax. Boston's property taxes, from which an inordinate amount of property is exempt, are among the highest in the nation and result in an extreme example of tax-created distortions. The study points out that many of Boston's problems will require regional solutions, "with the state providing the direction and most of the funds."

The Boston Metropolitan Area

The Boston Standard Metropolitan Statistical Area (SMSA) comprises 78 cities and towns embracing the whole of Suffolk County and parts of Essex, Middlesex, Norfolk, and Plymouth Counties. Its 17 cities and 61 towns have a total population of 2.6 million, more than half the total population of Massachusetts. It is the seventh largest SMSA in the country, but one of the slowest growing. Between 1950 and 1960, population increased 7.4 per cent contrasted with 22.6 per cent in other SMSAs. Boston, the central city, slipped in size from tenth in the United States in 1950 to thirteenth in 1960. The city's population as a proportion of the SMSA is only about 26 per cent, among the lowest for central cities in all major SMSAs. Its land area — 48 square miles — also is one of the smallest areas among core cities.

Social Characteristics

The 17 cities in the SMSA range in size from Boston with a population of over 600,000 to Melrose with 27,000 persons. Of the 61 towns, 25 have populations exceeding 13,500 (one has 55,000), while 12 have less than 5,000 persons; 24 communities have between 5,000 and 13,500.

The Boston SMSA has been a net exporter of population; it has not maintained its natural increase rate. There has been a continuing trend in population decentralization but the basic distribution of the SMSA has not fundamentally changed. One result of this pattern has been the reduction of population densities in the heavily settled core and an increase in the lightly populated suburbs.

Family incomes, labor force participation rates, age composition and levels of educational attainment bear a fairly close resemblance to patterns which prevail in many of the nation's largest urban centers. But the ethnic and racial composition differs considerably.

Based on census data, median incomes in the SMSA are substantially above the national average. Boston's own figure, however, is significantly below the SMSA average and is among the lowest of northern SMSA core cities. The city has tended to evolve into primarily a low-to-middle-income community. But it still contains a wider income spectrum than the smaller communities on its borders. Negroes represent about 3 per cent of the total SMSA population or less than 90,000. Although still a small fraction of the population, their numbers have increased rapidly.

The Boston SMSA's labor force is estimated at about 1.2 million persons. A major difference in occupational structure between the Boston SMSA and other major urban centers is Boston's strong emphasis on white collar occupations as compared to manufacturing employment. The two ends of the age spectrum — the young and the elderly — have increased more rapidly in the 1950-1960 decade than has the working age group. In the suburbs, there is a much larger proportion under 18.

Every community in the SMSA has its own school committee and a school district coterminous with its corporate limits. Although school committees have no separate taxing powers, statutes require cities and towns to appropriate whatever amounts school committees request. Failure to do so would result in a judicial decision compelling the appropriation of any deficiency plus a 25 per cent penalty. But the Boston school committee is limited. By statute, it can only appropriate a sum equal to the preceding year's expenditures plus an amount necessary to cover the full year's cost of any raises given in the preceding year. The Mayor and City Council are responsible for providing any additional sums needed above the appropriation limit.

County government in Massachusetts is relatively weak. County commissioners are elected, as are other officers such as treasurer. In most cases, counties are not natural and logical areas or units for administration of governmental services. They are basically judicial districts with some highway and correctional functions. Suffolk County, which includes Boston and three smaller communities, is quite different. The Mayor and City Council of Boston are the county commissioners while appointed city officers' such as the Collector-Treasurer also serve the county.

Metropolitan Services

Several services are administered on a metropolitan basis. In the field of public transportation, the Massachusetts Bay Transportation Authority, a political subdivision of the Commonwealth, embraces the entire SMSA. The Authority has general responsibility for development, financing, and operation of mass transportation facilities within its territory. It can improve, modify, or expand existing facilities, acquire or construct new facilities, and enter into agreements for providing mass transportation service with other public agencies or private companies, including railroads.

Water and sewerage are administered on a regional basis by the Metropolitan District Commission (MDC), a state agency. Communities in the water and sewerage districts pay assessments based on their use of these services. The MDC was organized just before the turn of the century. Thirty-eight communities of the SMSA belong to the sewerage district. Other SMSA communities operate with individual septic tank or cesspool systems. Thirty SMSA communities are in the water district; 24 are in both the water and sewerage districts. There is an MDC parks district which maintains, constructs, and polices the parks, beaches, and boulevards. Thirty-seven communities of the SMSA are in the parks district. The Metropolitan Air Pollution District consists of 30 communities in the SMSA closest to the core city.

The entire SMSA is in the metropolitan area planning district. The Metropolitan Area Planning Council provides regional planning and conducts research necessary to improve the physical, social, and economic conditions of the district. Its recommendations are advisory only.

Financial Characteristics

The relative wealth of the area, as well as disparities among communities, are apparent. Latest equalized valuation per capita in the SMSA averaged $5,364; in Boston it was $3,586. Only two communities had lower figures than Boston. The average equalized property tax rate for the SMSA in 1966 was $33.90 per $1000. Boston's, the second highest in the SMSA, was $60.90. The average 1966 property tax load per capita for the SMSA was $207.70; Boston's was $247. Thirteen communities had higher per capita property taxes than Boston, but each had more than twice the equalized valuation per capita.

Actual tax rates per $1000 of assessed value averaged $65.64 while Boston's was $101. The actual tax rate average is distorted, however, since 23 communities in 1966 were assessing at or close to the statutory "full and fair cash" level. Eleven of these had changed to the new standard in the past two years, indicating a growing trend.

The average proportion of the property tax devoted to schools in 1965 in the SMSA was 51.4 per cent. In Boston, the figure was 23 per cent, lowest of the SMSA. In general, communities in the inner ring had the lowest proportions.

Problems—Past and Present

Boston has long had property tax problems, expensive service levels, allegedly unfair cost burdens, and notorious assessment practices. Moreover, in the past, the suburbs and the legislature usually felt that Boston's problems were of its own making and that the city was not entitled to their aid in solving them.

Its present difficulties are still revenue-oriented, affecting such services as education, low-income housing, police protection, hospitals, health and welfare. In the future, services such as solid waste disposal will suffer.

Other SMSA communities, especially those outside the inner ring, face similar problems. In the decade prior to 1966, these communities began to experience property tax problems of a dimension relative to Boston's. Population growth with its effect on public school education was a major factor. At the same time Boston was able to stabilize its tax rate and tax levy.

According to 1962 census data, taxes—about 99 per cent of them property taxes—are the mainstay of general revenue for the SMSA. Taxes accounted for just over 60 per cent of general revenues for the central city area while accounting for almost 70 per cent in the balance of the SMSA. Between 1957 and 1962, property taxes for the central city area increased 22.5 per cent against 70.5 per cent for the balance of the SMSA. The percentage increases in property taxes per capita were 30.2 per cent and 58.5 per cent respectively.

Boston's Burdens

Immediately prior to 1960, Boston's property tax rate experienced several sharp increases. Between 1955 and 1959 the increase totaled $33 per $1,000 of assessed valuation, bringing the tax rate to over $100 for the first time. The trend in tax rate, tax base, and tax levy was halted and even reversed beginning in 1960 for two important reasons: first, Boston declared a moratorium on pay raises and fringe benefits, and second, the city adopted a strict no-hire, no-fire policy. In four years, more than a thousand permanent jobs were eliminated.

The city also sought to increase revenue through its own powers—by increasing fees and charges and by improving collections. It received authority to levy a sewer service charge in 1961, thus removing over $2 million in sewerage costs from the property tax. Parking fines and parking meter fees were increased as were fees at the city hospitals. The transit authority deficit—of which Boston paid 65 per cent—was stabilized because of increased fares and lower costs due to reduced service. There was some increase in the distribution of state-shared taxes due mainly to the establishment of a withholding system for personal income taxes and accelerated collection. Free cash, which developed because actual receipts exceeded estimated receipts, and the level of uncollected taxes were used for reducing the tax rate and for purposes for which appropriations might have been made.

Between 1959 and 1964 the property tax rate dropped from $101.20 to $96.00, while these taxes were increasing substantially in practically all other communities. The new atmosphere gave impetus to a massive urban renewal program which got underway in 1960.

Other state actions during the period both eased and increased Boston's burdens. Tuberculosis care and treatment became a state responsibility. A program of state aid for libraries amounting to 25 cents per capita was authorized as was a regional library system which the state would fund. School building assistance was increased to a minimum of 40 per cent of approved costs. Sums were distributed for local highway purposes from state highway bond issues. State sharing in half the local cost of urban renewal was passed on. On the other side of the ledger, new and higher minimum salaries for teachers were established. The poll tax, although amounting only to about $200,000 in revenue for Boston, was repealed. Pensions for public employees were liberalized. A lid was clamped on the motor vehicle excise tax rate which increased as average property tax rates in the state rose. Property tax abatements for certain persons over 70 were authorized to be funded solely through local revenues.

In 1965 Boston's tax stability was shattered and its property tax levy accounted for about one-third of the total 1965 increase in state-wide property taxes of close to $90 million. Several factors brought about the end to stability. The city had to use large amounts of free cash for tax rate reduction and recurring purposes. Major operating cost increases also took place. Police and fire personnel raises were mandated by a 1964 referendum. Larger welfare appropriations than normal had to be made because the city had to borrow to meet several million dollars in current welfare expense in 1964. This meant an automatic increase in 1965 welfare appropriations equal to the 1964 amount borrowed. Finally, in the 1965 tax rate computation certain receipts were estimated lower than necessary. Under the law these estimated receipts could have been as high as the actual receipts of 1964. By underestimating, the 1965 tax rate was higher than necessary. The benefit from the lower estimate was a large amount of free cash at the end of 1965 that could be used in 1966.

Although Boston and other SMSA communities have relied on property taxes for over 60 per cent of their general revenue, the city's property tax base has generally decreased for many years. Much of the loss has been due to the takeover of property for highways and urban renewal. In the last four years, however, there has been a net increase in Boston's base. Yet the effect on the city's finances has been minimal, since $1 million in new base only affects the tax rate by six cents, while $1 million in costs affects it by nearly 70 cents. Urban renewal projects are estimated to have a tax rate impact by 1970 of only about $3.50 per $1,000 of assessed valuation. In other words, the next effect on the tax rate of the renewal program between 1960 and 1970 should cause a $3.50 reduction. All but one of the other SMSA communities, another old central city, showed tax base increases in the last ten years.

Assessment Problems

Boston has had problems with assessing for many years. In fact, not too long ago its practices were notorious. The heavy reliance on property taxes for general revenue and the resulting fetish about the tax rate no doubt contributed substantially to these problems. Assessments were set which could not stand up under review. An equalization survey of income-producing properties, implemented in 1960, brought greater equity within classes of property. Abatements now are recognized more than before in setting subsequent assessments. The result has been fewer abatement applications and more confidence in the city's assessing.

At the same time, there is considerable doubt that all classes of property are assessed at the same ratio. It is alleged that commercial property is assessed at or near full and fair cash value while residential property is assessed at about one-half the commercial average. Further, the high property tax has resulted in taxing arrangements for new commercial-industrial construction based on a formula which insures the investor a proportional return.

Recent equalized valuations lists established by the state put Boston's total at almost twice the actual valuation set by the city assessor. The city disputed the state total, and recently Boston's appeal resulted in reduction of its equalized valuation to a figure only 20 per cent higher than the city's actual assessed valuation.

In the balance of the SMSA, although a few communities disputed the state's equalized figures, assessing revaluations have been taking place. For example, in the last two years, about a third of the communities have revalued and are assessing at the statutory level. This has been more prevalent in the bedroom communities where revaluation tends to shift tax loads among citizens. In Boston and inner-ring communities with substantial amounts of commercial-industrial real estate, revaluation would tend to shift the tax load from commercial to residential property. In Boston, the increase could amount to a substantial rise in property taxes for residential owners.

New court decisions and intolerable property taxes have prompted more and more taxpayer court action to hold up property tax bills until revaluation has been authorized. The trend is expected to continue, but it would appear that Boston will be one of the last to reach the revaluation stage, if it ever does.

Tax-Exempt Property

The amount of Boston's limited land devoted to tax-exempt purposes is a burden which few, if any, of the other communities in the SMSA share. Over $1 billion in values or over 40 per cent of total valuations are tax exempt. Over two-thirds of the exempt property is for governmental use. Tax-exempt property has economic benefits, however, as well as liabilities. Yet, no balance sheet has been drawn to measure either.

In a community with about 37 per cent of its small land area in tax-exempt use, further tax exemptions without some kind of payment in lieu of taxes must be viewed with skepticism. Several attempts have been made to get voluntary payments in lieu of taxes from educational institutions without success. In Cambridge, which has several tax-exempt institutions, both Harvard and the Massachusetts Institute of Technology (MIT) have made voluntary payments in lieu of taxes for many years.

County Costs

Boston, unlike communities in other counties, pays the entire cost of Suffolk County operations which now exceed $10 million. The three other communities in the County pay nothing as a result of a legislative arrangement that goes back to 1832. Past efforts to bring about a sharing of costs have met with failure. County costs—mostly for courts—are not locally controlled, even though the Mayor and City Councillors are the County Commissioners. Instead, cost hikes usually are the result of legislative action.

In other counties, the state legislature appropriates the county budgets and assesses the member communities for county costs. Major revenue proposals presented to the legislature by Governors have at times included provisions to have the state pay all county costs or at least all county court costs. None has succeeded.

Expenditure Disparities

Traditionally, Boston has had high and costly service levels. As the core city, its costs for practically all functional areas exceed those of other communities in the SMSA.

Census data of 1962 on general expenditure point up the disparities. General expenditures by the central city area (Suffolk County communities) in 1962 accounted for 35 per cent of the total general expenditures of the SMSA. The breakdown on a per capita basis was $323.18 for the central city area and $253.14 for the balance of the SMSA. Expenditures for public welfare exceeded those for any other function in the central city area, although education was not far behind. Outside the central city area, expenditures for local schools far exceeded those for any other function.

Total expenditures for local schools in the central city area amounted to 18 per cent of its total general expenditures contrasted to 40 per cent for the balance of the SMSA. On the other hand, total expenditures for welfare in the central city area were almost 20 per cent of its total general expenditures as opposed to 10 per cent for the rest of the SMSA. On a per capita basis expenditures for schools in the central city area and the suburbs were $62.17 and $100.68 respectively; for public welfare, $63.75 and $26.01 respectively.

Between 1957 and 1962 the percentage increase in per capita costs for public schools in the balance of the SMSA was twice that of the central city area while the percentage change in absolute expenditures was about three times greater. For public welfare, the reverse was true. Per capita percentage increases for public welfare in the central city area were more than twice those of the rest of the SMSA while percentage increases in absolute costs were 40 per cent higher. Other functional areas where direct expenditures of the central city area far exceeded the rest of the SMSA were hospitals, fire and police, and housing and urban renewal.

Census data on intergovernmental revenue shed more light on the welfare and local schools disparities. Total intergovernmental revenue amounted to only about one-fourth of total general revenue and practically all of this came from the state government. Included in the state government total, however, was the federal share of categorical welfare assistance. The central city area received almost twice as much as the balance of the SMSA on a per capita basis, largely because of its heavy welfare load.

On a functional basis, 40 per cent of intergovernmental revenue went for welfare, 12 per cent for education, and 20 per cent for general local support. Only in the areas of housing and urban renewal did the federal amounts exceed those of the state.

When related to all local government expenditure for corresponding functions, intergovernmental revenue for welfare in the central city area amounted to almost 83 per cent; for education less than 10 per cent; for housing and urban renewal 42 per cent. The proportions for the balance of the SMSA were 72 per cent, 9.7 per cent and 26.7 per cent respectively. The 1964 census data for the central city produced proportions of 80.4 per cent and 10.8 per cent respectively for welfare and education. Only recently did federal aid become significant in local expenditures and then mainly for urban renewal.

Local Public Schools

Local public education — its quality and its costs — has been a major issue for some time in the entire SMSA. Prior to 1966, local property taxes annually financed about 90 per cent of the cost of public elementary and secondary education. There were grant-in-aid programs for vocational education, special education for the handicapped, school lunches, school transportation, and several other minor programs. But school foundation aid which essentially was aimed at equalizing educational opportunity remained low.

In Boston, for example, the annual amount of foundation aid totaled less than $2 million or less than 5 per cent of average annual school costs. Failure of the State Legislature to up-date equalized valuations and the basic foundation amount per child since the 1940's resulted in smaller and smaller proportions of foundation aid for meeting local school costs. As will be described later, passage of a sales tax in 1966 with a new school aid formula and elimination of some of the separate grant-in-aid programs have increased the level of state aid for school purposes.

Communities with relatively more wealth have led in expenditures per pupil and in the level of teacher salaries. The poorer communities have been trying to catch up. But data also show that many poorer communities have made a greater financial effort in relation to wealth even though expenditures per pupil are not high. Overdependence on property taxes for school funds and competition for the property tax dollar among many functions in the inner ring communities help explain the disparities. In the outer SMSA communities, overcrowding and the need for new buildings and building additions have been major problems. The older communities are concerned with replacement of antiquated physical plant and teacher salaries. In Boston, the problems have been those of a deteriorating public school image worsened by alleged inferior teaching and by the large numbers of culturally and economically deprived pupils, many of whom are second and third generation Bostonians, as well as by antiquated physical plant.

It is difficult to know whether the quality of Boston's public school education has in fact slipped. Its spending levels per pupil and its teacher salaries have been high, as has its effort in relation to fiscal ability. Yet many believe that quality based on factors such as median grade reading ability has fallen. It may well be that our standards of measurement have changed. In the end, quality cannot be measured in simple terms.

With a relatively stable number of school pupils, Boston's school building problem has been largely one of replacing existing plant. World War II and the city's property tax problems in the 1950's deferred major replacement. Although a building program costing more than $115 million has recently started, a new factor has brought more delay. A 1965 law calls for correction of racial imbalance before state aid for school building can be given. More than 50 Boston schools have greater than a 50 per cent proportion of non-whites in their populations. It was not until 1967 that the State Department of Education accepted Boston's plan for correcting imbalance.

Public Welfare

As the census has shown, public welfare is a most expensive local function, especially in Boston. Total welfare costs in Boston approximated $85 million in 1967, with the local share amounting to about one-fifth of the total. Liberalization of eligibility, especially in the Aid to Families with Dependent Children category, the in-migration of low-income families, the basic economic composition of the population, and now medicaid have produced continual annual increases in total costs and total cases. Added to the welfare problem has been the lag in reimbursement by the state of its share of welfare expense. At various times during the year, the lag was as much as 24 months. The latter problem was solved with passage of the 1966 revenue measure which permits the state to be as current as possible.

Fire and police protection in Boston have been expensive services, not only because of the city's large day-time population and its amount of high value property to be protected, but also because of its traditionally high numbers of manpower in relation to area and population. Census data of 1964 showed $26.06 and $19.57 per capita spent for police and fire protection respectively in the central city area as opposed to $12.57 and $14.32 in the balance of the SMSA. The effect of population growth outside Boston was reflected in the growth of the police and fire protection problem in the suburbs. Between 1957 and 1962 the per cent change for police protection both in per capita amounts and absolute amounts in the suburbs substantially exceeded that of the central city area.

There are at least two other local functions — hospitals and highways — which have been major central city problems. Only two cities in addition to Boston in the SMSA have city hospitals. Boston's City Hospital has been in existence for more than a hundred years. More than 30,000 patients a year are admitted to its wards. More than 70 per cent of all patients are either unable to pay or are financed by welfare, compared to 15 per cent in the average hospital in the state. Income or hospital revenue has amounted to less than one-third hospital costs. In short, the hospital serves people of relatively low income.

But apart from this, Boston City Hospital is spread among 33 separate buildings, all built before 1940. Its age and attendant obsolescence have brought other problems. Investments in modernization, although steady, have been tempered by over-all municipal financial problems and have fallen far short of making any significant physical improvement. A $50 million rebuilding program has just been authorized. The 1962 census shows that hospitals are a major expense for the central city area with per capita expenditures amounting to $26.51 against $7.47 for the rest of the SMSA.

Although Boston has annual highway needs of $2 million to $3 million for its local streets and roadways, annual state aid for this function averages only about $500,000. Moreover, the aid formula fails to recognize the nature and density of the city's traffic. This annual state aid is supplemented at times by special distributions from state highway bond issues.

Major Policy Issues

One of the major policy issues of the Boston metropolitan region for many years was mass transportation. The major mass transportation system had long served only 14 cities and towns including Boston. Although the system became publicly owned in 1947, state statute limited it to operation within a transit district made up of the same 14 cities and towns, except under specified provisions of law.

The Metropolitan Transit Authority (MTA), the new state agency set up by law in 1947, owned and operated the system of rapid transit, street car and bus lines. It was supported by its own income — mostly fares — plus direct deficit claims against the cities and towns served. Boston was responsible for almost 65 per cent of the deficit. Three commuter railroads provided commuter service on lines radiating from all parts of the core city to the north, south, and west. No significant state assistance was available to the MTA. On the contrary, the state had imposed obligations that contributed to operating at a deficit.

The Mass Transportation Crisis

With a steady drop in ridership and rising labor costs, the system incurred increasingly larger annual deficits reaching about $20 million in 1960-61. The effect on the finances of transit district communities, and especially Boston, was obvious. The tax rate effect on Boston of an expense over which it had no control reached about $9 per $1,000 of assessed valuation.

The system had a poor image resulting from political interference and poor service. Millions were being spent by the state for highway construction. Yet there was no coordination among different forms of transportation, thus aggravating the mass transportation problem.

A solution came in 1964. There were many reasons for success, but two events of a crisis nature brought the problem to a head. One day late in December 1963, the rush hour produced the biggest traffic jam in Boston's history. An estimated 100,000 vehicles of immovable mass clogged downtown streets and expressways for hours. Secondly, the commuter railroads petitioned to abandon all or part of their commuter service. Public demand for a solution mounted. The Governor approved a feasible plan and campaigned for public support and the legislature enacted a new mass transportation law.

The plan itself resulted in almost complete public support. It introduced state financial assistance on a 90-10 basis for expansion of rapid transit lines along commuter rail lines. A new and enlarged transit district including all communities in the SMSA was set up. The new district members were not burdened with the old district's debt. New formulas for apportioning service deficits were devised. Cities and towns, especially Boston, which were ineligible for school transportation assistance were to receive reimbursement on account of school transportation costs attributable to use of public transportation facilities.

For the first time the mass transportation system would have to be planned and coordinated with the highway system. Most important, the financing plan was relatively painless because the state aid would come from an additional two cent tax on cigarettes.

Thus, a start was made in solving a problem that had long plagued the region. A $340 million expansion and modernization program has been approved by the region and is underway with major state aid and some federal funding.

State-Local Fiscal Relations

Another basic policy issue in the Boston SMSA and in the entire state for many years had been the antiquated and unfair state-local fiscal relationship. Massachusetts and its communities had a difficult time meeting twentieth century demands for new and increased governmental services because the already burdened property tax could not produce the required increased revenue without fiscal damage to communities.

Contrary to popular conception, the problem was not over-expenditure of public funds. Although Massachusetts is the tenth wealthiest state, 40 states spend more of their citizens' per capita income. Total expenditures for all Massachusetts governments combined ranked about twentieth in the country on a per capita basis. At the same time, the state was about fourth highest in per capita taxes, a disparity explained only by the shape of the state's revenue structure.

The problem was heavy dependence upon direct taxes for meeting total expenditures—more particularly an overdependence on a single tax source, the local real estate tax. As the census shows, local governments raised about two-thirds of the total tax burden, with practically all of that coming from property taxes.

As a consequence, property taxes in Massachusetts were second highest in the nation on a per capita basis. They were a direct deterrent to economic development, representing a penalty to investors who might otherwise take significant steps to construct or repair commercial property. Almost everyone in a position to judge agreed that property taxes were excessive and that more state help was needed.

Apart from their size, the most glaring fault of Massachusetts property taxes had been their unequal distribution among communities and among classes of property. One direct result was that the higher the rate of the property tax load, the greater the inducement for most local assessors to spare the homeowner at the expense of commercial property owners.

This was a key to the State Legislature's long inaction on a new revenue program. Home owners in the smaller and wealthier communities found their property tax bearable; home owners, and to some extent tenants in high-tax cities and towns had been spared the full brunt of the tax load.

There were two fundamental reasons for inaction. First was the separation of authority and responsibility between state and local government. Only the legislature has authority to open new tax sources for municipal use or through distribution of state-collected taxes to lighten the burden of local taxation. But aggrieved local taxpayers tended to look first to their city and town halls. Thus, taxpayer complaints were commonly misdirected to local officials.

Second was the open-ended character of the property tax. Taxpayers had come to accept the constant progression of local tax rates. They seemed unready or unwilling to believe that new revenues from the state would help relieve the property tax load. To the disbelieving taxpayer, the choice seemed to lie between a sales tax or increased income taxes and no new taxes when in fact the inescapable alternative was still higher property taxes.

Need for reform in state-local fiscal relations becomes even clearer with a brief examination of some elements of the state aid programs in effect prior to 1966. Portions of certain state-imposed, state-collected taxes were distributed among cities and towns. The largest of these were on personal incomes and corporations. After aid was provided for many special programs from the local share of the income tax, the remainder was distributed on an equalized valuation basis.

Although it had merit originally, this basis of distribution had become completely inequitable since equalized valuations had no relationship to need. The equalized valuation list in use had been established in 1945 and had remained unchanged until 1963. A community with a higher proportion of the state's total equalized valuation got a higher proportion of income tax proceeds distributed on this basis. The new list, moreover, was only a partial updating, but even an up-to-date list would not have solved the basic problem since distribution on the equalized valuation basis just made the rich richer.

School foundation aid also came from the local share of the income tax, and the 1945 equalized valuation list was used as an element of fiscal capacity in the formula. Thus, a community like Boston was in a sense cheated in school foundation aid since the city no longer had the larger proportion of equalized valuation shown on the 1945 list. But at the same time, it got more than it should have of any tax proceeds distributed on an equalized valuation basis.

Outdated formulas also applied to distribution of basic taxes collected by the state from business and manufacturing corporations. The first $9 million of the corporation tax distributed went by law to certain cities and towns named in a tabulation established in 1935 and 1936. This allocation was designed to compensate the listed cities and towns for property tax losses resulting from the exemption of machinery of manufacturing corporations in 1935. Although the formula for the $9 million was based on the 1935 tax loss and was designed to soften the impact of temporary loss on industrial communities, it was frozen into the statutes permanently. The remainder of the corporation tax distribution — the bulk of it — was distributed on an equalized valuation basis. Thus, not only did the state use the old equalized valuation basis of distribution but also an out-dated machinery exemption formula.

It is to be expected that communities will receive various forms of financial assistance from the state, but it was with respect to certain details of state aid in Massachusetts that questions arose and criticisms ensued. The amount of state aid, the purposes for which it should be granted, and the basis on which it should be shared or distributed were among the more significant matters of concern. And with the overworked property tax and lack of local authority for levying other taxes, there was cause for concern.

The 1966 Solution

Five times between 1957 and 1965 Massachusetts Governors submitted measures to raise new revenue and revise state-local fiscal relations. One of these called for major changes in the personal income tax; others involved the sales tax. A 1962 referendum to amend the Massachusetts Constitution to permit the legislature to enact a graduated income tax was turned down 5 to 1. Massachusetts is restricted to a flat-rate income tax with the rate based on source—not amount—of income. In 1965, during the 12 months that the legislature was in session, the Governor kept submitting revenue bills with a sales tax as the base which kept being defeated by the legislature. However, the opposition was unable to gain support for an alternative program which increased the personal income tax. Finally, in 1966 a law was passed effective in April imposing a limited sales tax and a new room occupancy tax, and increasing several existing taxes.

The entire proceeds of the sales tax less collection costs will be distributed to cities and towns. In 1967 when the full benefit of the tax program will be received by the cities and towns, an estimated $150 million of new revenue will be available for distribution. The sales tax exempts both food and clothing. Moreover, it allows credits in cash or against the personal income tax as offsets to the sales tax to low-income families with taxable incomes below $5,000.

Although the new law was temporary and due to expire at the end of two years, the 1967 General Court made it permanent. The legislature is expected to act favorably on the bill. Clearly, the new program introduces some long needed fiscal reforms. It sets up a local aid fund from which most state distributions and grants-in-aid to the communities (except highway aid) will be paid. The estimates of state aid sent to the cities and towns in advance of actual distributions will be much more inclusive than in the past. The procedure by which the state estimates the full or equalized values of taxable property for each city and town is improved and communities dissatisfied with the Tax Commission's proposed values have the right to contest them.

The new law provides major new state aid for local schools on an equalizing formula geared to the financial needs and efforts of each community. It replaces the long outdated formula and substitutes an estimated eventual $120 million in foundation aid for the former total of about $40 million.

The new program, however, retains the out-of-date equalized valuations of the past for all purposes except school aid, and keeps the antiquated "machinery distribution" for part of the corporation excise. It also continues the practice of making a large distribution solely on the equalized valuation basis. This continued distribution tends to nullify the equalizing effect of school aid grants.

Basically, the new school aid formula reimburses cities and towns for a portion of their actual expenditures per pupil on a sliding scale. The theoretical rate of reimbursement is 35 per cent, increased or decreased mathematically according to the wealth of the community. If the value of local taxable property per school child is above the state average the percentage drops in proportion, but not below 15 per cent. If the value of property per child is below the state average, the percentage rises, but not above 75 per cent.

This reimbursement percentage will be computed annually for each city and town using the latest figures for number of children attending school, public or private (kindergarten through grade 12) and certified school expenditures, and the latest state fixed values of local property. To guard against reimbursement of extravagant spending, no reimbursement is to be allowed for school expenditures which exceed 110 per cent of the average statewide expenditure per pupil.

To insure the lowest spending communities of the minimal level of state support, towns which are spending less than 80 per cent of the average statewide expenditure per child will be reimbursed as if they were spending at 80 per cent of the average state rate.

The state will not reimburse for school lunches, transportation, capital improvements, or classes for which special grants-in-aid are given. Vocational schools were first included in reimbursable expenditures replacing the former special reimbursements for this purpose. The 1967 General Court, however, restored the former special reimbursement for vocational education. Receipts from the federal government or other sources will be subtracted from total spending to determine the reimbursable portion.

A final limitation is the amount of money actually available. Of total sales tax proceeds, 80 per cent is allocated to school aid. Should this amount be less than the amount required to meet the formula, the amount payable to each city and town will be reduced proportionately.

The remaining 20 per cent of the sales tax proceeds also goes into the local aid fund but will be used to help pay for existing or new programs, or to be distributed on an equalized valuation basis. The entire proceeds of the personal income tax are also put into the local aid fund, as well as a portion of the corporation and meals taxes. These taxes, along with 20 per cent of the sales tax, will also be used to fund the existing and new programs and to be distributed on an equalized valuation basis. Equalized valuations in this case, however, means those last established by the legislature in 1963 which were only a partial updating of 1945 lists. These distributions will be inequitable unless the lists are brought up-to-date and kept so annually.

The Outlook

Support for the 1966 sales tax law came from several sources: those promoting more spending for local education; those seeking state aid for local services for which little or no state aid had been available; and those wanting new revenue to reduce or at least stabilize local property taxes. These seemingly contradictory purposes may be responsible for renewing the revenue crisis in a fairly short time.

There will continue to be demands that the new school foundation aid which goes into local general revenue funds be used to increase spending substantially for local elementary and secondary education. New school costs may result from the new and strengthened powers of the State Department of Education. The Department's power to establish standards such as pupil-teacher/administrator ratios could result in substantial cost hikes, especially in Boston.

Mandatory collective bargaining for teachers will further raise local costs above and beyond those normally resulting from school-community fiscal relationships. Teachers' salaries account for the major part of school budgets. Thus, significantly higher salaries and school costs can be expected. Until local communities get experience in bargaining, they will merely react to union proposals rather than offer their own. Inevitably, this lack of experience will further contribute to cost increases.

As Massachusetts finds it needs more revenue for its own purposes, it may well turn to diverting tax proceeds that go into the local aid fund. The personal income tax which has grown rapidly each year would be the logical source to which the state would turn. Under the 1966 tax law, the entire proceeds of the personal income tax went into the local aid fund. The 1967 General Court increased the personal income tax, among others, and allocated part of the increase for the State's General Fund. Equalized valuations as a distribution basis should eventually be eliminated, either through use of funds for particular programs or just as a reform measure.

The big question is how long the growth in tax proceeds going into the local aid fund will match local cost increases. It is estimated that by 1969 at the latest local property tax rates will begin to rise significantly again and that cries for changes in the state-local fiscal relationship will resume.

As local tax rates start to increase again and as the local aid fund becomes inadequate to meet rising local costs, it is expected that new revenue proposals will be offered. These will either include elimination of some of the sales tax exemptions or movement to a graduated personal income tax. The latter is more likely. Already one joint session of the legislature has approved a constitutional amendment that would permit a graduated income tax based on a percentage of the federal income tax. A graduated income tax measure could become law by 1969.

Local Public Schools

Of all the issues the most important in preventing Boston's decline is improving the school system. Rebuilding the image of quality education, replacing school plant and equipment, and complying with the racial imbalance law will continue to pose difficulties. Although Boston has provided its own funds for compensatory education programs and is spending its full allotment of funds available under the Federal Elementary and Secondary Education Act (ESEA), it will have to innovate and experiment even more with programs and with teacher salaries in order to bring about change.

The racial imbalance law complicates the Boston school problems. The School Committee at first failed to submit an acceptable plan to the state for dealing with imbalance. As a result, school foundation aid was withheld from Boston in 1966. A School Department plan was finally accepted early in 1967 and withheld funds were released.

The city's school building program was also held up since no state school building assistance can be given unless a racial balancing plan has been approved. The racial imbalance law provides state aid for 65 per cent of approved building costs where new buildings help to relieve imbalance.

The constitutionality of the law has been upheld. Thus Boston will have to submit plans annually for approval showing progress toward full compliance with the law. Such plans might include bussing, new district lines and new buildings. Disapproval of plans by state officials in any year could again result in withheld state aid.

Yet, there is considerable doubt that any plan or solution that calls for Boston to resolve imbalance within its own borders will be a lasting one. Thus, proposals for a metropolitan solution, i.e., a metropolitan school district, will continue to be made, and could be adopted.

The seeds of one such solution have already been planted. An experimental and voluntary metropolitan program of bussing is underway. A new private organization funded by federal ESEA monies and private foundations is transporting some 220, mainly low-income, non-white,

Boston children to seven suburban communities. The program should grow, at least as long as no local funds are required.

Other Issues

Demands on local revenue will continue for new, improved, or increased services. For example, with the concern over increasing crime both in the inner-ring and suburban communities, there will be increasing demands for better and more police protection. Yet, communities now have trouble retaining officers, as well as recruiting new ones. One solution emphasized by local officials is higher salaries.

The same is true with fire protection. In the metropolitan area with its many individual fire departments and hundreds of fire companies, many have inadequate personnel to handle working fires without off-shift personnel and mutual aid response. Again, higher salaries will be offered as an answer.

But improvement of recruiting and training must accompany pay increases. In the final analysis, a regional answer should be sought. It can be expected that new studies will stress such a response and that even suggestions for state aid for such specific functions will grow. Any state aid must recognize the special costs of such functions in the central city.

The heavy local burden of public welfare will be one of the first assumed by Massachusetts. Beginning July 1, 1968, the state will be responsible for the administration and financing of welfare. Personal income and corporation tax increases passed in 1967 will be used to pay for the present local share of welfare costs. Boston will be a major beneficiary; it will be relieved of costs of $17-$20 million.

Pressure should continue for state responsibility for total county costs, especially court costs, and many revenue proposals of the past have contained these provisions. The chances are much better for state assumption of court costs. If local aid funds are large enough, this reform can be expected in fairly short time, using funds that would have been returned to communities on an equalized valuation basis. Should local aid funds be insufficient, a much longer range solution—one dependent upon new revenue—will be inevitable.

Sewerage will become a major problem for communities now operating with individual septic tanks and cesspool systems. As the population increases, health considerations alone will force establishment of town sewerage systems and a tie-in with the Metropolitan District Commission's system. Even with present federal aid programs, a new sewerage system for smaller communities will be a major expense.

The problem of solid waste management will soon become one of major proportions for the entire Standard Metropolitan Statistical Area. The scarcity of dump space means that a regional system for handling solid waste must be found. A major study now underway by the Metropolitan Area Planning Council should provide an answer. One new method which may be adopted would call for hauling waste to the docks, loading it aboard ships to be hauled out to sea, incinerated, and then dumped in designated holes in the ocean floor.

The inability of communities in the inner core, and especially Boston, to build housing for low-income families has become and will continue to be a major problem. Boston's massive urban renewal program has removed many of the units which once housed low-income families. The new housing that has been created has been for high- and middle-income families. Even nonprofit and church groups, using existing federal aids, have produced middle-income units.

Given Boston's income and substandard housing data, the need for many units of new housing for low-income families, as well as for conserving and restoring existing housing, is evident.

A special state commission on low-income housing considered this problem in 1965 and many of its proposals have been enacted into law. They are designed to give financial incentive to low-income housing construction and to offer more flexible housing programs than are now available.

But as long as most low-income families remain in the core city, the attitude of many will be that low-income housing is a problem to be solved by the central city. Financial and other incentives, state and federal, could well be refused by other communities, since it could be in their best interests to do so. Creation of new low-income units in Boston would tend to attract more low-income families, thus continuing the need. Therefore, it would appear that a state-mandated solution on a regional basis is among the longer range prospects. The willingness of some suburbs to accept students from Boston's low-income families in their schools lends some degree of probability to this solution.

Beyond Local Capacity

Practically all of the problems discussed are beyond the capacity of any one or even several of the cities and towns to deal with, even if they had the fiscal capacity.

Money—its source and its control—will plague communities as it has in the past. Property taxes will remain the bulwark of local general revenue. Many vital services will have to be administered on a regional or state-wide basis. Boston, a core city that requires more and costlier services will continue to require special state attention.

Granting Boston special authorization to levy its own income and sales taxes will be debated. But in the small, compact, densely populated, geographical area of the SMSA, Boston would benefit more from state-levied, state-shared taxes, and much less from the power to levy its own.

Finally, it can be expected that the state will continue to play a dominant role in local affairs. The limited home rule powers recently obtained by cities and towns are welcome but do not include the power to solve the issues of the future. Thus, the state's role must be more positive, and no doubt it will be.

Lessons of Experience

It is difficult to point to lessons learned from the

experience of the Boston SMSA that can be useful to other metropolitan areas. The duration and intensity of the issues and the characteristics of each SMSA differ throughout the country.

However, Boston's experience does prove the old saw about an idea whose time has come. The two biggest issues in the Boston SMSA for many years were public transportation and new revenue. There were many studies of both subjects, much debate, and almost annual legislative bills for solution. Finally, in 1964 and 1966, legislation was enacted to attempt resolution of the issues. Why?

The mass transportation problem began to strike home in communities outside the transit district as well as becoming increasingly burdensome to those in the transit district. With the commuter railroads petitioning to go out of business and the public transit system deficit severely affecting local property tax rates, executive, legislative, and community leadership and support crystallized. The time was right, the plan was right, and the effort was right.

In the case of the revenue issue, the population increase and the demand for services in communities outside the central city area began to make their property taxes as intolerable as they were in Boston and inner-ring cities and towns. As court decisions and citizen action brought property revaluations, the situation worsened. Moreover, Massachusetts faced a revenue deficit of its own.

Again, executive, legislative, and community support materialized. It was no longer a question of whether a new revenue source was needed, but what revenue plan would be accepted. With the heavy dependence already on property, income and corporation taxes, the sales tax was the obvious new source. Despite party differences between the chief executive and the majority of the legislature, a revenue plan was agreed upon and enacted.

There is increasing recognition that the remaining issues are beyond the capacity of local communities alone to resolve. Attitudes about the problems of the central city reflected in suburban antagonism to Boston are beginning to change as a result. The willingness of seven school systems to accept low-income, non-white pupils from Boston is encouraging, and more communities are expected to participate in this attempt to deal with racial imbalance.

But even with incentives, the nature of most problems and the characteristics of the SMSA show the need for regional solutions with the state providing the direction and most of the funds.

LOUISVILLE:

Intergovernmental Reforms for Fiscal Progress

Roy W. Bahl

Post Doctoral Fellow
in Urban Economics

Syracuse University

92.

Louisville finds it difficult to finance its public services because of severe state restrictions imposed on its revenue raising power—and because its citizens rebel at having their taxes raised. This has adversely affected the city's school system (although reforms have recently been initiated). This study documents the difficulties in overcoming local government fragmentation and in planning for area-wide public services. Normal difficulties in these fields are compounded in the Louisville metropolitan area, because it straddles two states. But interstate cooperation— and the cooperation and consolidation of local governments —have speeded progress in planning and providing for area-wide services.

Without the substantial intergovernmental reforms which have taken place in the last five years in the Louisville Standard Metropolitan Statistical Area (SMSA), the fiscal position of that metropolitan area would be most critical. Among these reforms are (a) state action which has made the property tax a more viable source of local revenue; (b) elimination of disparities between city and county governments in their ability to finance services, which has resulted in a redistribution of functional responsibility among these local units; (c) broader use of a local occupational license tax; (d) some governmental consolidation and other movements toward area-wide financing and administration; (e) use of special financing arrangements to meet the immediate problems of extending adequate networks of sanitary sewers into the county; and (f) new machinery to insure a greater amount of interstate (Indiana and Kentucky) cooperation among local governments in the metropolitan area.

Distribution of Population and Local Government

Louisville is the central city of a two-state, tri-county SMSA of approximately 750,000 inhabitants. Table 1 shows the high concentration of this population in Jefferson County together with the relative distribution and growth rates of the population for the three counties and the City of Louisville. The table indicates that, while there was no significant change among counties in relative size over the decade, a significant redistribution of population did occur within Jefferson County.

The structure of local government within the metropolitan area is highly fragmented (see Table 2). The SMSA contains 129 local governments of which 105 have property taxing power, while 60 of 69 local governments in Jefferson County have the power to tax property. Including the City of Louisville, Jefferson County is overlapped by 49 municipalities, of which only eleven have populations in excess of a thousand.

Table 1   **Distribution of Population Within Louisville SMSA**

	1966	1960	Per Cent Increase 1960-1966
Jefferson County, Kentucky	83.6%	84.2%	9.5%
(Louisville Central City)	(48.8)	(53.9)	(−0.1)
Floyd County, Indiana	7.0	7.1	9.2
Clark County, Indiana	9.3	8.7	18.8
TOTAL SMSA			9.4%

SOURCE: U.S. Bureau of the Census, *Census of Population 1960* (Washington, D.C.: U.S. Government Printing Office); and Louisville Chamber of Commerce.

Table 2   **Distribution of Local Government Within Louisville SMSA**

	Jefferson County (Ky.)	Clark County (Ind.)	Floyd County (Ind.)	Total
All types, total	69	42	18	129
(With property taxing)	(60)	(34)	(11)	(105)
Municipal	49	5	3	57
(With population less than 1000)	(38)	(1)	(2)	(41)
County	1	1	1	3
Township	0	12	5	17
School districts	3	14	1	18
Special districts	16	10	8	34
(With property taxing power)	(7)	(2)	(1)	(10)

SOURCE: U.S. Bureau of the Census, *Local Government in Metropolitan Areas: Census of Governments: 1962,* Vol. V (Washington, D.C.: U.S. Government Printing Office, 1965).

Table 3   **Central City-Suburb Disparities**

	Louisville (Central City)	Jefferson County (Outside Central City)	Jefferson County (Total)
GENERAL POPULATION CHARACTERISTICS:			
Population (1966)	390,100	278,000	668,100
Population growth rate (1960-1966)	−0.1%	26.3%	n.a.
Mean income level (1960)	$6128	n.a.	$6831
Median school years completed (1966)	9.3	n.a.	9.9
Median value of owner occupied dwelling units (1960)	$10,400	n.a.	$11,800
POVERTY INDICATORS:			
Total welfare recipients (1965)	18,817	1,922	20,739
AFDC families (1965)	3,287	225	3,512
AFDC children (1965)	10,109	717	10,826
Per capita arrests (1966)	0.033	0.017	n.a.
Per capita juvenile arrests (1966)	0.017	0.005	n.a.
PER CAPITA CURRENT EXPENDITURES (1965):			
Police	$12.65	$6.41	$10.05
Fire	10.46	n.a.	6.09
Health	7.92	9.58	8.71
Streets	4.74	4.45	4.62
Sanitation	5.68	6.17	5.88

Central City-Suburb Disparities

Louisville affords an excellent example of the stereo-type central city-suburb[1] relationship (see Table 3). The core city is suffering population stagnation while the suburbs are growing rapidly. Income levels and housing values are substantially lower in the central city. These data also show wide central city-suburb disparities in the level of poverty (as measured by welfare case loads) and in the incidence of crime.

Finally, the fiscal data included in Table 3 indicate that per capita expenditures in the central city for certain func-

---

[1] Suburbs are defined here to include only that area outside the Louisville central city in Jefferson County, Kentucky. Where data are available, the Clark and Floyd County, Indiana areas are also considered.

tions (Police, Streets, Fire) are higher than in the outlying area. This results at least partially from two factors: (a) the drain on city services created by nonresident commuting into the central city to place of employment, to shopping facilities, to the University of Louisville, etc.; and (b) the higher incidence of poverty in the central city which requires a high per resident cost to provide acceptable levels of certain types of public services.[2]

Disparities Within the Central City

In addition to central city-suburb differences, there are broad disparities in the level of economic well-being within the Louisville central city area. Louisville's Model City program is designed to reduce these disparities through redevelopment of the worst slum area of the city. This area (which contains 39 per cent of the city population) contains 95 per cent of all central city nonwhites. One-third of its 40,000 families have incomes below $3,000; over half the housing units are sub-standard; the infant death rate is one-third higher than for the city as a whole; the unemployment rate is 50 per cent higher; and the percentage of persons receiving welfare is double the city-wide rate. The data in Table 4 show these disparities in more detail.

The original Model City proposal was a five-year plan designed to remake approximately one-fourth of the central city. But this was reduced by approximately three-fourths by the Department of Housing and Urban Development. Louisville's proposal called for the development and improvement of educational, vocational, health, recreational, cultural, and social services in the Model City area. Great emphasis was placed on developing multipurpose educational, health, and community centers. However, Louisville was not one of the 63 cities chosen in the first round of the Model Cities program.

---

[2] A third possibility is that these statistical data are distorted by either interlocal differences in the degree of public and private provision of services, e.g., garbage collection, or by inaccurate measurement. It is especially difficult to estimate the level of public spending by the 50 small municipalities located in Jefferson County.

In addition, there are six Urban Renewal Projects presently in execution and two in the planning phase — involving both clearance and rehabilitation and covering about one-fifth of the area. The area presently contains 4,990 units of low-rent public housing while 305 additional units for the elderly are now being constructed.

Table 4 **Disparities Within the Louisville Central City: 1965**

	City Total	Model Neighborhood Total	Model Neighborhood Total as a Per Cent of City Total
Substandard housing units	35,900	27,590	76.9%
Per cent of persons 25 and over with less than 8 years of education	24.2	33.2	—
Infant deaths as a per cent of births per year	2.5	3.2	—
Per cent of males 14 and over who are unemployed	6.4	9.3	—
Per cent of persons under 21 receiving AFDC payments	6.9	12.4	—
Number of juvenile arrests	6,665	4,250	63.8
Nonwhite population	78,327	73,982	94.5
Number of families with incomes less than $3,000	21,717	13,545	62.4

SOURCE: University of Louisville Urban Studies Center.

State Actions to Relieve Fiscal Pressures on Local Government

The state government in Kentucky has provided a partial solution to the fiscal problems of the Louisville metropolitan area through action taken at a special session of the state legislature in September 1965. The special session was called to consider two major problems: (1) The State Court of

Appeals had ordered one year earlier that all property in the state be assessed at 100 per cent of fair market value, instead of the existing median state ratio of 27 per cent (34 to 38 per cent in Jefferson County). (2) The Jefferson County school systems were facing a serious financial crisis after local residents had twice defeated proposals to raise additional revenues for the education function.

Property Tax

The Kentucky statutes limit the property tax rate of all school districts and cities to $1.50 per $100 of assessed valuation, and the rate of county governments to $.50 per $100 of assessed valuation. Since property was assessed at approximately one-third of full value prior to the court decision, effective property tax rates of local governments in the Louisville SMSA varied roughly between $.50 and $.17 and there existed no upward flexibility in these rates.

The court ordered local assessors to inflate assessed valuation by the reciprocal of the existing assessment ratio (e.g., 2.63 is the reciprocal of a 38 per cent assessment ratio). At the same time, local governments were ordered to reduce property tax rates by the same multiple, so that the property tax yield would be the same before and after the 100 per cent ruling. Local units would then have the option of raising the rate, provided that the estimated yield from the property tax would not increase by more than 10 per cent. Both the Louisville City and Jefferson County school districts, and the Louisville city government exercised this option in 1966, while the Jefferson County government did not choose to increase rates. The same 10 per cent maximum yield increment is in effect for 1967. What action the local units will be allowed to take on property tax rates after 1967 has not been decided at this writing.

The effects of this court decision on local finances in the Louisville area may be seen from the data in Tables 5 and 6 which indicate the actual increments in assessed value and tax rates.

Table 5   **Effects of 100 Per Cent Assessment on**
Assessed Valuations in Jefferson County
(in dollars)

	Louisville (Central City)	Jefferson County (Outside Central City)	Jefferson County (Total)
Total assessed valuation			
1966	1,595,525,750	1,528,207,600	3,123,733,350
1965	535,002,240	504,262,059	1,039,264,299
1964	529,518,760	472,563,000	1,002,081,760
Per capita assessed value			
1966	4,090	5,497	4,669
1965	1,373	1,849	1,569
1964	1,361	1,807	1,540
Average annual rate of increase in total assessed valuation			
1957-1965	0.021	0.055	0.042
1965-1966	1.980	2.030	2.005

Table 6   **Effect of 100 Per Cent Assessment on**
Actual Property Tax Rates in Jefferson County

	Actual Rate 1965 per $100	Actual Rate 1966 per $100
City of Louisville	$1.50	$0.501
City school district	$1.50	$0.547
Jefferson County	$0.50	$0.171
County school district	$1.50	$0.570

Occupational Tax

A second purpose of the special legislative session of 1965 was to consider the problem of financing education in the Louisville Metropolitan Area. The result of the session was that the legislature authorized school districts to impose an occupational license fee, not to exceed one-half of 1 per cent of (a) salaries, wages, commissions, and other compensations earned by persons within the county; and (b) the net profits of all businesses, trades, occupations, and professions, for activities conducted within the county. The revenues are to be shared by the two school districts in proportion to the number of pupils in average daily attendance.

This license tax (at a rate of 1.25 per cent) has been levied by the Louisville city government since 1949 and by the Jefferson County government since 1961 and accounts for over one-fourth of all general revenues of both the city and the county. In all cases the revenue collection is administered by a Sinking Fund Commission.

Workers employed within the city are not subject to the county tax and in cases where income is earned in both the city and county the tax is prorated between the units. Employees whose residence is not in Jefferson County are exempted from the levy for the education function.

Financing Education in Louisville-Jefferson County

The educational system of the area is administered primarily by an independent city school district and an independent county school district whose boundaries are not coterminous with the incorporated city limits. There is a third, relatively small independent school district, operating in the municipality of Anchorage which is located in Jefferson County. Enrollment in parochial schools in both the central city and in Jefferson County outside the central city is considerable; in 1966 approximately 33 per cent of enrollment in the central city was in parochial schools while the corresponding figure for Jefferson County outside the central city was about 21 per cent.

As suggested above, the problems of financing education had reached a critical level by 1965. The consequences of local voter resistance to alternative solutions was a gradual worsening of the quality of education offered students in both the city and county school systems.

Quality of the Program

In 1952 the City of Louisville school district was spending $279 per pupil, $23 above the national average — but in 1964, it spent $298 per pupil, $69 below the national average. The expenditures of the Jefferson County school system were $63 per pupil below the national average in 1964.

The acuteness of the problem in the city system evolved primarily from a level of current funds insufficient either to carry out an adequate program of services or to pay competitive teachers' salaries. The extent of the financial difficulties was such that in 1956 the city system eliminated kindergartens, reduced visiting teacher services, cut the city-wide remedial reading staff to one specialist, limited building maintenance and curtailed the allotment of school supplies. Among the first results of the diminished quality of services were an increase in dropouts and a doubling of first grade failures after the abandonment of city kindergartens.

While the problem of the city schools was deficient current revenues, the county schools were plagued by insufficient funds for necessary expansions of the physical plant. In 1963, 5,800 county students were on double sessions. The number grew to 19,000 in 1964 and at that time was projected to grow to about 49,000 or 60 per cent of the total county enrollment by 1970. Consequently, the county elementary schools were not accredited in 1965 and the high schools faced the loss of accreditation because of overcrowding and inadequate library facilities.

School District Financing

The Kentucky statutes limit the property tax rate of all school districts to $1.50 per $100 of assessed valuation. In 1965, this had the effect of limiting the school districts to approximately $.50 per $100 of full valuation of property within the taxing jurisdiction. Both the city and county districts were at the $1.50 rate limit, making an increase in property tax revenues possible only with the consent of the voters by general referendum. In 1952 each system was voted a special building tax of $.50 per $100 of assessed valuation, to be used exclusively for the financing of capital improvements. This building tax will terminate in 1972.

Aid to the school districts under the state minimum foundation program has represented an increasing proportion of school district receipts, presently constituting approximately 40 per cent of all revenues for the two systems combined. In the period 1956-1966, the ratio of state to local support of each of the Louisville and Jefferson County school systems more than doubled.

Alternative Solutions

Twice between 1962 and 1965, the city and county school boards went to the voters with proposals to increase revenues, and on each occasion the proposals were defeated.

In November 1963, the city school board proposed a two-fold program to meet the revenue deficiency. First, the special building tax would have been reduced from $.50 to $.25 per $100 of assessed valuation, but the termination date of the program would be extended from 1972 to 1997. This measure was proposed to enable the school board to continue its program of financing capital improvements through revenue bonds. Second, the board proposed the authorization of a new tax for general school purposes at a rate of $.64 per $100 of assessed valuation. In total the two measures would have resulted in a net rate increase of $.39. The referendum was defeated 2 to 1 in the city, just as a similar proposal by the county had been defeated 3 to 1 only seven months earlier.

Again in 1964 the school boards offered the voters a solution to the fiscal problem. This revenue program would have given both the city and county school districts authority to levy an occupational tax with a rate up to 3 per cent. Further, it provided for a property tax increase of $.32 per $100 of assessed valuation. This plan would have increased revenues by $3.7 million in the county and $4.2 million in the city, but again the referendum was defeated. A public opinion survey revealed general discontent with the quality of the fiscal management of the school districts. It revealed, further, a strong feeling that the existence of two school districts spawned inefficiency through duplication of functions, and that consolidation should therefore be considered.

Three other possible solutions to the Louisville school fiscal crisis, involving local resources, were suggested. The first proposal was for a 1 per cent county-wide occupational license to be used exclusively for the education function. (This would be in addition to the existing 1.25 per cent countywide occupational license, none of the funds of which is currently used for school purposes.) This proposal would produce an additional $14 million per year to be distributed between the school districts on the basis of distribution of students — not on the basis of contribution from each district. A second proposal would require a legislative act to permit the school boards to increase the property tax rate above the present statutory limit of $1.50. Still within the purview of local resources, the revenue problem could be alleviated by a legislative act permitting the county, by referendum of the voters, to impose a sales tax not to exceed 1 per cent. This tax would be collected by the state (which presently has a 3 per cent sales tax) and returned to the school districts on the basis of average daily attendance. School districts using this method of financing would continue to be limited to the present property tax rate ceiling of $1.50.

Of these three possibilities for increasing school tax receipts from local sources, the alternative involving an increment in the property tax rate above the legal limit appeared to be the least feasible (without constitutional revision) because of strong public sentiment against any adjustment in the property tax rate. The sales tax alternative is less satisfactory than the occupational tax because (a) it would produce less revenue, (b) it would be more difficult to administer, and (c) it would be strongly opposed by labor. The primary criticism of the occupational tax was the questionable legality of this method of raising additional revenues for education and the legal problems of devising a method of distributing proceeds between the two districts.

County officials suggested yet another method of coping with the fiscal problem of the county schools. The plan called for Jefferson County to pay $700,000 a year in rent to the school system for use of school buildings and playgrounds in the county recreation program. The school board would then spend the $700,000 to underwrite 25 year bonds for construction of new schools and additions to existing buildings, thereby eliminating double sessions within two years. The county government proposed to raise the money through an across-the-board cut in the county's next annual budget. This plan has many serious drawbacks: (1) Community action would be required to provide funds for equipment and increased operating expenses. (2) The plan does not provide for the salary raises which would be needed to attract new teachers to the system. (3) The bond issue would have to be approved by the state Department of Education. (4) A buyer for the bonds, at some reasonable interest rate, would have to be procured.

It was proposed that the state government could aid in alleviating the school finance problem either by sharing an existing state tax, or by legislative actions which would enable local governments to solve the crisis. The state could authorize an increment of 1 per cent in the existing 3 per cent state sales tax. If the receipts from this surtax were distributed among the school districts in the state on the same basis as present state aids to education, the combined revenues to the two school districts would total about $6.5 million as compared with $14 million from the proposed 1 per cent occupational tax. An alternative to the state-wide rate increase is a bill sanctioning the application of the present sales tax to services now exempted—thus diverting a portion of the revenue to school use.

State Action

As described above, the special session of 1965 resulted in a 100 per cent assessment of property with a compensating reduction in rates, and the authorization of a county-wide occupational tax for education purposes. This state action is a first step in the long-run solution to the problems of financing education in the Louisville SMSA.

Though property tax rates were ordered reduced to compensate for the full value assessment, local governments were permitted to readjust rates so that revenues could be increased by 10 per cent. Local governments may also elect to take a 10 per cent increment in revenues during the second year, but no decision has been made as to the long-run restrictions on rate increments.[3]

The school boards were authorized to impose a county-wide occupational tax not to exceed one-half of 1 per cent, and to divide the proceeds of this tax on the basis of average daily attendance. This source of revenue for the education function was given to school systems in any Kentucky county having more than 300,000 residents.[4]

Financing Sewage Disposal in Louisville-Jefferson County

Inadequate sewage disposal—both the servicing of existing residential development and the extension of the city system into undeveloped sections—has been a growing problem in Jefferson County for years. Many areas were originally developed with septic tanks which have experienced notable failure, while other municipalities within the county but outside the Metropolitan Sewer District are finding problems not satisfactorily solved even though they provide treatment plants or distribution systems. These limited facilities have in some cases been rapidly outgrown, uncoordinated, and poorly maintained and operated. Sewage from malfunctioning septic tanks and small treatment plants has, in some instances, discharged into ditches and gutters of built-up areas, creating hazards to the health of the community and odor that becomes a public nuisance. An ultimate result is devaluation of property in these areas. In addition to these adverse effects on public health and quality of

---

[3] These 10 per cent revenue increments are over and above the "natural" increase in the property tax base.

[4] Fayette County (Lexington) is the second largest in the state, having less than 200,000 residents.

service, there are considerable disparities in the cost of services, as the rate assessed in suburban areas is usually higher than that in the central city. Finally, the topographic features of certain parts of the county have resulted in a county board of health prohibition of the use of septic tanks in these areas. Therefore, inadequate disposal facilities may have had a dampening effect on the rate of suburban expansion into undeveloped areas around the city of Louisville.

However, in the past two years the Louisville Metropolitan Sewer District (MSD) has taken steps to remedy these problems. The MSD now maintains and operates 37 of the smaller treatment plants in the county. This has substantially raised the quality of service in these suburban areas and has reduced the wide service level variations among suburban units. Disposal facilities have been extended into certain of the county areas where the prohibition of septic tanks had stymied urban expansion. In addition, a consolidation of water districts in Jefferson County has resulted in a reduction of water and sewer rates outside the central city, though county rates still exceed those in the central city.

Extending the Existing System

The maintenance, operation, and extension of sewer facilities are the responsibility of the Louisville and Jefferson County Metropolitan Sewer District. Approximately 90 per cent of operating revenues of the MSD are derived from metered service charges of the Louisville Water Company.

The effectiveness of the MSD has been limited by restrictions placed on its powers in areas beyond the Louisville city limits. Prior to 1964 legislation, the Metropolitan Sewer District was limited to contracting for sewer extensions into unincorporated areas of the county. In order to make feasible an extension (which would be financed by special assessments), full financial participation by the property owners was needed. Thus, a minority in a given area could effectively block an attempt to extend the city sewer system.

A 1964 bill, drafted by legislators of both parties, author-izes the MSD to set up construction subdistricts and build sewers within the confines of those areas. The extensions are to be financed by revenue bonds tied to user rentals and charges in the subdistrict. The bill provides for alternative methods of financing: (a) sewer assessments based on either area or assessed valuation, and (b) payment to the sewer district by the subdivider who in turn passes the cost on to home buyers. Placing the initiative and the burden of the cost on the benefited parties removes the objections of central city residents who have reacted against suggestions of area-wide financing of extensions of the existing system into the county.

Since 1965, 23 construction subdistricts have been created in Jefferson County to finance the extension of sewage disposal facilities. These subdistricts have been utilized generally in the construction of sewer trunks while the subdividers have constructed the laterals.

While the construction subdistrict is created to facil-itate financing of sewer laterals and trunks, the 1964 bill also provides another method for financing the extension of more costly trunk sewers into various watersheds, and the con-struction of needed treatment plants. It enables the creation of sanitation tax districts with the authority to levy a property tax to finance this more costly phase of the program.

A recent study of county needs estimates a cost of ap-proximately $280 million to sewer the county adequately, with over half of this amount needed for the construction of costly trunks and new treatment plants. This need offers a test of the effectiveness of the 1964 legislation in providing a method of financing the county-wide program. While the issuance of revenue bonds tied to user-charges in the con-struction subdistricts appears to be an adequate method of financing the construction of laterals and some trunks, the use of the sanitation tax district is likely to be an ineffective way of financing the more costly trunks and treatment plants, primarily because of voter opposition. Conceivably, a home could lie within the taxing jurisdiction of both a construction subdistrict and a sanitation tax district and thus would be subject to the charges of both.

An alternative to the tax district method is the issuance of a general obligation bond by the county. The feasibility of this alternative is limited by two factors: (1) A county general obligation bond requires approval of two-thirds of the voters. The strong objections of city voters to paying for county sewers suggests that passage would be improbable. (2) General obligation debt of Kentucky counties is limited to 2 per cent of total assessed valuation, or in the case of Jefferson County, approximately $24 million.[5] Thus, county debt would seemingly provide an inadequate source of financing a project of this magnitude.

Future Planning

While the ultimate aim of the Metropolitan Sewer District is a county-wide, fiscally integrated system, the immediate objective is the extension of sanitary sewers in the county. In accordance with these goals, these general policy objectives have been established: (a) that all existing sewer systems outside Louisville be acquired by the Metropolitan Sewer District, (b) that sewers be extended into the county in accordance with a long-range land use and development plan, and (c) that advance planning should begin for financing two large treatment plants.

The first of these objectives has been accomplished during the past two years in the sense that the MSD has assumed, by contractual arrangement, the operation and maintenance of 37 county sewer systems. The potential for achieving the second of these objectives is greatly enhanced by the creation of 23 construction subdistricts during the past two years. However, there remains the problem of finding a method for financing the costly capital improvements necessary to sewer the county properly and simultaneously to construct an adequate drainage system.

---

[5] How the full valuation of property will affect debt limits has not yet been determined.

Shift of Functions Between City and County

Prior to 1960, the City of Louisville had been saddled with responsibility for a number of what might ordinarily be county government functions. The basic reason for this division of financial responsibility was the limited fiscal abilities of the county. The primary source of revenue was the property tax, the rates of which are limited by the state constitution to $.50 per $100 of assessed valuation — a ceiling which was reached by the county government more than a decade ago.

Though receipts from the property tax did increase substantially over the decade because of a rapid increase in population outside the central city, there remained a need for additional funds. Consequently, in 1959 the county enacted a 1.25 per cent business and occupational license tax to be administered along with that of the city by the Sinking Fund Commission. Workers employed within the city are not subject to the county tax and, in cases where income is earned in both the city and county, the tax is prorated between the units. Table 7 shows the relative importance of the occupational license tax as a source of revenue in both the city and the county.

As a result of the increased revenues of the county government from the occupational license, there occurred a shift in the degree to which the city and county shared in the financing of certain functions. The county immediately assumed major responsibility for the local welfare function, and the county appropriation to the University of Louisville rose from $40,000 in 1961 to $570,400 by 1963. Similarly, the county appropriation for the City-County Board of Health and Public Libraries increased by a significant amount.

Table 7 **Occupational License and Property Tax Revenues of Louisville City Government and Jefferson County Government: 1966** [a]

	Louisville City	Jefferson County
Occupational License Tax Collections:		
Total	$13,809,959	$6,482,260
Per capita	35.40	23.32[b]
Per cent of total revenue	.21[c]	.33[c]
Property Tax Collections:		
Total	9,209,342	5,596,500
Per capita	23.61	8.36
Per cent of total revenue	.39	.37

[a] Fiscal year.

[b] Per capita occupational license collections for county government are on a basis of population in Jefferson County but outside the Central City. For county government property taxes, the per capita base is the entire population of the county.

[c] The occupational license is administered and collected by the City of Louisville Sinking Fund and not all collections in a given year are transferred to the city and county general funds. Therefore, occupational license *revenues* as a per cent of total general revenues is lower than would be a comparable statistic computed on a basis of occupational license *collections*.

Consolidation and Merger

As noted in Table 2, the Louisville Standard Metropolitan Statistical Area is fragmented politically by 129 local governments (67 of which are located in Jefferson County). A comparison of Census of Governments statistics indicates a growth in this fragmentation over the 1957-1962 period.[6] These data reveal that Jefferson County was overlapped by 48 local governments in 1957, which means a net increase of 21 local units over the five-year period. Most of this increment was due to the creation of 15 incorporated municipalities (nine of which had 1957 populations of less than a thousand) outside the central city in Jefferson County.

In the very recent past, certain movements have been made toward consolidation and merger with respect to the

[6] U.S. Bureau of the Census, *Local Government in Standard Metropolitan Areas: 1957 Census of Governments,* Vol. I, No. 2 (Washington, D.C.: U.S. Government Printing Office, 1957) and U.S. Bureau of the Census, *Local Government in Metropolitan Areas: Census of Governments: 1962,* Vol. V (Washington, D.C.: U.S. Government Printing Office, 1965).

education and water supply in Jefferson County.

Up to 1965, the Louisville Water Company furnished a relatively high quality and low cost service to residents of the central city and some suburbs, while a number of small distributor systems in the suburbs furnished a generally lower quality service at higher rates. However, in the past two years, the Louisville Water Company has purchased the distributor systems in the county. Though this consolidation has probably resulted in a reduction of variations in the quality of services and in a reduction of water rates in the county, the rates remain lower inside than outside the central city area.

In addition to the fiscal problems which have plagued the school systems in Jefferson County, there are wide disparities in output and fiscal capacity between the city and county school systems. It has been suggested that reorganization of the county school system might partially correct these imbalances.[7]

Most of the disparities in question grow out of a difference in income level between the central city and the balance of the county. Income level and the value of housing units are lower in the central city and general levels of extreme poverty are higher (per capita welfare recipients outside the central city amount to 0.007 while the corresponding figure inside the central city is 0.048). In addition, the per cent of nonwhite population in the central city is approximately seven times that of the suburban areas.

The result of this imbalance is reflected in the output of the local school systems. In 1966, approximately 77 per cent of 9th graders were going on to complete high school in the county school system, while only 64.2 per cent were completing the 12th grade in the central city system; 51 per cent of the 1966 graduates of the county system entered college while only 35 per cent graduating from city schools did so; less than 1 per cent of 1965 graduates from county high schools are estimated to be unemployed while

---

[7] See *Preliminary Evaluation Report on Louisville and Jefferson County Public Schools,* University of Louisville Urban Studies Center, April 1967.

the estimate for central city graduates is over 9 per cent.[8] It would appear that these disparities have been accentuated rather than reduced by the state and local fisc. It may be seen that *both* per student revenues from local sources and per student state aids are higher outside the central city (see Table 8). However, these data also show that Louisville central city residents exert less fiscal effort than do residents outside the central city.

A merger of the school system would provide a method of reducing at least the fiscal disparities. Other opportunities for correcting the over-all imbalances are being presented to the community in the form of the Charter Committee for Reorganization via an "umbrella" system.[9] Under this arrangement, the consolidated district would be segmented into a small number of pie-shaped units with each wedge having its apex in the central city and extending into the county. A result of administrative units of this type could be a sharp reduction in racial and class imbalance in school enrollments within the SMSA, i.e., a given pie-shaped unit would include both the poor in the central city and the relatively affluent in the suburbs.

Table 8 **Public School Finances: Selected Statistics for 1966**

	Louisville City School District	Jefferson County School District
Average daily attendance	45,774	65,843
Per student assessed value	$12,430	$12,668
Effective tax rate	.542	.724
Per student state revenue	$154	$161
Per student local revenue	$209	$262

SOURCE: *Public School Financial Analysis,* Bureau of Administration and Finance, Kentucky Department of Education, October 1966.

[8] *Holding Power and Graduates,* Division of Research, State Department of Education, Frankfort, Kentucky, March 1967.

[9] *Preliminary Evaluation Report on Louisville and Jefferson County Public Schools, op. cit.,* p. 4.

Cooperation Among Local Governments

Because of the fragmented nature of local government in Jefferson County, Kentucky, and because the Louisville Standard Metropolitan Statistical Area lies partially in two Indiana counties (Clark and Floyd), the need for cooperation among local governments in the solution of urban problems is especially complex. However, much progress has been made since early 1965 in the cooperation among states and local governments in area-wide planning, and in the area-wide provision of certain public services.

Interstate Cooperation Among Local Governments

Even though the Kentucky and Indiana portions of the Louisville SMSA are physically separated by the Ohio River, the interaction is substantial and has important implications for the provision of public services. It is estimated that approximately 9 per cent of Jefferson County employees commute from the Indiana counties, while approximately 8 per cent of Clark County and 7 per cent of Floyd County employees reside in Jefferson County.[10] In addition to net in-commuting to place of employment, it is probable that there is a net inflow to the Kentucky side of the SMSA for other purposes—shopping, entertainment, commuting to the University of Louisville, etc.

These interactions suggest immediately that a major role to be played in the interstate cooperation of local governments is that of developing and coordinating an adequate transportation network. Highway departments of the two states have long had an agreement on the division of responsibility for the maintenance of the bridges over the Ohio River. A comprehensive metropolitan area transportation study is now underway, which has been jointly undertaken by local governments in the SMSA and the highway departments of the two states.

---

[10] Charles Garrison: *Intercounty Commuting in Kentucky,* Bureau of Business Research, University of Kentucky, Lexington, 1961.

For public functions other than transportation, the inter-action between the states has proceeded on an informal basis in such areas as law enforcement and fire fighting. Recently a more formal organization has been established to promote cooperation among local governments in the metropolitan area. The Falls of the Ohio Metropolitan Council of Govern-ments is a newly established organization having a broad mandate for study, planning, and action. Its organization is partially an outgrowth of a new federal requirement of com-prehensive regional planning on a metropolitan level as a prerequisite for continued and expanded grants to local communities. In this regard the function of the council is to serve in an advisory and coordinating capacity in evaluating and defining the planning need of an area, establishing policies in regard to the planning program, and designing a continuing planning program.

Cooperation Among Local Governments in the Jefferson County Area

The City of Louisville and Jefferson County govern-ments jointly finance a number of agencies providing area-wide services. Among these are the Youth Commission, the Public Libraries, an Air Pollution Control District, and a Department of Traffic Engineering. In almost all cases, the city government contribution is substantially larger. Sanitary sewage services are now provided on an area-wide basis; the Metropolitan Sewer District has assumed the maintenance and operation of 37 small treatment plants and distribution systems in the county. Ninety per cent of the MSD's operating revenues comes from user-charges.

Finally, new enabling legislation enacted by the 1966 Kentucky General Assembly will facilitate local planning programs and the coordination of joint local government long-range planning efforts. Basically, the act makes the establishment of regional and county-wide planning programs more feasible, defines the minimum requirements of a com-prehensive plan, and sets forth administrative and enforce-ment procedures and penalties.

Conclusions

The general conclusion to be drawn from the Louisville experience is that the solution to the local fiscal problem will require the resources of all levels of government. Moreover, the role of the state government is not only to supplement local revenues, but also to take whatever action is necessary to improve and coordinate the abilities of local governments to finance public services.

It is apparent that the fiscal ability of local units was adequate to resolve the serious financial crisis in education. However, state action was required to make the property tax an effective method of financing, and to authorize the use of revenues from an occupational license tax for education. In addition, the pressures on central city government revenues have been relieved substantially in recent years by increased revenues of the county government which resulted from the levy of a 1.25 per cent occupational license tax in the county. Therefore, in the Louisville case it may be concluded that local governments have used neither their own resources nor the property tax to their full potential.

On the other hand, there are major problems which face the Louisville area which, because of the magnitude of needs, may not be resolved entirely with local funds but may require state and federal assistance. The first of these is the transportation problem which is complicated by the fact that the SMSA lies in two states and is physically divided by the Ohio River. A metropolitan area transportation study is now underway to identify long-run needs and to suggest a plan for financing an adequate transportation network. The problem of planning for transportation is becoming particularly acute in the Jefferson County area with the increasing tendency of new firms to locate outside the central city, and for many existing firms to move to suburban or rural areas in the county. Regardless of the nature of the transportation plan much federal assistance will probably be needed.

A second problem facing the Jefferson County area involves developing an adequate sewer and drainage system.

Though special district financing methods have generally proven sufficient in the extension of the city sewer system into the county, the costs of enlarging central city facilities and constructing treatment plants are such that federal assistance will be required.

A third problem is the serious central city-suburb disparities which are largely a result of the decline of the core city. While the outlying areas have generally flourished with rapidly growing population, high and rising income levels, and growing tax bases, the central city has been losing population and is experiencing declining income and high poverty levels. Further, these imbalances may be self-perpetuating. For example, school dropout rates and the per cent of unemployed high school graduates are both higher in the central city than in the outlying areas of Jefferson County. The local fisc is such that per student revenues from local sources are higher in the county than in the central city. Moreover, state policy would appear to be accentuating rather than reducing these imbalances since per student state aids to the county school system are greater than those to the city school system. An additional factor which may work in the direction of creating a substantial fiscal disparity is the decentralization in the location of industry in the SMSA. This pattern of movement of firms results in denying the central city this industrial component of the property tax base, and also the proceeds from the occupational license which are collected at the place of employment rather than at the place of residence.

There would appear to be two factors which may result in reducing these disparities — the Model City proposal and a consolidation plan for the education system. The Model City proposal would reduce disparities by concentrating on redevelopment of the worst slum area in the central city with emphasis on the improvement of educational, vocational, health, recreational, cultural, and social services. Though local cooperation is needed, this program is to be financed primarily with federal money made available through the Department of Housing and Urban Development (HUD).

A second possibility for the long-run reduction in disparities involves consolidation of the local school systems and the formation of a small number of administrative units within the single school system. These smaller units would be wedge-shaped with the point in the central city and extending out into the county. Enrollment at high schools in these wedge-shaped units would then be a mixture of the central city poor and the wealthier from the suburbs. The long-run objective of this plan would be a reduction of racial and class imbalances. An additional result of school district consolidation would be the elimination of differences in the resources available for the central city and county educational function.

Federal-Local Relations

On the question of the future role of the federal government in assisting local units, the Louisville experience suggests that the major problem areas are those for which federal grant programs now exist, such as costs of improving the sewer and drainage system, the urban renewal and Model City programs, and the development of an adequate transportation system. Further, it is not at all apparent that local governments in the area are incapable of financing adequate levels of urban services given the yield of the occupational license, the renewal of the property tax brought about by the full value assessment ruling, and the balancing of the revenue raising potentials of Louisville City government, the Jefferson County government, and the Louisville City and Jefferson County school districts. Thus, there would appear to be little justification for a program of unconditional federal aids.

State-Local Relations

In Kentucky, state grants are made for education, while the state government assumes the major share of highways, public welfare, health, and hospitals.

As was suggested above, state education aids are greater on a per student basis in the county area than in the central city — though a comparison of the output of the two school systems suggests that relative need is greater in the central city. Despite the distribution of these aids, both the Louisville and Jefferson County school districts rank low among the 200 Kentucky school districts in per capita state aids received (187th and 179th respectively). Further, the proportion of state to total education revenues is 38.4 per cent in Louisville and 35.9 per cent in Jefferson County as compared to a state-wide average of 50.6 per cent. Therefore, it would appear that for education, at least, a state allocation decision results in a redistribution of public revenues from Jefferson County toward the lower-income counties.

Given that existing state aid and direct expenditure programs do not coincide with the major problem areas in the Louisville SMSA, there would seem to be little to recommend a program of increased federal aid to be distributed through the state government. Further, experience with the state education grants program suggests that urban areas, such as Louisville, may benefit less under a state distribution of federal money than under a direct federal-local arrangement.

TOPEKA:

The Local Impact of Grants-in-Aid

Darwin W. Daicoff

Associate Professor
Department of Economics

The University of Kansas

■

*A large proportion of the Topeka metropolitan popu-
lation lives within the central city and the entire metropolitan area consists of a single county. Moreover, the number
of overlapping governments has been reduced through
annexation. But Topeka, and the state of Kansas, make an
interesting study primarily for their experiences with federal
categorical grants-in-aid and their effects on initiative at
the state and local level. This shows up in the state's efforts
to improve its mental health facilities, where it is revealed
that such grants do not aid, but are at the expense of the
state. If grants were less restrictive, the study shows, they
presumably could be used more efficiently and flexibly
by the state. The study also reveals that "on the basis of
recent Kansas history, it would be reasonable to assume that
the major impact of general aid would be to reduce the
local property tax."*

The Metropolitan Area

The Topeka Standard Metropolitan Statistical Area (SMSA) consists of only one county — Shawnee County, Kansas. The 1960 county population was 141,000, ranking the Topeka SMSA 154th among the 212 SMSAs in the United States. Topeka, the major city, had a population of 119,000. The population of the other three cities totaled less than 1,300. The remaining 21,000 inhabitants of the metropolitan area resided in the unincorporated area of the county.

In 1960, 85 per cent of Shawnee County's population was located in Topeka; among the 190 largest SMSAs, the comparable figure was 57 per cent. As a further example of the exceptionally large concentration of population in the central city, it should be noted that only five of the 190 SMSAs, all larger than Topeka, had a more concentrated population in 1960. It is interesting that four of these cities are in Texas, a state with notably liberal annexation statutes.

The portion of the economy represented by the central city can be an important factor in the financial condition of the governmental units in the metropolitan area. Just as the population of the SMSA is concentrated in Topeka, so do most other measures of economic activity illustrate a high degree of concentration. Topeka accounts for over 90 per cent of the total retail, wholesale, and service activity in the county. Manufacturing activity in Shawnee County is also concentrated in Topeka, although to a lesser extent.

The Topeka SMSA contained 66 units of government in 1964. A majority of these were school districts but there were also 13 special districts, five cities, and 12 townships.

Since 1964 there has been a major decrease in the number of school districts and a small increase in the number of special districts.

As to governmental finances, the municipalities, special districts, and townships are comparatively less important in the Topeka SMSA than they are in other SMSAs of the same size. Topeka received more per capita general revenue and makes a somewhat greater use of taxes (more use of the property tax and less use of other taxes) and a much greater use of charges. There are major differences in intergovernmental aid. The amount of state aid to Topeka is relatively small, but the amount of federal aid relatively large compared with other areas. Capital outlays are much more important in Topeka, particularly for housing and urban renewal, and highways. Current expenditures are particularly high for public welfare, libraries, health, fire protection, and highways. Debt is rather large in Topeka; there is more short-term, more full faith and credit, and more school-associated debt.

Property Tax

For each of the major governmental units of the Topeka SMSA, the property tax provides the major source of general revenue. In the City of Topeka, the proportion is less than 40 per cent; for the county government and for all other units combined a majority of the general revenue is property tax revenue. Intergovernmental revenue, providing about 30 per cent of all general revenue, accounts for between a quarter and a third of all general revenue for each major class of government. The state provides three times as much intergovernmental revenue as the federal government. However, this ratio is not constant among governmental units. Although the county receives a significant amount of state aid and no federal funds, the central city receives only slightly more state aid than federal aid. In the Topeka SMSA, school districts and special districts accounted for the largest single amount of general revenue in 1962, the City of Topeka for the second largest, and Shawnee

County for the third largest. The remainder of the governmental units received very small shares.

The dominance of the central city is borne out by special data provided by the Bureau of the Census covering the finances of Topeka's central city area as distinct from the "balance of the SMSA." Over 85 per cent of the revenues and expenditures is attributed to the central city area. This exceeds the concentration of central city population. Thus, per capita revenues and expenditures are greater in the central city area than in the rest of the SMSA. On the revenue side, the balance of the SMSA in per capita or absolute terms shows somewhat less taxes, much less charges, much greater federal aid, and somewhat greater state aid. Per capita capital outlays are larger in the balance of the SMSA.

As expected, there are many urban services not provided by the balance of the SMSA. But per capita local school expenditures are twice as high in the balance of the SMSA as in the central city area. These high educational expenditures are 78 per cent of the total expenditures in the balance of the SMSA; another 18 per cent is added by public welfare and highway expenditures. Thus, about 97 per cent of the total is accounted for by these three functions. In the central city area only 45 per cent is spent on local education and only two-thirds on the three functions. With the exception of a large school debt in the balance of the SMSA, debt for all categories is larger in the central city area. Between 1957 and 1962, in both absolute and per capita terms, almost all the growth of revenue, expenditures, and debt occurred in the central city area. The balance of the SMSA has been increasing its use of charges, its capital outlays (primarily educational), and its current expenditures on parks.

On a per capita basis the balance of the SMSA received 22 per cent more intergovernmental revenue than the central city area in 1962. This was true even though Topeka received a large urban renewal grant in that year. While all the federal funds going to the balance of the SMSA went to support education, 64 per cent of the state funds went to education and 29 per cent to public welfare. In the central city area one-quarter of all federal aid supported education, and the remaining three-quarters assisted urban renewal. State funds were more evenly distributed with 33 per cent for education, 30 per cent for public welfare, and 26 per cent for highways. Per capita differences between the central city area and the balance of the SMSA are explained by the fact that the balance of the SMSA received three times as much per capita aid for education, twice as much from the state, and 7.4 times as much from the federal government. Per capita aid to both areas was approximately equal for public welfare.

There are measurements which reveal the changing ability of Shawnee County's local governments to finance their operations. Recently the rate of population increase in Shawnee County has been greater than the rate of population increase for the United States. In contrast, the rate of increase in employment in Shawnee County has lagged behind the rate of the national employment growth. Since unemployment in the county has been low and relatively unchanged in recent years, an increasing proportion of the population is evidently not in the labor force. The implication for local finances is that a decreasing percentage of income earners must provide the financial resources for the expanding population and its subsequently increasing level of public spending. There is some evidence to suggest that the expansion of the nonworking population has occurred at both ends of the age range. This has required a relative increase in spending for both public schools and assistance to the aged.

Problems And Issues

The Topeka SMSA's major source of revenue is the property tax. This creates financial problems resulting from the disparity between growth of the property tax and the increase of local public needs. Between 1956 and 1961, the assessed value of property in the county rose by 19 per cent. Over the same period the county population increased by 18 per cent. As a result, Shawnee County's per capita assessed value of taxable property rose by a modest 0.8 per cent, an increase which, because of rising price levels, was inadequate to maintain a constant level of public spending in real terms. However, local governmental aid from both the state and federal governments more than doubled over the same five-year period, and the use of non-property taxes and charges also increased. Nonetheless, property tax collections rose by 67 per cent — 43 per cent in per capita terms. Thus, only a slightly larger value per capita has been called upon to support a considerably increased amount of public services. As a result, between 1956 and 1961 the mill rate based on assessed value rose by over 42 per cent. In 1961 the estimated effective property tax rate, based on the estimated actual market value of property, was 1.8 per cent. Thus, while the property tax is not extraordinarily high, it has been rising rapidly. This gives evidence of the fiscal problem of the Topeka SMSA.

Annexation

Topeka has greatly curtailed metropolitan fragmentation through a series of annexations. In 1950 the city's area comprised only 14.1 square miles. By 1960 the city had more than doubled its size to 36.4 square miles. The annexation of Highland Park by Topeka became a heated political issue. Highland Park residents are said to have had a close sense of identity. They were fearful that their school system might deteriorate, and they were not sure that the tax system could be adjusted satisfactorily. However, from the point of view of local fiscal relations, the resulting annexation has been judged a success.

Although the city has successfully annexed residential areas, it has not done as well in annexing industrial areas. Some of the largest employers in the metropolitan area are located in the unincorporated districts near Topeka. These industrial firms, although they are users of many public services, make no direct contribution to support Topeka government. If one projects city growth to a time when these industries are at the city boundaries, the issue of annexation doubtless will be raised. It is by no means certain, however, that these industries will then be annexed by the city. For there is considerable feeling that they deserve the special tax treatment they are now enjoying.

There are a number of reasons for Topeka's success in annexation. First, Topeka is authorized to control subdivisions within three miles from the city limits. Thus, the city is able to set standards for these subdivisions and to help them make an easy transition to city status. Second, the Kansas annexation statutes allow subdivided areas to be annexed without the consent of their residents. When unsubdivided, up to 20 acres may be annexed by the city commission. When the major part of the boundary of an area is represented by the city boundary, the area also may be annexed by the city commission. Third, annexation is often encouraged by the city's reluctance to provide utilities outside its limits. This frequently discourages the contractor-developer from going outside the city limits for his subdivision developments. Although Topeka currently supplies water service to some township water districts, its reluctance to do so has aided annexation. Many contractors argue that this has prevented suburban incorporation in competition with the core city. Finally, incorporations within the county are subject to county commission approval. It has been fortunate and a credit to local planning that incorporated cities have not bounded Topeka.

In many metropolitan areas the multiplicity of governmental bodies and, hence, area fragmentation is the result of a multiplicity of school districts. In Kansas this problem is being solved in two ways: first, by financial inducements through state aid for education, and second, by a "mandatory" school consolidation law, which provides for a considerable reduction in the number of school districts. As a result of school district consolidations now under way, few districts will remain in each county. Topeka has recently completed its school consolidation. The consolidation plan reduced Shawnee County's 35 school districts to five. This nearly halved the over-all number of governmental units in the Topeka SMSA. Often the multiplicity of governmental units found in many metropolitan areas results in special functional districts. This, however, is not the case in the Topeka SMSA. Since there are relatively few people outside the central city, Shawnee County has little need for special districts. Moreover, when annexation occurs, special districts usually are absorbed into the city government and are no longer separate governmental bodies.

Home Rule

The history of home rule in Kansas is one of local frustration. In 1960, Kansas passed a home-rule amendment to the state Constitution. Most Kansans presumed that they were voting to allow cities to determine their own affairs, and to eliminate the need for the legislature to consider special bills on issues of concern only to individual units of government. A peculiarity of the amendment enabled the legislature almost to prohibit home rule. The 1961 legislature prohibited a local sales tax, a local excise tax on cigarettes, gasoline, and motor vehicle registration, and a local income tax, but it did allow the municipalities to levy occupational taxes so long as the basis of taxation was neither sales nor income. Some cities in Kansas have made use of occupation taxes; Topeka has not. At present, the main result of the home rule amendment is that it allows the municipalities to avoid statutory property tax levy limitations. The irony of the situation is that although the home rule amendment was initially proposed as a means of reducing the property tax, its net effect has been to increase this tax.

The county and other political units in the Topeka SMSA coordinate their activities in many different ways. For example, there are joint city-county health, planning, and civil defense arrangements. Furthermore, county personnel sometimes assist local units in budget preparation and sometimes provide engineering services for local government. Finally, the assessment and collection of the property tax is a county function. This eliminates the problem of competitive underassessment so common in some metropolitan areas in other states.

Although the Topeka SMSA has fortunately avoided some metropolitan area problems, not all local fiscal problems have been solved. For instance, a major complaint heard in the cities is that property tax levies to support some county expenditures are largely borne by city residents. Since most of these expenditures are made in the non-city portion of the county, city dwellers argue that their tax burden is disproportionate in comparison to the benefits received.

State-Local Fiscal Policies

Shared taxes are an important source of local revenue in Kansas. All of the state intangible property tax is distributed to local units at a fixed ratio; the motor carrier property tax is distributed on the basis of the school census; and 5 per cent of the inheritance tax is retained in the county where the tax is collected. In addition, part of the motor fuel tax and most of the liquor sales tax are returned to the counties and cities; county treasurers retain a small part of the motor vehicle registration fees; and part of the cigarette tax is distributed to the cities and counties on the basis of population. Almost all fire and lightening premium tax revenue is allocated to the firemen's relief association of the locality where the insured property is located.

In the last three sessions of the Kansas legislature, a Topeka Senator has proposed that Shawnee County be authorized to impose a local sales tax to supplement the state sales tax. This bill died in committee each time it was proposed. The attitude which weakened the home rule amendment was still present in the legislature and may explain the failure of this tax supplement. The Kansas Livestock Association and other major farm groups have attempted to provide property tax relief through a local income tax supplement.

The state accepted a different solution to the local financial problem. Kansas reduced the property tax support for local education by adopting the state-assisted school foundation program. This program necessitated an increase in the state income and sales taxes. Although not literally earmarked, the sales tax increase provided most of the revenue.

It was recognized that since the Livestock Association income tax proposal would have had only a residential basis, the place where the income was earned would receive no consideration. The dilemma posed by having to choose between a residential-based tax and an earnings-based tax is well known in metropolitan finance and is relevant to Topeka. It also was recognized that in an economy dependent upon agriculture, there is an additional problem. Since agricultural income is so variable, an income tax rate required to support local education would also have to be extraordinarily variable. Thus, within any county the relative burden on the urban-nonfarm income recipients would be subject to extreme fluctuation. Finally, an income tax supplement for each school district would have created such administrative difficulties as to render the Livestock Association proposal unsatisfactory.

The sharing of state taxes with local governments in Kansas was largely frozen between 1949 and 1965. During that time, the increase in revenue accruing to the local government through state aid resulted from economic growth rather than from an increase in the apportionment of existing taxes or from any new or expanded revenue sources. For example, when the cigarette tax (a shared tax) was raised, the revenue distribution formula was altered. While the new distribution formula returned the same dollar amount to the local units, it reduced the proportion of the tax they received. On the other hand, in 1965, when state taxes were dramatically increased, local governments shared in the increased revenue. The distribution formula for the cigarette tax was not changed and, as a result, although local units received the same proportion, they realized a larger dollar amount of shared tax revenue.

General state financial aid to local units is distributed in Kansas according to varied criteria. In some cases, population is the sole determinant; in others, property values are given equal weight. The population data is taken from the annual Kansas census; the property values are sometimes based on full value as computed by an annual assessment-ratio study. Under some aid formulas, larger property values result in larger state aid; in others, when local ability to finance public expenditures is included, more property value results in less aid. Education, highway, public welfare, hospital and health functions are aided on the basis of specific criteria established under each program. For example, highway aid is distributed on the basis of population, secondary road mileage, assessed value, miles of city streets, and, in part, on the basis of an equal division among the counties. Within the county, the aid is often further distributed to local units on the basis of population, assessed value, or the amount of the property tax levy. A small amount is distributed on the basis of collection.

Prior to 1965 the major increases in state assistance to local units came through increases in state grants. These grant increases have been primarily associated with special education programs, general education aid, and hospital construction aid. In 1965, the adoption of a foundation program for education greatly increased the amount of state aid accruing to local government to support local education. State aid has not been looked upon as an unqualified blessing by Topeka. Since the metropolitan areas pay a large share of state taxes, they have been concerned with the distribution of state aid. Underrepresented in the state legislature, metropolitan areas feel discriminated against, although they admit that the degree of discrimination has been reduced in recent years.

One of the ways the state has assisted Topeka is via state aid in support of the municipal university. In Kansas and other states there has been a tendency to absorb municipal universities into the state higher education system. This has recently been done for Wichita University. Washburn Municipal University of Topeka is the next likely candidate to join the state system. The consequences would be to reduce the local property tax burden and to finance the university through state taxes.

Federal-Local Fiscal Relations

Federal aid to local governmental units in Shawnee County more than doubled from 1957 to 1964. Most of the increase financed a limited number of new or expanded activities. Of prime importance has been the increase in federal aid for social welfare. Major new federal aid was received in the form of hospital construction grants and aid for vocational education. Of considerably less importance has been the growth of federal programs associated with flood control, the National Defense Education Act, civil defense, and public health.

Topeka has taken advantage of most federal assistance — for urban renewal, education, and many other services. Occasionally, one hears complaints of possible federal interference in local affairs, but these complaints have been few and ineffectual. Most of the vocal opposition has been associated with special interest groups. The real estate groups, for example, have argued against federally-assisted low-income housing in Topeka.

The position taken by public officials on federal aid to local government reflects to a considerable extent their state or local orientation. Those who advocate that the state receive and then apportion the funds see an advantage in state coordination of such matters as administration, planning, and legal services. Efficiency is better achieved, they argue, by the use of the state administrative procedure. On the other hand, those who oppose the state's handling of funds for local needs argue that such practice creates an unnecessary duplication of effort which adds to administrative costs. Finally, those who advocate state participation in federal grants assert that it is desirable for the state to retain administrative control over functions such as education, in which it has traditionally been involved.

State and local government officials in Kansas have one serious complaint about federal aid, which centers on the use of conditional grants by the federal government. Largely because of Kansas' experience with federal grants for public and mental health care, many state and local officials object to the fact that the federal government sets minimum national standards for the support of a particular public service, without taking into consideration the special efforts of individual states. Not too many years ago Kansas had one of the poorest mental health programs in the nation. Kansas now has moved to nearly the top of the states in terms of the quality of its mental health program. Kansas has committed a disproportionately large part of its resources to this public service. As a consequence, other important public services have received proportionately less support. This was a conscious state choice. If the federal government now is to assist other states to reach the quality of mental health services that Kansas already has achieved, Kansas gains nothing. In fact, Kansas would lose because it chose to solve this problem on its own initiative. Kansas' argument is simple: Why not return to Kansas the amount it would have received had it allocated its resources as the other states did?

The Outlook

There has been progress in solving fiscal problems in the Topeka SMSA. And in Topeka and throughout Kansas there is an important ingredient for further progress — an increased awareness of the problems. This new awareness finds expression in policy statements and proposals of many individuals and groups. The recent creation of a Governor's assistant for urban and community affairs is further evidence of this awareness. The step now underway involves a sifting of proposals and developing a course of action. It is impossible to judge which solution will be adopted. But it is likely that major decisions will be made in the next few sessions of the state legislature. Proposals affecting the Topeka SMSA that seem to have a chance for adoption are outlined in the following discussion.

A number of proposals have been put forward that are aimed at improving the efficiency of providing local services. Recently the Urban Affairs Study Committee, a group of local representatives appointed by the Governor, and the

League of Kansas Municipalities have proposed that cities and counties be authorized to undertake much broader cooperative actions. The proposal would extend joint undertaking authority from the currently authorized areas of public improvements, utilities, and fire protection to such areas as joint purchasing, ownership, and use of property. The two groups also have proposed allowing further intergovernmental contracting for services. Particular concern has been expressed about contracting for highway construction and maintenance. The League of Kansas Municipalities has also called for some reallocation of the responsibility for providing highways within city limits. As noted earlier, annexations have been successful in Topeka. Because some cities have had difficulties, the Kansas Legislative Council has approved a new uniform annexation statute which would make annexation still easier.

Many groups have sought to enable the cities to solve their own fiscal problems, largely through the expanded use of nonproperty taxes. In the recommendations of the Urban Affairs Study Committee and of the League of Kansas Municipalities, the cities would be freed from the restrictive statutes preventing effective home rule; the Governor-elect and the Kansas County Commissioners Association would extend home rule to counties. A number of restricted grants of local authority have also been proposed. The Topeka City Commission, the Urban Affairs Study Committee, the Kansas State Chamber of Commerce, and the League of Kansas Municipalities all have recommended that the state allow a county-wide supplement to the state sales tax. This state administered tax would be shared by the cities and the county. Some disagreement as to whether this should be a city or a county tax has been voiced. Almost every possible local tax finds some supporters and some opponents. For example, the Chamber favors and the Topeka City Commission opposes a local supplement to the state income tax. The League generally favors a wide number of local taxes if other solutions to local fiscal problems cannot be obtained. An increased use of fees and charges also finds support; the form most often mentioned is a municipal and county motor vehicle license fee.

Improvements in the property tax have been viewed as a means of strengthening the tax and of increasing local receipts. Various proposals have been made by the state Chamber of Commerce, the County Commissioners Association, the League of Kansas Municipalities, the Topeka City Commission and others that would lead to the appointment of professionally-qualified assessors rather than the current method of election. General agreement has been expressed in favor of repealing some of the exemptions under the property tax. In Topeka there are particularly strong feelings on this matter. In addition the City Commission is seeking payments from the state for the cost of providing public services to state facilities.

The surplus which has been accumulated by the state is viewed with envy by local officials. Various proposals have been made to share additional state revenue with local governments. Sharing of state income tax has been recommended by the Urban Affairs Study Committee and the League of Kansas Municipalities. The desire for increased state aid has extended to the proposals that would require an increase in state taxes. Such a consequence would result from the various proposals to increase the shared gasoline tax and insurance tax revenue.

Conclusions

The need for property tax relief has been stated time and again in Kansas. This is partly because the farmer and the aged feel this tax most severely. When combined with a stable or falling income, the increasing property tax becomes a very burdensome tax to be paid out of current income. This explains the partial distribution of sales tax revenue to local units so as to ease the property tax burden. It also explains the Livestock Association's attempt to substitute a state income tax for a major part of the property tax, as well as the limit put on the expansion of local education expenditures under the education foundation program.

There are lessons to be learned from the experience of

the Topeka SMSA in dealing with its fiscal problems. Paramount has been the experience with annexations. This method of solving, or at least preventing, fiscal problems has worked. Other methods of achieving metropolitan cooperation have been successfully employed and seem to be expanding. Positive as these actions have been, it is clear that additional steps must be taken to solve the local problem. A straight-jacketing of the local governments in the SMSA has proved that substantial nontax revenue can be produced. It has proved further that the property tax can be called on to produce ever-increasing revenues.

More general solutions to the fiscal problems of the SMSA have been tried or are being considered. Some of these involve expanding locally raised revenues. Since home rule has not been allowed, the direction of current policy seems to be toward permitting a local supplement to an existing state tax — probably a county-wide sales tax supplement. By most criteria this would be a reasonable partial solution. Increased state aid has been received in the SMSA. Its form, a school foundation program, has solved one crucial fiscal problem. Although the financial problems of the schools are not likely to be severe in the near future, it remains to be seen how long this solution will be effective. It works when state revenue is increasing rapidly; it is unclear how well it will work when Kansas enters one of its periodic financial crises.

It has been argued that, if permitted, the Topeka SMSA could solve some of its problems. For example, the property tax could be made more equitable and more productive. There are further gains to be realized through direct state assistance. However, the extent to which state aid can be effective in the SMSA depends on the ability of the entire state to support the level of public services the citizens expect. There remains a crucial role for the federal government. A state with large net out-migration, such as Kansas, suffers a large spillout of public expenditures that properly could be financed by the federal government.

What would happen if there were federal block grants? On the basis of recent Kansas history, it would be reasonable to assume that the major impact of general aid would be to reduce the local property tax. If the aid were conditional, Kansas would have its misgivings. Yet, it would accept rather than reject any reasonable program.

II.

The Potential Impact of
General Aid in Four Selected States

Richard P. Nathan
Research Associate
The Brookings Institution

138.

The material presented in this paper was the basis of the author's Ph.D. dissertation in Political Economy and Government awarded by Harvard University in March of 1967. The field research was carried out from May to August of 1965 under the auspices of the Federal-State-Local Fiscal Relations Subcommittee of the Committee for Economic Development. Lawrence R. Kegan, Director of Special Studies of the Committee for Economic Development, supervised this research and provided valuable advice and guidance. In addition to the Committee for Economic Development, the State-Local Finances Project at The George Washington University under the direction of Dr. Selma J. Mushkin also provided financial assistance for this research.

Professors Samuel H. Beer and Dan Throop Smith of Harvard University read the author's dissertation and made many suggestions which were extremely useful in the preparation of this paper. Others who provided assistance are Joseph A. Pechman, James A. Maxwell, L. L. Ecker-Racz, Dick Netzer, Allen D. Manvel. Stuart Urbach, and Arnold H. Raphaelson.

The views and conclusions presented in this paper are those of the author and do not purport to represent the views of other staff members, officers, or trustees of The Brookings Institution.

Introduction

Today, more than any time in our history, the fiscal relationships of federal, state, and local governments are being seriously questioned. Among the most important recent developments in the field of intergovernmental fiscal relations was the proposal in 1964, by Walter W. Heller, then Chairman of the President's Council of Economic Advisers, for general and essentially unconditional federal aid to the states. Joseph A. Pechman, Director of Economic Studies of The Brookings Institution, headed the President's Task Force which studied the Heller proposal and recommended its adoption to the President.

Coming when it did in the spring of 1964, Heller's proposal was seen mainly in terms of national fiscal policy. The tax cut of 1964, signed in February, was enacted as a means of curtailing "fiscal drag" by stimulating the private sector of the economy. The basic idea behind Heller's new proposal for general aid to the states was that "fiscal drag" would continue to be a factor in economic policy and that the next step to reduce its impact should stimulate the *public* sector of the economy. Relatively little consideration was given at this time to the other side of the equation, namely the impact of general aid from the point of view of the states.

This research project is an attempt to look at the other side of the equation. It is an assessment of the general aid approach as seen from the state house. Its essential aim is to develop a research method for evaluating the potential impact of general federal aid on the public finances and governmental machinery of the states. The information and data contained in this paper, as well as the analytical framework used to present this material, should be especially helpful to persons interested in future federal aid policy directions. It also has special relevance for those concerned with designing new federal aid instruments, and particularly for those who may be formulating broad conditions of a general aid or any other new and broader grant-in-aid program affecting the states.

Because state-local public finance systems vary widely and because averages for the states tend to conceal and blur these variations, the decision was made early in the planning of this research to concentrate on four individual lower-income states. The four selected states are Georgia, Maine, Mississippi, and South Dakota.

One reason for the focus on *lower-income* states relates to an essential facet of the general aid approach—*equalization.* In any general aid plan for the states, careful consideration must be given to the extent to which the plan takes into account inequalities in fiscal capacity among the states. This requires an understanding of the special financial problems and needs of the lower-income states.

A more important reason for concentrating on the lower-income states involves the nature of the public debate thus far on the Heller-Pechman plan. A frequent argument against the plan has been that certain states are not sufficiently "progressive" or "innovative" to utilize effectively general and basically unconditional federal aid. There appear to be more examples among the lower-income states of so-called "un-progressive" governments. Therefore, selecting lower-income states as the focus gives special recognition to whether these states are in a position to utilize effectively general and basically unconditional federal aid.

For purposes of this study, lower-income states were defined as the lowest 16 states in 1963 per capita income. The four states chosen were selected to achieve a reasonable geographical cross section. Two Southern states have been included because of the preponderance of lower-income states in the South. An effort was also made to have sufficient differences in levels of per capita income so as to reflect some variation in degree of economic need. Maine ranked second from the highest in 1963 per capita income among the 16 states, South Dakota fifth, Georgia eighth, and Mississippi at the very bottom. Finally, differences in the structure of state-local finances were taken into account in the selection process. In the two Southern states selected, state governments play a prominent role in state-local public finances. In the other two selected states, state governments play a much more limited role in state-local public finances.

The research findings for the four states presented in summary form in Sections 1-3 of this paper are divided into four parts.

Part A deals with the impact of existing federal aids. This consists of a description of the fiscal, administrative, and policy-making impact of existing grants-in-aid by major functional area. Fiscal impact refers to federal aid as a percentage of total state spending in the aided functional area. While the administrative and policy-making impacts of federal aid cannot be defined as sharply, an effort is made in this paper to factor out the effects of aid on the on-going administrative processess of state government and on the policy-making roles of elected and major appointive state officials.

Part B deals with public finance. Since the general aid approach is based in part on the assumption that the states will make the "right" expenditure choices, an attempt is made in this study to identify recent expenditure priority trends for each of the selected states. This is done to determine what, in comparison to recent federal domestic spending policies, would be considered priority public expenditure needs by states under a general aid program. The study does not suggest that current state expenditure priorities should be exactly the same as those of the federal government. Indeed, if federal and state expenditure priorities were exactly the same, there would be little argument for providing federal aid on a new and more flexible basis. What is involved here is a general assessment of state expenditure priorities in broad functional areas in order to compare these priorities with those of the federal government and the states as a whole. In addition to expenditure trends and needs, Part B also analyzes revenue effort and tax policy issues for the selected states.

Part C deals with state-local relations. Here again, the purpose is to examine the selected states in relation to basic assumptions underlying the general aid approach as embodied in the Heller-Pechman and similar proposals. Central issues are: (1) whether the state government has been active in helping localities meet their expenditure needs: (2) whether, in the distribution of intergovernmental aid funds to localities, there is a reasonably equitable relationship between urban and rural communities; and (3) whether the state is exercising leadership in major areas of intergovernmental relations.

Part D deals with the machinery of state government, particularly the role of the governor. State governments have been widely criticized for not moving fast enough in modernizing and revising the machinery of state government to meet the new and more complex governmental responsibilities of the postwar period. For purposes of a general aid plan, it is clearly desirable to have state governmental systems in which the governor can give central direction in the assessment of priorities and in the implementation of a program for which his administration is held accountable. A governmental system in which the office of the governor is relatively weak makes it much more difficult to develop and affect centrally planned policies designed to concentrate on priority areas of public need. There is a tendency for each department to go off in its own direction, limited in its activities by what it can secure in state appropriations and federal aid. Despite progress made in recent years in state governmental reorganization and reform, many states, particularly the smaller states, fall quite short of the model.

To summarize, this study assesses the potential impact of general federal aid — as opposed to existing categorical-type aids — with emphasis on seven major factors:

1. The administrative and policy-making impact of existing categorical federal aids;

2. The extent to which the state has been utilizing its own financial resources to satisfy major state-local public needs;

3. Whether the state could be expected to devote unconditional general aid funds from the federal government to priority needs, as opposed to tax reduction or expenditure increases which in terms of federal domestic spending policies would be considered lower priority expenditures;

4. Whether the state could be expected to allocate a part of these new and additional resources to localities in a way that involves an equitable relationship between urban and rural areas;

5. Whether the state government has been playing a leadership role of its own in key areas of joint state-local responsibility;

6. Whether the powers of the office of the governor are sufficient to enable him to develop and implement a centrally-planned and coordinated state expenditure program; and

7. Whether the state has executive staff machinery for determining expenditure needs at the state level on a basis which takes into account the various relevant economic and demographic factors.

In the research on the four selected states, data on public finances from the United States Bureau of the Census and state budget documents were supplemented by a field investigation conducted in the summer of 1965. The field work consisted of interviews with state officials, representatives of major interest groups, and university and other state fiscal and governmental experts.

An obvious problem for the reader in going through this report is that the story cuts off in late 1965 and only on major points refers to developments since then. But more important is the effort made here to develop an analytical approach for assessing the potential impact of general aid on state governments *per se.* Increasingly, the need is to synthesize and analyze data about state-local finances and administrative machinery in some consistent way so as to make intelligent and informed judgments about the potential impact of future policy directions in the field of intergovernmental fiscal relations. This is the kind of contribution which was intended when this study was conceived. One could surely argue that the need for such a comparative analytical framework is even greater today than it was when the Heller-Pechman plan surfaced in 1964.

1. Maine

Of the four states selected for this study, Maine had the highest per capita income in 1963 — $2,008. Maine ranked second among the lowest 16 states in per capita income. Maine's population is just a little under one million. The state experienced a net out-migration of 66,000 in the decade 1950-60.[1] Contributing to this out-migration is the fact that jobs have been increasing by less than 1 per cent a year in recent years.

A. Impact of Existing Federal Aids

Maine received $48 million in intergovernmental revenue from the federal government in 1964, accounting for 25.7 per cent of total state general expenditures. This was $48.69 per capita, slightly above the national average of $47.48 per capita.

Table 1

Intergovernmental Revenue from the Federal Government: Maine, 1964
(Thousands of dollars)

Education	$ 2,898
Highways	22,377
Public welfare	16,991
Health and hospitals	816
Natural resources	2,069
Employment Security Administration	2,218
Other	786
TOTAL	$48,155

SOURCE: U.S. Bureau of the Census, *Compendium of State Government Finances in 1964* (Washington, D.C.: U.S. Government Printing Office, 1965).

---

[1] James A. Storer, "Maine's Economic Structure," *Understanding Maine's Economic and Social Environment.* Proceedings of the Annual Winter Cooperative Extension Service Conference (Orono, Maine: January 1965), p. 15.

Education

Federal aid for education had a very small fiscal impact in Maine in 1964. Federal aid plus the required state matching funds accounted for approximately 7 per cent of total state educational expenditures, although this figure is now close to 25 per cent as a result of federal aid received post-1964 under the Elementary and Secondary Education Act of 1965.

The subject of federal aid for education was found to be a controversial one in Maine due to the administrative impact of federal aid on certain school programs and on the role of State Department of Education officials in federally aided fields. And even beyond this administrative impact, the subject of federal school aid was important because of widespread support for additional federal aid funds. Maine faced in 1965, and continues to face a major financial dilemma in the education field. Property taxes, long the principal support of education, are at such high levels that funds to meet rising school costs must increasingly be provided from other than local sources, i.e., the federal government and/or the state.

In terms of their administrative impact, the federal grants-in-aid cited as the best illustration of the basis on which federal school aid should be provided were payments made to local schools in federally impacted areas under P.L. 815 and P.L. 874. Federal conditions are at a minimum. As long as a federally affected school is approved by the State Department of Education, it qualifies to receive aid. Maine has a fairly large number of defense facilities. Thus, in recent years the state has received proportionately larger amounts of school aid for federally affected areas than many other states. In 1964 Maine received $2.52 per capita for maintenance, operation, and construction of schools under this program, as compared to a national average of $1.69 per capita. In 1964 aid under this program ($2.5 million) approximately equaled the amount of federal aid received by the state for all other educational purposes as shown in Table 2.

Table 2   **State Revenue from Federal Government
for Education by Program: Maine, 1964
(Thousands of dollars)**

School lunch and special milk	$ 996
Cooperative vocational education and defense educational activities	710
Vocational rehabilitation	392
Manpower development and training and area redevelopment training activities	356
Amounts received by state universities (not included elsewhere)	358
Other	86
TOTAL	$2,898

SOURCE: Based on data from worksheets of the U.S. Bureau of the Census, Governments Division.

The most widely criticized federal aid program in terms of the administrative impact of federal aid was Title III of the National Defense Education Act (NDEA). Title III provides 50 per cent matching funds for laboratory and other special equipment and materials for strengthening instruction in science, mathematics, and modern foreign languages.[2] The basic criticism of this program was that local school officials have been forced to master the art of "grantsmanship" in order to find ways to use these funds, in some cases distorting school program priorities, and in most cases wasting the valuable time of school officials on complex bookkeeping procedures.

The federal vocational education grant-in-aid program was found to be much more popular with school administrators in Maine than NDEA. The principal reason for this is that under revisions made by the Vocational Education Act of 1963 state and local school officials were given authority to transfer funds among the various vocational education categories. Prior to 1963, federal aid was allocated by narrowly defined subject matter categories, causing much the same kind of concern among state and local school officials as under NDEA Title III.

---

[2] Title III was amended in 1964 to include "other critical subjects."

Employment Security

As in all states, the Maine Bureau of Employment Security stands out as the state agency which receives the highest degree of financial support and administrative direction from the federal government. The Bureau administers the employment service and unemployment compensation programs. The federal government provides 100 per cent grants for administrative costs under both of these programs. In 1964 Maine received $2.2 million for employment security administration — 4.6 per cent of total intergovernmental revenues from the federal government.

As would be expected, the administrative impact of this federal grant-in-aid is substantial. Federal requirements regarding the administration of employment service and unemployment compensation programs are detailed and extensive. State agency plans must be approved by the United States Secretary of Labor. Grants for administration are based on the cost of "proper and efficient" administration as determined by the Secretary, and all state employment security personnel must be covered by a federally approved employee merit system.

Health and Hospitals

An important distinction must be made between two major kinds of federal aid for health and hospitals. The federal government provides aid to the states for health and hospital facilities *construction* (primarily under the Hill-Burton Act of 1946) and for various public health *services.*

As for construction, the entire amount of Hill-Burton funds received by the State of Maine in recent years has been directly apportioned to nonprofit hospital corporations by the Maine Division of Hospital Construction. These funds do not appear in the state budget. The 50 per cent matching funds required are provided by the participating institutions.

The Bureau of Health in the Maine Department of Health and Welfare administers the public health service programs under which funds are received from the United States Public Health Service (PHS) and the Children's Bureau. The fiscal impact of this aid is quite significant. In 1964 the Bureau of Health received $627 thousand (41 per cent of its total revenues) from the federal government. With the required matching funds included, approximately two-thirds of the Bureau's activities were directly financed or determined by federal aid.

Over half of 1964 federal aid to Maine for public health services was received *via* the eight narrowly defined PHS grant-in-aid programs under which aid is distributed to the states according to a uniform national formula. (These categories have since been combined.) The other half was in the form of aid for specific public health projects. Project aid is available for a wide variety of narrowly defined health services at both the state and local levels.

The policy-making impact of public health service grants in Maine was found to be of special interest. These grants (as structured in 1965) significantly limited the area in which the Governor and legislature could shape and affect policies and programs in this field. The expenditure of federal aid funds in Maine is subject to "allotment approval" by the Governor and the Executive Council. However, this approval is virtually automatic. State administrative officials can decide *not* to take advantage of certain federal aid funds, but their decision, if they decide to accept federal aid, is final as far as the state is concerned. With few exceptions, state health officials in Maine have attempted to utilize fully available federal grants. They appear thereby to have gained considerable political leverage within the state government in terms of their ability to achieve major health program goals without having to rely heavily on the legislature and elected state officials for program authority and financial support.

The administrative impact of federal aid for health and hospitals was found to be essentially the same for both public health service and construction grants. The requirements for approved state plans, the specificity of aided categories, and the coverage of state personnel under a federally-approved employee merit system tend to produce close personal and professional relationships between regional federal aid administrators and state health officials.

Highways

The largest amount of federal aid received for a major state function in Maine in 1964 was for highway construction. Sixty-four per cent of state highway construction expenditures in 1964 were financed with federal aid.[3] Of the total amount of aid received, 65 per cent was in the form of 90-10 matching funds for interstate highways, and the remainder in 50-50 matching funds for primary, secondary, and urban highways.

There is no question that federal highway aid has a major impact on state budget policies. In some quarters in the state, there is concern that federal highway aid may be over-stimulative. It is noted that while highways have been well financed other programs have been limited by the lack of state funds.

The use of earmarked state revenues for highways accounted for an important difference in Maine between the policy-making impact of federal aid for highways as compared with other areas where federal aid accounts for a significant proportion of departmental revenues. In the health field, federal grants-in-aid and the attendant conditions appeared to be the most important factor in reducing the effective policy-making discretion of the Governor and the legislature. Federal aid for highways likewise enhances the independence of state highway administrators, but this is in addition to the earmarking of state highway revenues which also contribute materially to the autonomy of the Highway Commission vis-a-vis the Governor and the legislature. Although in Maine the legislature must officially allocate State Highway Fund revenues to the Highway Commission, the effective power of the legislature over the Commission is limited by the fact that these funds cannot be used for other purposes.

Within the Maine State Highway Commission, federal aid has a significant administrative impact. The supervision of highway construction projects is to a large extent influenced by the various regulations of the United States

---

[3] Maine State Highway Commission, *Fifty-first Report,* 1964, p. 64.

Bureau of Public Roads. The relationship between federal and state highway officials was described by the Chairman of the Maine State Commission at a hearing of the Maine Intergovernmental Relations Commission in 1963:

> The Commission is required to work very closely with the federal Bureau of Public Roads which must approve all phases of construction projects involving federal funds, including preliminary plans, acquisition of right-of-way, construction plans and construction procedures. The federal Bureau personnel audit each project before final payment of federal funds is made to the state and exceptions are taken where indicated.[4]

In his testimony the Chairman characterized current relations between federal and state highway officials as "generally good." At the same time, he expressed concern about strengthened procedures of the United States Bureau of Public Roads and the "resulting increase in paper work to satisfy federal requirements." These strengthened procedures are seen as a result of "isolated instances of funds used improperly in other states," which have put the United States Bureau of Public Roads in the unwanted position of having to increase its regulatory functions to the point where they infringe in some cases on what are regarded as the administrative responsibilities of state highway officials.[5]

Natural Resources

Maine received $2.1 million from the federal government for natural resources in 1964. This was 18.9 per cent of total natural resource expenditures as classified by the United States Bureau of the Census. Half of these funds were for agriculture, over 80 per cent of which were for two programs—the State Agricultural Experiment Station and the Cooperative Extension Service.[6] Both of these programs

---

[4] *Summary of Statement* by David H. Stevans, Chairman, Maine State Highway Commission, before Intergovernmental Relations Commission, Augusta, December 31, 1963, p. 1.

[5] *Ibid.,* pp. 1-2.

[6] Data on amounts of intergovernmental revenues from the federal government for various natural resource purposes were provided in worksheets of the U.S. Bureau of the Census, Governments Division.

are operated as part of the State University. In Maine, as in most states, the State University has considerable independence in comparison to other activities of the state government. Thus, federal aid for these two agricultural educational activities does not have a direct and important policy-making impact on the state government as such. The remaining relatively small agricultural grants-in-aid are received by the Maine Department of Agriculture for poultry inspection and various special marketing projects.

Under natural resources, federal grants-in-aid for forestry are of special importance in Maine, as forestry is a major industry. In 1964 Maine received $538,000 for such specific forestry purposes as maintaining timber growing stocks, fire protection, pest and insect control, and tree planting. This was approximately 57 per cent of the expenditures of the Maine Department of Forestry. Adding in the required matching funds, the fiscal impact of this aid is substantial.

The remaining major functional category under natural resources for which federal aid is received is fish and game. In 1964 Maine received $287,000 for fish and game research and development. Although its fiscal impact is relatively small (8.7 per cent of state expenditures for fish and game), the impact of this federal aid on state administrative machinery in these areas tends to be significant. While there is no general merit system requirement, the narrowness of the aided categories and the role of federal aid officials in the approval and oversight of state plans for aided programs fosters close federal-state working relationships at the program administration level.

Public Welfare

In two-thirds of the states federally aided public welfare programs are directly administered by the state. In the remaining third, the state government merely acts as a conduit, receiving federal public assistance funds and then passing them along to the local welfare officials who actually administer the federally aided programs. Maine is in the first group. The state government directly administers the major public assistance programs for which federal aid is provided: Old Age Assistance (OAA), Aid to the Families of Dependent Children (AFDC), Aid to the Blind (AB), Aid to the Permanently and Totally Disabled (APTD), and Medical Assistance for the Aged (MAA).

As for the required matching funds, the state provides the matching funds for all but the AFDC program, in which case the state and locality share the cost of matching on an approximately equal basis. This sharing arrangement for AFDC costs often involves troublesome problems in state-local relations, especially when determining a recipient's "place of residence."

Under all federally aided public assistance programs, the states have considerable policy-making discretion. This applies primarily to the establishment of eligibility standards and benefit levels. It must be stressed, however, that even though state elective officials have considerable policy-making discretion in these two important respects, they do not as a practical matter have the policy option of refusing to operate programs. To do so would mean a substantial sacrifice in financial aid from the federal government. Put another way, federal aid under these programs strongly induces the states to respond to the federal stimulus, while giving them wide policy-making discretion as to *how* they respond.

In 1964 federal aid to Maine for public welfare accounted for 61 per cent of total state public welfare expenditures as classified by the United States Bureau of the Census. This is exclusive of required federal matching funds.

Federal aid in the public welfare field is highly stimulative. This is illustrated in Maine (as in the three other selected states) by the sharp contrast between the relatively higher benefits and uniform standards under the federally aided programs and the lower level of benefits and lack of administrative standards for general relief (payments to non-federally qualified recipients). General relief in Maine is provided by cities and towns on a limited and diverse basis. Total cash assistance in Maine, other than under the federally aided public assistance categories, amounted to 10 per cent of the payments under the aided categories in 1962.[7] If a needy person cannot be qualified under one of the aided federal categories, then in Maine, as in most states, the amount of public support he can obtain is likely to be very small.

The stimulative effect of federal aid is also experienced under the program of aid for dependent children (AFDC). Under this program a needy family in which the father is absent, disabled, or deceased can receive aid for the children. The program is widely criticized in all four of the states studied on two grounds:

1. that it encourages a father to desert (permanently or temporarily), and in so doing undermines moral standards in a community; and
2. that it provides fairly substantial subsidies to able-bodied adults, which in low wage areas can result in having families on welfare with higher incomes than families headed by employed workers.

There have been periodic attempts in the Maine legislature to place strict limitations on AFDC eligibility, but the very strong federal financial inducement has been sufficient to overcome opposition. (It should be noted here that the legislature has thus far declined to provide funds to take advantage of the AFDC amendments enacted in 1962 to permit the payment of benefits for the children of unemployed parents.)

The other federally aided public assistance categories are much more widely accepted. In fact, the largest federally aided category, that for old age recipients (OAA), is quite popular in Maine. The remaining three categories (aid to the blind, the disabled, and medical assistance for the aged) are much smaller than OAA or AFDC. These three categories accounted for approximately 15 per cent of total federal aid to Maine for public welfare in 1964.

As for its administrative impact, public assistance program administrators must comply with federal standards and regulations, and the state must operate under a federally

---

[7] U.S. Bureau of the Census, *Compendium of Government Finance: 1962 Census of Governments,* Vol. IV, No. 4 (Washington, D.C.: U.S. Government Printing Office, 1964), p. 95.

approved plan. Likewise, all public welfare personnel must be under an approved employee merit system.

B. Public Finance

Maine state-local public finances follow a pattern quite typical of New England, high local property tax rates and relatively low-level state financial support to local governments. Based on 1960 data, Maine and Massachusetts had the highest effective property tax rates of all of the states — 2.4 per cent of estimated market value.[8] Using 1964 Census Bureau data, Maine was 58 per cent below the national average in state intergovernmental aid to localities relative to income.

Financial aid to localities is one of the most important public finance issues in Maine. The heavy reliance on property taxation, plus the fact that property tax rates have reached what are widely regarded as their practical limits, have produced a situation in which the state is under considerable pressure to increase its traditionally low level of financial support to localities.

The area in which local expenditures have been rising most rapidly and in which demands for further state aid have been greatest is education. From 1960 to 1965, an amount equal to approximately 90 per cent of the increase in property tax revenues was devoted to increased local school expenditures. Even with these increases, average per pupil expenditures and teachers' salaries in Maine are the lowest in New England. In fiscal 1965 Maine spent $371 per pupil in average daily attendance.[9] This was $112 below the national average and $67 per pupil below Vermont, the next lowest New England state. The gap between average yearly teachers' salaries in Maine and those in both Massachusetts and Connecticut was over $1,500, causing a drain of well

---

[8] Advisory Commission on Intergovernmental Relations, *Measures of State and Local Fiscal Capacity and Tax Effort,* Washington, D.C., October 1962, p. 125.

[9] National Education Association, *Ranking of the States, 1965,* Washington, D.C., 1966, p. 49. (Future reference to the National Education Association as a source for school data refer to this publication).

qualified teachers out of the state. Not only does Maine lose teachers to neighboring high education expenditure states, but it is affected by school financing in these states in that their example tends to give meaning and impetus to efforts to raise school expenditures in Maine. The pressures for increased school spending in Maine are probably greater than those in most lower-income states because of the large discrepancy in educational financing between Maine and its neighboring states.

1965-67 Budget — Major Increases for Education

Over three-fourths of the total increase in state spending for the 1965-67 biennium was for education. This includes items in the January 1965 biennial budget and in the January 1967 supplemental budget.

With state school aid increases totaling $15 million during 1965-67, the state's share of local school costs will increase from approximately 21 per cent in fiscal 1965 to between 26 per cent and 28 per cent in fiscal 1967, depending on the growth in local educational expenditures. This is still considerably short of the 40 per cent goal adopted by a number of major organizations, including the Maine Teacher's Association, the School Superintendents' Association and the Maine Municipal Association. The 40 per cent goal (which would have required additional yearly expenditures of another $18 million) is equal to the average state share of total public elementary and secondary school costs for the nation as a whole, according to estimates by the National Education Association.

The 1965-67 increase in appropriations for the University of Maine was even larger than that for local schools. Appropriations for the State University, including capital items, were increased $16 million over the two-year period.

Besides education, appropriations for the Department of Health and Welfare and for the Department of Mental Health and Corrections were raised by $5.6 million and $4.8 million respectively for the 1965-67 period.

When the 1965-67 budget was voted, needed additional revenues to cover these increased educational, health, and welfare expenditures were obtained in two ways: (1) by raising selective sales taxes — on cigarettes from $.06 to $.08 per pack and on alcoholic beverages by 5 per cent; and (2) by simply raising the state's revenue estimates. The $.08 per pack tax on cigarettes put Maine among the 13 states in the nation which have an $.08 tax, the top levy on cigarettes in 1964.

Proposed Tax Increases

In recent years, there have been efforts in Maine to vote new taxes in recognition of the eventual need for additional revenues. The League of Women Voters, the Maine Municipal Association, and the School Superintendents' Association have organized support for a state personal income tax. (The personal income tax is the only major new state tax source still available in Maine, as the state already has a general sales tax.) Others have proposed increasing and/or expanding the state's general sales tax, which is the largest single state tax source in Maine at the present time. The general sales tax was first enacted in 1951. It began at 2 per cent, was raised to 3 per cent in 1957, and again to 4 per cent in 1963. In 1964 the general sales tax produced $40.8 million — 37 per cent of total state tax revenues. Although the rate of Maine's sales tax is high compared to other states (only five states had rates of 4 per cent or more in 1964), its coverage is quite narrow. The sales tax in Maine on a per capita basis was the lowest of the five states which in 1964 had state sales taxes of 4 per cent or above.

Among the various steps which have been proposed to expand the general sales tax, the largest revenue producer would be removal of the food exemption. It was estimated in 1965 that this would yield approximately $12 million annually.[10] This alternative, however, is widely opposed in Maine by those who feel that broadening the sales tax to

---

[10]John D. Coupe, "Prospects in Taxation in Maine," in *Understanding Maine's Economic and Social Environment,* p. 107.

include food would make it unduly regressive. Neither of the two other New England states which had general sales taxes in 1965 (Connecticut and Rhode Island) covers food. Other possibilities for expanding the sales tax to include such items as fuel, automobile trade-ins, and major services would yield considerably smaller amounts of new revenue than removing the food exemption.[11] A more likely major alternative than removing the food exemption would be to raise the general sales tax rate from 4 per cent to 5 per cent. It was estimated in 1965 that this would yield an additional $10 million annually.

Tax Effort and Major Expenditure Needs

Underlying the political issue of whether to raise state taxes and, if so, by how much, is the basic economic question of whether Maine compared to other states can and should increase the share of the state's total income which is devoted to the public sector. In Maine the determination as to the appropriate level of tax effort is basically the responsibility of the state government. Property taxation as a major tax source has reached what is widely regarded as its practical limit. Thus, to increase state-local tax revenues beyond normal growth, the state must either grant localities the authority to levy nonproperty taxes (which it has refused to do in recent years) or increase state taxes, using its broader fiscal base to provide resources for unmet needs at the local level. This decision involves an assessment of the extent and priority of unmet needs at both the state and local level in Maine.

Evidence available in 1965 suggests that Maine has significant unmet needs in several major areas. On the basis of the comparative data on per pupil school expenditures and teachers' salaries cited above, it appears that substantial needs exist in the field of public elementary and secondary education.

---

[11] In the 1967 Supplemental Budget, removal of the exemption on auto trade-ins was proposed, as was removal of the exemptions on rental, repair, service, and installation of tangible personal property.

There was also widespread concern in Maine about needs for new and expanded public higher education facilities. A recent state-by-state study of future public spending needs for higher education by the Council of State Governments indicates that Maine must increase public spending for higher education much faster than the nation as a whole between 1962 and 1970. It was estimated that Maine would require a 260 per cent increase in state and local expenditures between 1962 and 1970 in order to meet projected student higher education expenditure goals, after account is taken of tuition and fees and income from endowments, gifts, and other sources.[12] This is compared to an increase of 150 per cent for the nation as a whole. Using this index, Maine has relatively greater needs in the field of higher education than the other three selected states.

In the health field state officials estimated that as much as $3 million in additional funds was needed annually for the operation of health facilities. It was also noted that there are sizable needs for the construction of new health facilities (especially for mental health) in addition to these operating expenditure needs.

General relief was also cited by some state officials as an area in which additional funds are needed in Maine, as in many states.

Still another major area of public need in Maine is water pollution control. Maine's rivers and streams have long been an asset in attracting industry. But industrial growth along the state's waterways has also had its liabilities. Industrial waste products plus public sewage have caused quite serious problems of water pollution. In 1963 a $25 million state bond issue was voted for water pollution control. Added to available federal aids to localities for waste treatment, these new state funds will appreciably assist cities and towns in the construction of pollution control facilities. However, additional funds are likely to be needed in this area.

Many communities in Maine were also found to have major capital needs for streets and roads, new and expanded

---

[12] Selma J. Mushkin and Eugene P. McLoone, *Public Spending for Higher Education in 1970* (Chicago: Council of State Governments, February, 1965), p. 58.

public facilities, and urban renewal in general. With more increased local revenues going for education in recent years, capital needs have been building up rapidly. In many communities the problems of financing new construction are compounded by the out-migration of people and industry, thus narrowing the local tax base.

Against this array of public needs, it is necessary to weigh the effect of increased tax effort on the state's competitive position in attracting and holding industry. Compared to other states Maine is already making a relatively high tax effort. Using as an index of tax effort, state and local taxes per $1,000 of personal income, Maine (with $108.48 per $1,000 of personal income) ranked second in tax effort to Vermont in New England, and was 4.8 per cent above the national average in fiscal 1964. Basing tax effort on the index of the Advisory Commission on Intergovernmental Relations comparing 1960 state taxes to the estimated yield under a "representative tax system," Maine had a relatively higher rating. Maine again ranked second to Vermont in New England, but with this index was 26 per cent above the national average, ranking fourth among all of the states.[13]

Expenditure Effort by Major Function

Data from the 1957 and 1962 five-year Census of Governments permit a comparison of expenditure effort by major function as a rough index of the way in which states assess the relative priority of major governmental functions. Expenditure effort is defined here as state-local expenditures per $1,000 of personal income.

Table 3 shows that total expenditure effort in Maine in 1957 was $4.32 above the national average, and that Maine was above average in two areas—highways and public welfare. Five years later, Maine's expenditure effort was above the U. S. average in the same two categories as in 1957, plus education. In 1957 Maine had been below average in

---

[13] Advisory Commission on Intergovernmental Relations, *Measures of State and Local Fiscal Capacity and Tax Effort, op. cit., p. 75.*

expenditure effort for education by $4.58. In 1962 Maine was above average by $3.47. Table 4 converts these changes into percentages, which is the best basis of comparison in using these data. It shows that for education (the functional area in which expenditure effort grew the fastest for the nation as a whole) Maine's rate of increase was *twice* the national average from 1957 to 1962. Maine's rate of increase in expenditure effort was above average for the three other major functional areas and below average for "all other" expenditures.

Table 3

Expenditure Effort by Function:
Maine and the United States, Average, 1957 and 1962
(General expenditure per $1,000 of personal income)

	1957			1962		
	(1)	(2)	(3)	(4)	(5)	(6)
	Maine	U.S.	(1−2)	Maine	U.S.	(4−5)
Education	$ 35.95	$ 40.53	$− 4.58	$ 53.99	$ 50.52	$+ 3.47
Highways	33.41	22.41	+11.00	36.21	23.55	+12.66
Public welfare	11.96	9.99	+ 1.97	13.81	11.56	+ 2.25
Health and hosp.	6.89	8.95	− 2.06	7.92	9.87	− 1.95
All other	31.89	33.90	− 2.01	36.57	41.41	− 4.84
TOTAL	$120.10	$115.78	$+ 4.32	$148.51	$136.91	$+11.60

NOTE: Detail will not necessarily add to totals because of rounding.

SOURCE: U.S. Bureau of the Census, *Historical Statistics on Governmental Finances and Employment, Census of Governments, 1962*, Vol. VI, No. 4 (Washington, D.C.: U.S. Government Printing Office, 1964).

While these findings are somewhat limited for comparative purposes, there is some basis for drawing conclusions about Maine's capacity for making the "right" expenditure choices in the future as to the use of general and unconditional aid from the federal government. These data, along with the more qualitative findings on state public finances above, suggest that Maine's current expenditure priorities are reasonably in line with the current (since 1960) domestic spending priorities of the federal government. In Washington, education in recent years has received major stress, with public welfare spending (anti-poverty funds included) and health probably next in order of magnitude in terms of new and expanding federal domestic spending priorities.

As stated earlier, this does not suggest that current state expenditure priorities be exactly the same as those of the federal government. The study's general assessment of state expenditure priorities in broad functional areas is designed to provide a means of comparing these priorities with those of the federal government and the states as a whole.

Table 4   **Percentage Increase in Expenditure Effort by Function: Maine and the United States Average, 1957 to 1962**

	Maine % change	U.S. Average % change
Education	52.0	24.6
Highways	8.4	5.0
Public welfare	15.4	5.7
Health and hospitals	14.9	10.4
All other	14.7	34.0
TOTAL	23.6	18.4

SOURCE: U.S. Bureau of the Census, *Historical Statistics on Governmental Finances and Employment, Census of Governments, 1962,* Vol. IV, No. 4 (Washington, D.C.: U.S. Government Printing Office, 1964).

C. State-Local Relations

The central issues in state-local relations are (1) whether the state government has been active in helping localities meet their expenditure needs; (2) whether, in the distribution of intergovernmental aid funds to localities, there is a reasonably equitable relationship between urban and rural communities; and (3) whether the state is exercising leadership in major areas of intergovernmental relations.

State financial support to help meet local needs has been treated in Part B above on public finances, since one of the principal public finance issues in Maine at present is the extent to which the state is relieving the pressure on local property tax resources by shifting part of the local tax burden to its broader tax base. The recent increases in state school aid and the bond issue for water pollution control represent substantial steps in the assumption of greater financial responsibility at the state level. These steps are all the more significant in Maine because they involve moving away from a tradition (common to New England) of limited state financial support for localities.

While these forward steps stand out, it would be a mistake to overstate their significance. The fact remains that Maine is still among the lowest states in the nation in the relative level of state intergovernmental expenditures. Furthermore, both the Governor and the legislature in 1965 and again in 1967 were unwilling to vote major new taxes to help finance local schools and provide funds for needed expenditure increases in other areas. The legislature in the past has also refused to grant localities the necessary non-property taxing authority to meet these needs on their own. This issue came to a head in 1963 when the legislature in a major tax battle declined to grant authority for Portland, the state's largest city, to levy a 1.5 per cent gross receipts tax as a substitute for the tax on personal property.

Distribution of State Intergovernmental Expenditures

The answer to the question of whether there is reasonable equity in the distribution of state funds to localities in Maine requires an examination of the formula for distributing state school aid. The only other substantial category of intergovernmental payments by the state is for highways. On the basis of 1964 United States Bureau of the Census data, education accounted for 76 per cent of total state intergovernmental expenditures in Maine, and highways 14 per cent.

State aid for highways is provided to cities and towns for state-aided construction, town road improvements, and plowing. The largest proportionate shares of these funds tend to go to the more sparsely populated towns. However, the distribution of highway aid is not nearly as important a political issue between the representatives of urban and rural communities as that involving the distribution of school aid. First of all, the total amount of highway aid is considerably smaller than for schools. In addition, the fact that there are significantly more highway miles per capita in rural areas makes it difficult for the cities to argue against the present distribution system.

1965 School Aid Distribution Formula

Prior to 1965 the Maine school aid distribution formula equalized for differences in *taxing capacity* among localities, but not for differences in *tax effort*. The new formula, contained in the Uniform Effort Education Act of 1965, introduces a tax effort factor in the distribution of state school aid. This Act sets the minimum tax effort of local school districts at 20 mills (2 per cent) on state property valuation. State valuation is roughly 50 per cent of market value. This means that the standard for every community is a local property tax of 1 per cent of market value for education. Above the yield of a property tax of 1 per cent of market value (or 20 mills on state valuation), the new school aid formula provides 100 per cent aid up to certain ceilings defining the foundation school program which the state will support. Thus, the basic elements of the formula are: (1) the 20 mill school tax; and (2) the state defined foundation program, with the state paying the difference between the two to each school district.

For urban areas, however, the 20 mill tax effort factor presents problems. A 20 mill tax effort on state valuation for some of the larger cities and towns is more than enough to meet the full costs of the foundation program. Portland, the state's largest school district and which contains 18 per cent of the state's population, currently makes a tax effort for education of between 12 and 14 mills on state valuation, and out of this tax finances per pupil school expenditures well above state foundation levels.

To avoid a complete cut-off of aid to Portland and other more prosperous communities, two features were written into the 1965 law. The first provides that no school district in the state is to receive *less than 20 per cent* of the cost of the foundation program per pupil, and the second provides that all school districts must receive *at least 5 per cent more* than in the previous year (1964).

The 1967 allotment to Portland under the new formula illustrates how these two features operate. Under the old law, Portland was receiving 18 per cent of the cost of the minimum foundation program per pupil. The new law increases its allotment from 18 per cent to 20 per cent. As this amounts to more than a 5 per cent increase over Portland's 1964 allotment, the city is unaffected by the 5 per cent increase feature.

In 1964 Portland received $60.04 per pupil in state aid as compared to $102.73 for the state as a whole.[14] This is 58 per cent of the average per pupil state aid payment, a lower proportionate share of state school aid than that of the largest cities in the other three states selected for this study — Georgia, Mississippi, and South Dakota. This 58 per cent figure will increase, but only slightly, under the new aid distribution formula.

The question of whether this is a reasonably equitable distribution depends on an evaluation of differences in educational needs and economic capacity among the various communities in the state. Portland is considerably more prosperous than many other communities in Maine. On a per pupil basis, Portland had $14,592 in state valuation per local school pupil in 1965, whereas the average for the state is $8,671. To summarize, Portland had roughly 1.7 times as much property valuation (an indication of its taxing capacity) than the per pupil state average. At the same time, school districts in the state on the average receive 1.7 times as much school aid as Portland.

Portland city officials are not satisfied with this relationship. They contend that higher costs for other public ser-

---

[14] Data provided by the Maine Department of Education

vices warrant their receiving a larger proportionate share of state school aid. Their argument that Portland has urban needs different from those of the smaller towns and that for this reason state school aid should not be equalized strictly on the basis of property tax capacity has thus far received relatively little recognition in Maine. There is considerable evidence, however, that in the future the state will use school aid more as an instrument to supplement local taxing powers and less as an equalization device.

Role of the State Department of Education

Since education is the largest area of state intergovernmental expenditure, the role of the State Department of Education is an important indicator of the state's willingness to exercise leadership in major program areas. In Maine, the Commissioner of Education is an appointive position, unlike the other three states studied in which the chief state school official is elected. The appointment of the Commissioner appears to give the Department of Education in Maine a more professional and less political orientation than the departments of education in the other three selected states.

In Maine the State Department of Education plays a dominant role in the determination of school policies and programs, despite its relatively small contribution to local school costs.[15] Besides setting standards for teachers' salaries and other major expenditures as conditions for the distribution of state school aid (practices common to most states), leadership has been exercised by the Department in the field of school district consolidation. This subject was of central importance in all four of the selected states. It is widely held that to obtain maximum efficiency and quality in education school districts must be large enough so that they can be managed by qualified school administrators.

Under the state's Sinclair Act of 1957 the Maine Department of Education was empowered to set standards for

---

[15] Maine ranked thirty-fourth among the states in 1964-65 in the percentage of elementary and secondary public school revenues from the state government. National Education Association, *op. cit.,* p. 42.

school district consolidation as a condition for the distribution of state school aid allotments for capital purposes. School construction funds are distributed in the same proportion as state foundation school aid. For example, if the state pays 30 per cent of the cost of the foundation program in a given district, it also pays 30 per cent of school construction costs, assuming that the district meets state school consolidation standards. It is estimated that since the Sinclair Act was put into effect, state-approved School Administrative Districts have been established that include over 75 per cent of the state's public school pupils. There are, however, a number of relatively wealthy communities which have resisted school consolidation because it would increase school taxes for these communities to take in less prosperous outlying districts. In recognition of the fact that these communities are not sufficiently motivated under present law to consolidate, the legislature in 1965 enacted a bill requested by the Department of Education to give the Department authority to mandate school consolidation. There is some question as to the deadline for voluntary compliance before the state can act, but it is clear that at some future point the Department will be in a position to mandate school consolidations among the remaining recalcitrant localities. The new Governor elected in 1966 has announced this as one of his priority objectives.

A related area of intergovernmental relations in which states are in a position to exercise needed leadership is the consolidation of small and relatively inefficient local governmental units. The situation in Maine was described by one expert in the following terms:

> ... many towns are simply too small in population and too lacking in tax valuation to furnish adequately the municipal services expected or needed. The result in many instances is a high per capita cost for substandard performance. Over and over again within a radius of a few miles towns are duplicating the purchase and use of supplies and police and fire protection, and the general responsibilities of administration.[16]

---

[16] Eugene A. Mawhinney, "Should Maine's Small Towns be Consolidated?" *Maine Managers' Newsletter,* Vol. XII, No. 8 (April, 1964), p. 2.

In 1963 the legislature enacted a law to facilitate (but not direct) the consolidation of major governmental functions by two or more towns. The Maine Intergovernmental Relations Commission has also taken an active interest in this area, and there are indications that it will step up its efforts.

State Role in Property Tax Administration

A final subject which is a useful index of a state's leadership in state-local relations is its role in property tax administration. To date, property tax assessment practices have been highly disparate among Maine's 494 local taxing jurisdictions. Moreover, the state has done very little to unify and improve property tax assessment and administration. Each jurisdiction has its own assessor or assessors, many of whom are part-time workers with little special training.

According to the State Tax Assessor, the basic problem is that of inequalities in assessment within municipalities, that is, "properties within any given municipality assessed at widely varying ratios in comparison to actual worth.[17]

Although the state government in Maine has not been active in this area to date, the issue has been receiving increasing attention in recent years. In 1965 the legislature enacted a measure to enable the newly established Bureau of Public Administration at the University of Maine to conduct a study of property taxation in Maine. The property tax study constitutes the first recognition of the role of the state government in strengthening the property tax. Whether the state government will play an active role in this area in the future will depend in large part on the outcome of this study and on the work of a task force on the state tax system and local tax assessing appointed by the new Governor early in 1967.[18]

---

[17] Maine Department of Taxation and Finance, Bureau of Taxation, *Suggestions toward the Improvement of Property Tax Administration,* July 27, 1964, p. 1.

[18] State of Maine Budget Document, 1968-69.

D. State Government

The role of Governor is a quite central consideration in assessing the likely effect of general and unconditional federal aid. State governments have been widely criticized for not moving fast enough in modernizing and revising the machinery of state government. For purposes of a general aid plan, it is clearly desirable to have state governmental systems in which the Governor can give central direction in the assessment of priorities and in the implementation of programs.

Probably the outstanding characteristic of state government in Maine is the weakness of the formal powers of the office of the Governor. Professor Eugene A. Mawhinney of the University of Maine has termed the State Constitution as "legislatively overbalanced."[19] He said:

> The spirit and power allotment of the Maine State Constitution is primarily a product of the Jeffersonian philosophy of government....It is historically close to those first state constitutions prior to the turn of the nineteenth century which reflected worry of excessive executive power.[20]

Mawhinney further maintains that "the major goal of an integrated executive is still unfulfilled."[21] Among the principal steps to achieve this objective, he urges state agency consolidation, giving the Governor the item veto (Maine is one of eight states that does not have the item veto), and increasing the power of the Governor over appointments.

The most important factor in constricting the appointive power of the Governor is the Executive Council. The Council is composed of seven members, each representing a different region of the state and each chosen by a majority of the legislature, so that all seven are of the same political party. The Council has approval power over most major

---

[19] Eugene A. Mawhinney, Statement before the Maine Constitutional Commission, Augusta, March 21, 1962, p. 3.

[20] *Ibid.*

[21] *Ibid.,* p. 5.

appointments and also has a wide range of other lesser responsibilities that in most states are exclusively executive powers.[22]

The Governor in Maine is further constricted in his appointive power by two major factors: (1) the exceptionally wide coverage of the state's employee merit system; and (2) the tradition that major programs heads are not removed by newly elected governors.

The tendency to keep state program administrative heads in office on what amounts to a nonpartisan basis is based on purely practical considerations. In a small state, such as Maine, there is a limit to the number of administrators qualified to direct increasingly more specialized and complex public programs. The result is that at the agency head level the responsible state officials often do not have close political ties to the Governor and do not necessarily associate themselves with the goals of his administration. Although the positions of these program administrators are not classified under the state's merit system, many of the incumbents have been in office for long periods and have served under both Republican and Democratic Governors. It is likely that in a number of these cases the practical consideration of a limited supply of qualified administrators is even more restrictive of the powers of the Governor than the approval power of the Executive Council over major appointments.

Added to these essentially political limitations, the impact of federal grants-in-aid in restricting the area for executive decision-making further reduces the Governor's role in major program areas. This factor undoubtedly has a greater impact in lower-income states, as many of these states tend to receive proportionately more revenues from the federal government than do wealthier states. In the latter, federal aid is more easily absorbed for matching purposes, leaving room for the state to place major stress on the program areas which it regards as most essential.

---

[22] In the area of fiscal policy, changes in the budget as enacted by the legislature must be approved by the Executive Council. The Executive Council also shares with the Governor the power to allot "gifts and grants" (including federal grants-in-aid) to the various recipient state agencies.

Budget Process

The budget process is of special interest in relation to a general aid program, since it is the central point in the machinery of government at which competing expenditure needs are evaluated and decisions reached as to their relative priorities. All but six states (one of which is Mississippi) have executive budget systems. State budget systems vary in the relationship between the budget office and the Governor and in the extent to which the budget office is equipped with the professional staff and authority necessary to effectively carry out its functions.

In Maine the Division of the Budget is located in the Department of Finance and Administration. As of 1965, it had a four-man professional staff, including the State Budget Officer, although there were plans to expand the staff by at least two professional positions. The Division did not have a management office or the staff to perform fiscal planning functions. Long-range fiscal policy planning, to the extent that it exists in Maine, is the responsibility of the Department of Economic Development. The Department has as a major objective the development of economic development plans for the state, although fiscal planning for public expenditure needs is not emphasized as an aspect of the planning process. Various departments of the state government also have their own long-range program plans. Many of these plans have been prepared because of federal agency requirements (as in the case of highways, public health, and welfare and under the newly established federal Land and Water Conservation Fund).

The actual workings of the budget process in Maine reflect the institutional organization of state government. Although the Division of the Budget is formally under the Governor in the Executive Department, there is a close working relationship between the State Budget Officer and the Chairman of the Committee on Appropriations in the legislature. (Legislative committees in Maine are joint.) The Appropriations Committee is a powerful agency of state government in Maine, often taking major initiatives in revising and shaping the Governor's budget to fit its assessments of the state's needs. It is likely that the already noted restrictions on the powers of the Governor are a major factor underlying the considerable initiative taken by the legislature on fiscal matters.

E. Summary Analysis

Press accounts of the report of the Pechman Task Force indicated that the Task Force proposal involved the distribution to the states of 1 per cent of the federal personal income tax base after exemptions and deductions. For the nation, this would have meant about $2.5 billion, or $13 per capita in 1964. Maine would have received $13 million on a straight per capita basis, and with an equalization and a tax effort adjustment, a larger amount depending on the formula. Aid to Maine in any event would have been roughly two-thirds of the amount estimated as required in 1965-67 to raise the state's share of total public elementary and secondary school costs to the magic 40 per cent goal.

It is, of course, not possible to establish in advance how these new and additional federal funds would be used in any given state, but there is a strong likelihood that education at all levels would receive by far the largest share in Maine. Other major areas in which the state might be expected to expand its activities are health facilities operation and construction (including water pollution control and mental health), welfare, and perhaps local support for capital purposes. There is also a possibility that some general aid funds would be transferred from the state's General Fund to the Highway Fund, instead of continuing the current policy of borrowing to finance highway spending in excess of available earmarked state and federal funds.

A further prospect in some states is that general aid would be used to reduce local property taxes. There does not appear to be strong sentiment in Maine at present for state aid on a basis that would offset local property tax reductions. Nevertheless, in a state such as Maine where there is a substantial awareness of high real property tax rates, it is quite possible that part of a general aid grant could be used in this way.

Besides its effect on the expenditure side of the public finance ledger, a general aid program on the order of the Heller-Pechman plan in Maine would also have a significant impact on the revenue side. It is predicted by many that there will eventually have to be a major tax increase in Maine to meet growing state and local public expenditure needs. A fundamental economic policy question is whether the federal government should take all or part of the tax burden off the state-local tax base of states such as Maine. Maine presently does not use one of the two principal tax sources available to state governments, the individual income tax, although the state's over-all tax effort is above the national average. One of the most frequent arguments against raising the state's tax effort further under present circumstances is that an increase would jeopardize Maine's economic development goals in light of the competition that the state faces from wealthier and better located states with more highly skilled labor forces. Proponents of the tax credit approach, by which taxpayers would receive a federal tax credit for a certain proportion of their state income taxes, would be expected to disagree with this line of reasoning. They would probably argue that Maine should have a personal income tax; thus, the credit approach is more appropriate than the general aid approach.

To sum up, Maine has high-level unmet needs, has *generally* allocated its resources in accord with the priorities reflected in recent federal domestic policies and programs, and already makes a relatively high tax effort. Supplementary general aid from the federal government in excess of $10 million would enable the state to meet major public needs on a more adequate basis without raising its tax effort. Furthermore, Maine's competitive position vis-a-vis other states would be improved to the extent that equalization provided additional funds. Even without equalization, general aid by upgrading basic services in Maine (such as education) could improve Maine's over-all economic position more than the same proportional amount of general aid to wealthier states, which might be inclined to use this aid for somewhat more marginal types of public services, having less effect on their economic base.

The major questions or potential problem areas affecting a general aid program in Maine are: (1) the apparent political power of smaller and more rural communities, which results in low relative amounts of state aid for urban areas; and (2) the weakness of Maine's executive machinery, which makes it difficult for the governor to undertake centralized planning and program direction.

As to the distribution of state aid, there are indications that changes will be made in this area. Until recently the basic concept of state school aid has been equalization, and the amount of aid has been fairly limited. With reapportionment and with the prospect of further increases in state school aid, it is likely that the concept of supplemental financial support will receive relatively more emphasis in the future resulting in an increase in the share of aid to urban areas. But, even without any change, it can be argued that the significant differences in fiscal capacity among communities in Maine warrant the present distribution of school aid. Maine's inclusion among the 16 lowest income states is largely due to the fact that certain areas in the northern and central part of the state are economically depressed. Compared to Portland and other wealthier communities in the southern and coastal regions, it may be that these areas are sufficiently depressed to warrant the present distribution of state school aid.

As to the problem of relatively weak executive powers; this has not hampered the state in recent years from putting increasing stress on what are widely considered priority needs, such as those in the education field. Therefore, while Maine's state governmental machinery may be far from ideal, one might argue that this factor would not appear to be sufficiently important as to prevent general aid from achieving its basic objectives in Maine.

2. South Dakota

Of South Dakota's 1960 population of 681,000, 30 per cent was classified as farm, 30 per cent as nonfarm rural, and the remaining 40 per cent as urban. Agriculture is by far the state's largest industry. Although South Dakota was fifth among the bottom 16 states in 1963 per capita income, the state has few really serious poverty areas. The major exceptions are the Indian areas.

The fact that there are comparatively few poverty areas in South Dakota despite the state's low level per capita income may be attributable in part to the way in which personal income is defined by the Office of Business Economics of the United States Department of Commerce. It is widely held that Commerce Department per capita income data understate the economic well-being of farm residents due to the relatively low values assigned to the rental of farm dwellings and the prices of food and fuel consumed on the farm. Besides these internal characteristics of available per capita income data, high per capita property values (which are not reflected in personal income)[23] and the generally lower living costs of farm families add to the difficulty of making comparisons of economic well-being between farm and nonfarm areas.

A. Impact of Existing Federal Aids

In 1964 South Dakota received $57.2 million in intergovernmental revenues from the federal government. This was 36.8 per cent of total state general expenditures. On a

---

[23] The Advisory Commission on Intergovernmental Relations Staff Report on *Measures of State and Local Fiscal Capacity and Tax Effort* shows South Dakota ranking first among the states in the ratio of estimated non-residential property value to personal income. In South Dakota, where farm property constitutes 82.6 per cent of total nonresidential property value, nonresidential property values were 4.36 times personal income in 1959. In New York the ratio was 1.10:1. Advisory Commission on Intergovernmental Relations, *Measures of State and Local Fiscal Capacity and Tax Effort, op. cit.,* p. 66.

per capita basis South Dakota received significantly more intergovernmental revenue from the federal government in 1964 than any of the other three selected states.

Table 5   **Per Capita Amounts of Intergovernmental Revenue from the Federal Government: 1964 (dollars)**

Maine	$48.69
Georgia	49.88
Mississippi	53.29
South Dakota	79.97
50 State average	$47.78

SOURCE: U.S. Bureau of the Census, *Compendium of State Government Finances in 1964* (Washington, D.C.: U.S. Government Printing Office, 1965).

Table 6   **Intergovernmental Revenue from the Federal Government: South Dakota, 1964 (Thousands of dollars)**

Education	$ 5,378	9.4%
Highways	37,065	64.8%
Public welfare	9,590	16.8%
Health and hospitals	1,016	1.8%
Natural resources	1,662	2.9%
Employment Security Administration	1,220	2.1%
Other	1,250	2.2%
TOTAL	$57,181	100.0%

SOURCE: U.S. Bureau of the Census, *Compendium of State Government Finances in 1964* (Washington, D.C.: U.S. Government Printing Office, 1965).

The chief reason for the high proportionate amount of federal intergovernmental revenue to South Dakota is the relatively larger amounts of highway aid received by sparsely populated states. In 1964 intergovernmental revenue from the federal government for highways accounted for 65 per cent of total federal intergovernmental revenues received by South Dakota, compared with a 50 state average of 39 per cent.

Despite the high level of federal aid to South Dakota, there is considerable opposition to federal aid in the state stemming in large part from the fiscal conservatism of South Dakota politics. For instance, Governor Archie Gubbrud in his 1965 budget message justified proposed increases in state spending on the grounds that "to refuse to move ahead at the state level is tantamount to inviting still more federal intervention."[24] This attitude was expressed in all four of the selected states but appeared to be most pronounced in South Dakota.

Especially important for the administrative impact of federal aid in South Dakota is the requirement in three areas (health, welfare, and employment security) that state employees assigned to these programs be covered under an approved employee merit system. Thirty states have general merit systems, which in most cases also cover employees in these three federally aided program areas.[25] South Dakota does not have a general merit system. Thus, a separate Merit System Council is maintained for federal grant-in-aid personnel. Employees in the covered areas tend to regard themselves as being in a better position than other state employees because of the various protections and benefits afforded them through the Merit System Council.

Education

Prevailing attitudes toward federal education aid in

---

[24]State of South Dakota, *Governor's Budget Report, Fiscal Biennium July 1, 1965 to June 30, 1967.*

[25] *The Book of the States, 1964-65,* Council of State Governments, Chicago; pp. 178-81.

South Dakota are very similar to those in Maine. Opposition to federal aid has tended to focus on federal controls. But, like Maine, the state government of South Dakota currently faces mounting demands for further state school aid which have brought about a change in attitude toward federal aid for education. Education officials in the state see a need for further federal aid in addition to that received under the 1965 Elementary and Secondary Education Act. As in Maine, they stress that this should be general school aid.

A major argument for additional federal school aid in South Dakota is that to a high degree the state is educating for export. Many of its best educated young people leave the state when they complete their education, thus burdening the state with educational expenses, the benefits of which accrue to other states.

In 1964 South Dakota received $5.4 million in federal aid for educational purposes. As in Maine, the fiscal impact of this aid is limited. Federal aid accounted for 14.6 per cent of total state spending for education.

On a per capita basis, the State of South Dakota received more federal aid for education in 1964 than any of the other

Table 7   **Revenue from the Federal Government for Education by Program: South Dakota, 1964 (Thousands of dollars)**

School lunch and special milk program	$ 946
Cooperative vocational education	461
Vocation rehabilitation	516
Defense education activities	419
Manpower development and training and area redevelopment training activities	276
Amounts received by state universities (not included elsewhere)	2,241
Bureau of Indian Affairs — Education of Indians	519
TOTAL	$5,378

SOURCE: Based on data from the worksheets of the U.S. Bureau of the Census, Governments Division.

three selected states.[26] South Dakota school districts also received significantly above average per capita aid under P.L. 815 and P.L. 874 (school aid for federally impacted areas), as a number of Minuteman missile sites and Army Corps of Engineers public works projects have recently been constructed in the state.[27] In 1964 South Dakota received $5.54 per capita for schools in federally affected areas, compared to a national average of $1.69. This was a larger per capita share than that received by any of the other three selected states.

Under the distribution formulas in the Elementary and Secondary Education Act of 1965, South Dakota also receives a relatively large share of federal aid. Of the four selected states only Mississippi receives more on a per capita basis than South Dakota. Estimated annual payments to Mississippi under the Act in 1965 were $13.27 per capita, and to South Dakota $10.00 per capita. The national average per capita payment was $6.32.

Employment Security

South Dakota received $1.2 million in 1964 for employment security administration. As was pointed out for Maine, the administration of these programs is entirely supported by federal aid and is extensively influenced by federal standards and regulations.

Health and Hospitals

In South Dakota hospital and health facility construction funds (principally those received under the Hill-Burton Act) are distributed to local governments and nonprofit hospital corporations by the Division of Hospitals in the

---

[26] This is primarily due to the inclusion of federal payments to state universities in this category as defined by the U.S. Bureau of the Census. As shown in Table 7, South Dakota received $2.2 million under this heading in 1964, 42% of total intergovernmental revenues from the federal government for education.

[27] School aid for federally affected areas is not included in Table 7 as it is disbursed directly to local school districts.

Department of Health. In a larger number of cases than in Maine, local governments in South Dakota operate their own hospitals. However, these federal aid funds have much less effect on the administrative and policy-making machinery of the state government than do federal grants to the states for public health services.

The fiscal impact of federal aid for public health services is very large in South Dakota. Practically the entire 1965 budget of the Health Department was financed by, or determined by, federal grants-in-aid. This was clearly reflected in the policy-making impact of federal grants-in-aid for public health services, which was found to be of special interest in South Dakota.

Public health services are highly controversial in South Dakota primarily because of the opposition of private physicians to publicly financed activities in this field. Their influence is felt in the legislature, which has consistently made sharp cuts in requests for health appropriations. In 1965 the Department of Health requested $754,000. The Governor reduced this request by 10 per cent, and the legislature cut it by another 14 per cent. On top of these cuts, the legislature in 1965 for the first time imposed a flat ceiling ($560,000) on the amount of funds from "other" sources which the department could expend. "Other" sources for all practical purposes means federal aid. The legislative ceiling was aimed at federal "grantsmanship," by which the Health Department can amplify its influence using funds from local governments (and in some cases from private groups) to match federal funds, then returning both the federal aid and local funds for programs at the local level. South Dakota health officials noted that federal aid ceilings of this kind had been adopted in one or two Western states, but that the practice is otherwise limited.

Under-matching (the failure to put up sufficient state funds to take full advantage of available federal aids) in the health field in South Dakota in 1964 was much larger than in the other three selected states. In most of the cases where it occurred, the under-matching of formula-type grants for public health services in South Dakota involved an administrative determination by Health Department officials made necessary as a consequence of cuts in Departmental appropriation requests. South Dakota under-matched four of the eight United States Public Health Service formula grant-in-aid programs in 1964.[28] The state used only 8.5 per cent of its cancer control allocation, 29.6 per cent of its allocation for heart disease control, 43 per cent of funds available for the chronically ill and aged, and 70.3 per cent of the funds allocated for radiological health.

Highways

Federal aid for highways amounted to $50.33 per capita in South Dakota in 1964, compared to a national average of $19.24 per capita. South Dakota's per capita share of highway aid was more than twice as large as that of any of the other three selected states.

As in Maine, the fiscal impact of federal highway aid is substantial. Federal aid accounted for 63 per cent of state highway construction spending in 1964.[29] Interstate highways are a particularly big factor in South Dakota. Over 40 per cent of state highway construction spending in 1964 was for federally aided interstate highways. Planned interstate highways to be completed in 1972 (the year in which the 1956 Federal Highway Act program is scheduled to end) will span the state both north-south and east-west. To complete these and other scheduled federal aid highways by 1972 will require increasingly larger amounts of federal aid over the next five years.

For highway needs beyond 1972, all states were required in 1965 to submit estimates of their 1972-82 highway needs to the United States Bureau of Public Roads. The character and direction of the federal highway program after 1972 is of considerable importance to South Dakota. If greater emphasis in the future is placed on federal aid for urban and metropolitan highways, as seems possible, there could

---

[28] Data provided by the U.S. Department of Health, Education and Welfare, Public Health Service, Bureau of State Services.

[29] South Dakota Department of Highways, *Biennial Report for Fiscal Years 1963 and 1964,* pp. 21-22.

be a reduction in South Dakota's relative advantage over other states in the distribution of federal highway aid.

As in Maine, current levels of federal highway aid have caused concern in some quarters in South Dakota that this program has over-stimulated highway spending at the expense of other areas in which needs are not being adequately met.

Also as in Maine, highway aid in South Dakota tends to strengthen the position of the Department of Highways, adding to the autonomy within state government which the Department derives by virtue of the earmarking of state gasoline tax revenues for highway purposes. However, the fact that the Department has a high degree of autonomy within the state government does not remove it from the political process. Political appointments tend to be more common in the Department of Highways in South Dakota than in other state agencies which also receive a significant proportion of their revenues in the form of federal aid. One reason is that, unlike other federally aided programs, there is no federal requirement that state highway personnel be under an employee merit system. As noted above, South Dakota does not have an across-the-board state employee merit system.

Natural Resources

South Dakota received $1,662,000 from the federal government for natural resources in 1964, 18.3 per cent of total state expenditures in this area. Of the total amount, 70 per cent was for agricultural programs, mainly the Experiment Station and Extension Service at the University of South Dakota. Approximately two-thirds of the expenditures of the State University's Experiment Station and Extension Service were financed directly with, or determined by, federal aid. The state also received $503,000 for fish and game research and development (24.2 per cent of state fish and game expenditures).

Public Welfare

In South Dakota the state directly administers and finances the federally aided public assistance programs.[30] Federal aid in 1964 accounted for 64 per cent of total state expenditures for public welfare as classified by the United States Bureau of the Census. As in Maine, the highly stimulative effect of this aid is illustrated by (1) the sharp contrast between benefits under the federally aided categories and general relief; and (2) South Dakota's experience under the Aid for Families with Dependent Children (AFDC) program.

General relief is a very small factor in total state and local public welfare spending in South Dakota. According to the 1962 Census of Governments, cash assistance for other than the federal categorical programs amounted to 1.4 per cent of total benefits under the federally aided categories.

By far the least popular federally aided public assistance program in South Dakota is AFDC. The reasons given are much the same as in Maine. South Dakota is a relatively low income state in which there is a strong tendency towards fiscal conservatism. Under AFDC it is possible for able-bodied adults to receive incomes as high or higher than people working full-time in lower wage areas of the state. When this happens, it tends to create resentment toward the AFDC program. Another factor underlying the unpopularity of AFDC is that a large proportion of the receipients are Indians against whom there is a certain amount of prejudice and also resentment. This resentment stems from the fact that Indians living on federally owned lands have a special economic status as a result of the services available through the United States Bureau of Indian Affairs. Data from the State Department of Public Welfare for September 1964 indicate that, while Indians in South Dakota account for only 4 per cent of the state's population, 46 per cent of

---

[30] In addition to Old Age Assistance (OAA), Aid for Families with Dependent Children (AFDC), Aid for the Blind (AB), and Aid for the Permanently and Totally Disabled (APTD), South Dakota in 1963 established a program under the Kerr-Mills Act (1960) for Medical Assistance for the Aged (MAA). The state has not taken advantage of the 1962 Social Security Act amendments to provide AFDC benefits in cases where parents are unemployed.

the recipients of AFDC are nonwhite.[31] One out of every four nonwhites under 18 in South Dakota was receiving benefits under AFDC in September of 1964, compared to a ratio of three out of every 100 persons under 18 for the state as a whole.

The unpopularity of AFDC was made clear in fiscal 1964 when the State Welfare Commission was faced with the need to cut back public assistance benefit levels because insufficient funds were available out of the lump sum appropriated at the beginning of the biennium. The Commission made an initial determination to pro-rate the three adult programs (OAA, AB, APTD) at 92 per cent of then existing benefit levels. The AFDC program was not included because it had already been prorated at 92 per cent. Protests from a number of key groups (hospital, medical, and nursing home groups) as well as some legislators forced the Commission to change its position and prorate AFDC at 80 per cent, leaving the other three program benefit levels unaffected.[32]

While the AFDC program has had its difficult moments, it does not appear to be as unpopular with the legislature as federal grants-in-aid for public health services. In fact, the legislature in 1965 voted to raise the ceiling on AFDC benefits from $30 monthly (then the ceiling up to which federal matching aid was provided) to $35.

State welfare officials indicate that South Dakota is currently taking full advantage of available aid under all of the federally aided public assistance categories and that the state's eligibility requirements are reasonably in line with those of other states.

In addition to the federally aided public assistance categories, South Dakota in 1964 received 33.4 per cent of its total budget for child welfare services ($121,000) in federal aid. The state received an approximately equal amount from

---

[31] The vast majority of nonwhites in South Dakota are Indians. Data here provided by South Dakota Department of Public Welfare.

[32] South Dakota Department of Public Welfare, *Annual Report,* July 1, 1963 —June 30, 1964, p. 10.

the United States Bureau of Indian Affairs for foster home care.

B. Public Finance

The characteristics of South Dakota public finances that stand out are (1) low level state aid to local governments; (2) a correspondingly low proportion of state-local taxes collected at the state level; and (3) a general fiscal conservatism, as illustrated by the fact that South Dakota is one of only eight states in the nation with no full faith and credit state debt outstanding.

South Dakota's level of state aid to localities is extremely low. With $20.73 per capita in state intergovernmental expenditures in 1964, the state ranked forty-ninth among the states. In South Dakota, as in Maine, the limited role of the state government in state-local finances is a basic factor underlying recent developments in the field of public finance.

Recent Developments

In the past several sessions of the legislature, there has been steadily rising pressure for increased school support as well as for other forms of financial aid to localities, including local property tax relief. Until 1965, the legislature had for the most part resisted these pressures. Conservative Republicans from the western ranching areas of the state have tended to dominate state politics, and their view favoring a limited fiscal role for the state government had generally prevailed.

In the 1965 session of the legislature, the cities and the politically more liberal farming areas in the eastern part of the state, where there is more support for higher state financial aid, scored significant gains. The incumbent Governor (Nils Boe, re-elected in 1966) is from Sioux Falls, the state's largest city, located in the state's eastern farming region. One of the major planks in Governor Boe's 1964 campaign was the promise that state aid for local schools would be substantially increased.

The legislature made two major strides in 1965 to raise state financial support for localities. It increased the state appropriation for school aid by 50 per cent, and it adopted a plan for the reinbursement of localities for the elimination of the personal property tax on household goods. The total amount of increased appropriations during 1965-67 was $24 million — a 20 per cent rise in General Fund spending. Of this amount, $8 million was for the tax refund plan, $7 million for the state universities and colleges, $7 million for increased state aid for local schools, and the remainder for various general and miscellaneous increases.

Taking school aid first, the additional $7 million increased the state's contribution from $10 million in 1963-65 to $17 million in 1965-67. This raised the state's share of local school costs from the 1964 level of about 8 per cent to between 11 per cent and 12 per cent in the 1965-67 biennium. In 1967, when the state budget was converted to an annual basis, the Governor requested $10 million for school aid, an annual increase of another $1.5 million.[33] This would raise the state's share of school spending still further to upwards of 15 per cent of total elementary and secondary public school expenditures. This is still considerably short of the state Education Association goal of 40 per cent (the same as in Maine).

The second major form of increased financial support for localities passed in the 1965-67 biennial budget was the $8 million program to reimburse local taxing jurisdictions for the elimination of the personal property tax on household goods, an extremely difficult and costly tax to administer. An appropriation for this purpose passed the legislature in 1965, but was later vetoed by the Governor in a complicated parliamentary battle.[34]

---

[33] Message of Governor Nils Boe, South Dakota Legislature, Forty-Second Regular Session, 1967, p. 5.

[34] In the legislative session following the field work on this study, the legislature passed a revised version of the 1965 tax reimbursement plan. The 1966 plan appropriated $5 million for property tax relief on an across-the-board basis. The Governor signed this bill, resulting in a 3-1/2 per cent to 5 per cent tax reduction for all taxpayers. Further property tax relief was mentioned in the Governor's 1967 Message, but no specific proposals were made.

Two aspects of the personal property tax reimbursement plan are of special interest for purposes of this report. First, it is notable that despite steady pressure for more state aid for local schools, the legislature in 1965 put more funds into tax relief than into school aid. The question of tax reduction versus increased expenditures is highly relevant in assessing the impact of general aid on state-local public finances.

It should also be noted in reference to the 1965 property tax reimbursement plan that it was directly linked to the major state tax increase enacted in 1965. The legislature voted to raise the state's general sales tax (its major revenue producer) from 2 per cent to 3 per cent and broadened its coverage to include services previously excluded. It was estimated that these changes would yield $19 million for the 1965-67 period. In turn, the $8 million needed to reimburse localities for the elimination of the personal property tax on household goods was to be financed out of the revenues from the sales tax increase. In addition to the increase in the sales tax in 1965, the legislature raised the tax on cigarettes from $.06 to $.08 per pack. It was estimated that the cigarette tax increase would yield $1.3 million annually. In 1967, no increases in taxes or new taxes were recommended by the Governor.

Tax Effort and Major Expenditure Needs

In Section I above, an analysis was made of tax effort and expenditure needs in Maine. It was found that Maine has an array of major public service needs (education at all levels, water pollution control facilities, local capital expenditures, welfare, and public health) and that at the same time the state and localities are making a somewhat above average tax effort to meet these needs.

Looking first at public service needs in South Dakota, education needs appear to be less extensive than in Maine where education stands out as the principal area of public need. In 1964-65, per pupil expenditures for public elementary and secondary schools in South Dakota ($416) were 12 per cent above Maine ($371), although still 14 per cent below the national average ($483).[35] Among the seven Plains states, South Dakota ranked sixth in per pupil expenditures, but the differences between South Dakota and its neighbors in per pupil expenditures are not nearly so great as those between Maine and the other New England states.

The University of South Dakota, like other state universities of the Midwest, already maintains a much more liberal admissions policy than the University of Maine. Thus, needs for new and expanded higher education facilities are not as large as those of the University of Maine. The Council of State Governments study of future education needs, referred to in Section I, estimated that Maine will require a 260 per cent increase in state and local expenditures for the teaching of students in higher education from 1962 to 1970. Using the same index for South Dakota, the state was found to require an estimated increase of approximately 100 per cent during this eight-year period, below the national average requirement of 150 per cent.[36]

Estimates are not presently available for South Dakota as to future needs in other public expenditure areas. The most useful comparative indication of state public service needs is per capita expenditures by major function. It is notable that in 1964 South Dakota state-local per capita expenditures for health and hospitals were the *lowest of any state in the nation.* The state was also 36 per cent below the national average in per capita expenditures for public welfare, which suggests that there may be fairly sizable levels of unmet need in this field, as well as in the health field.

At the local level South Dakota, like Maine, appears to have major public needs for capital items in the larger towns and cities. A number of localities have reached the state ceiling on property tax mill rates and have therefore deferred major capital expenditures.

Set against these indications of areas of major expenditure need, South Dakota's tax effort is high measured on the basis of state and local taxes per $1,000 of personal income.

---

[35] National Education Association, *op. cit.,* p. 49.

[36] Mushkin and McLoone, *op. cit.,* p. 58.

Using this index, South Dakota ranked third among the 16 lowest income states and tenth in the nation in 1963-64, with a tax effort 13 per cent above the national average. However, there is evidence that this index overstates South Dakota's relative position among the states in tax effort. As already noted, personal income statistics as presently compiled may not adequately adjust for the rental value of farm dwellings and the cost of food and fuel consumed on the farm. In the development of the index of tax effort of the Advisory Commission on Intergovernmental Relations, which is based on the yield of a "representative tax system," adjustments were made for these data. Using this index South Dakota was 8 per cent *below* the national average in 1960.[37] For the same year the state was 40 per cent *above* the national average measuring tax effort relative to personal income. In light of this discrepancy, the question of relative tax effort in South Dakota must be deferred until more data have been assembled.

Expenditure Effort by Major Function

Also of relevance for a general aid program is the pattern of state expenditure priorities. For Maine it was found that public expenditure priorities correlate quite closely with those of the federal government as reflected in the current emphasis on new education and public welfare measures. Similar data for South Dakota are presented here, although it should be stressed that it is much more difficult to make a comparative analysis in the case of South Dakota than in the case of Maine.

Table 8 shows that in 1962 South Dakota's expenditure effort for health and welfare was comparatively low, while its expenditure effort for education was considerably higher. Its expenditure effort for highways was more than twice the national average, although a proportionally high level of federal aid to rural states makes this a limited basis of comparison. Table 9 converts the above data into percentage

---

[37] Advisory Commission on Intergovernmental Relations, *Measures of State and Local Fiscal Capacity and Tax Effort, op. cit.,* p. 75.

changes. It can be seen from this table that South Dakota's expenditure effort did not rise as fast as the national average from 1957 to 1962 in the areas of health, welfare, and education, whereas for Maine expenditure effort grew faster than the national average for all three of these functional areas.

Table 8

Expenditure Effort by Function: South Dakota and the United States Average, 1962 (General expenditures per \$1,000 of personal income)

	(1) So. Dak.	(2) U.S.	(3) (1−2)
Education	\$ 57.05	\$ 50.52	\$+ 6.53
Highways	54.92	23.55	+31.37
Public welfare	10.61	11.56	− .95
Health and hospitals	4.98	9.87	− 4.89
All other	33.49	41.41	− 7.92
TOTAL	\$161.05	\$136.91	\$+24.14

SOURCE: U.S. Bureau of the Census, *Historical Statistics on Governmental Finances and Employment, 1962 Census of Governments,* Vol. VI, No. 4 (Washington, D.C.: U.S. Government Printing Office, 1964).

Table 9

Percentage Change in Expenditure Effort by Function: South Dakota and the United States Average, 1957 to 1962

	South Dakota % change	U.S. Average % change
Education	+ 5.2	+24.6
Highways	+10.0	+ 5.0
Public welfare	− a	+ 5.7
Health and hospitals	(− .8)	+10.4
All other	(− 6.1)	+34.0
TOTAL	+ 3.7	+18.4

a Less than .5 per cent.

SOURCE: U.S. Bureau of the Census, *Historical Statistics on Governmental Finances and Employment, 1962 Census of Governments,* Vol. VI, No. 4 (Washington, D.C.: U.S. Government Printing Office, 1964).

For several reasons, the data in Tables 8 and 9 are limited for comparative purposes. To the extent that United States Office of Business Economics figures understate personal income, this would be reflected in a tendency to overstate South Dakota's expenditure effort defined in terms of expenditures per $1,000 of personal income. Furthermore, the figures on highway expenditure effort are of limited value for comparative purposes because of South Dakota's relatively large needs in this area (due to low population density) and because of its well above average level of federal highway aid in relation to personal income. It is also quite possible that the public needs of rural states are sufficiently different for health and welfare that even in these areas a comparative analysis would be misleading.

Despite limitations in the comparability of these data, general conclusions can still be drawn. South Dakota expenditure priorities, for whatever reason, differ markedly from those of other and generally more urban states, as well as from those of the federal government as reflected in recent federal domestic expenditure policies. This is not to say that these priorities are "wrong" for South Dakota. It may well be that they merely reflect the fact that rural and predominantly farm states have different problems and needs than urban states. Nevertheless, it is quite likely that a general aid program would result in a different pattern of expenditures (and possibly also tax reduction) in South Dakota than would be the case if the same funds were allocated by the federal government for narrowly defined federal aid purposes, as has been the practice under the more traditional forms of federal aid.

C. State-Local Relations

The principal intergovernmental fiscal issue in South Dakota at the present time involves the amount of state financial aid to localities (*i.e.* for schools). This issue is covered in Part B, as it is a central consideration in the analysis of recent public finance developments in the state. Closely related to this issue is the question of whether existing state financial aid is distributed on a reasonably equitable basis between the larger, more urban communities and the state's smaller towns and rural areas. Four-fifths of South Dakota intergovernmental expenditures in 1964 as classified by the United States Bureau of the Census were for education and highways. The distribution of both education and highway aid is of interest for this report.

Distribution of State Aid for Local Schools

The present school aid distribution formula has been in effect for the past five years. In 1964-65 Sioux Falls School District Number 1 (the largest in the state) received state aid for education equivalent to 82 per cent of the average per pupil school aid payment in the state.[38] This is a much larger share than the 58 per cent of the per pupil state average received by Portland, Maine in fiscal 1965.

As indicated for Maine, a basic consideration in evaluating whether a school aid distribution formula is reasonably equitable are differences in tax capacity among localities. Sioux Falls School District Number 1 in 1964-65 had an adjusted assessed valuation per classroom unit 59 per cent *above* the state average. At the same time, its share of state school aid was 18 per cent below the state average, indicating that the distribution of state aid does not involve an especially high degree of equalization for differences in taxing capacity among school districts in South Dakota.

State Aid for Highways

The second major form of state intergovernmental expenditures in South Dakota is aid for highways in the form of shared taxes. Shared taxes for highways in 1964 totaled $2.5 million, 17 per cent of total state intergovernmental expenditures. The state shares with the counties one-half of the proceeds of the motor fuel tax distributed in propor-

---

[38] *South Dakota School Statistics, 1963-64,* State Superintendent of Public Instruction, Research Bulletin 45.3. The Sioux Falls School District contains approximately 10 per cent of the state's total public school enrollment.

tion to county assessed valuation. In addition 10 per cent of the proceeds from the sale of hunting and fishing licenses is returned to the counties for highway purposes.

Cities tend to be critical of this arrangement in that no funds are provided for city streets and roads. However, this situation is likely to be materially affected by pending legal action. The State Supreme Court in 1966 ordered the reapportionment of the Board of Supervisors of Minnehaha County (which contains the city of Sioux Falls). Until then, the majority of the board had been elected by the one-third of the people in the county who live outside of the city. Should the Minnehaha case lead to the reapportionment of other county boards, as is likely, the urban-rural distribution of state highway aid could be significantly altered.

Aside from intergovernmental expenditures for schools and highways, other forms of state aid are paid to cities and towns — but not to counties. The largest single category of state payments to local governments other than for education and highways is the shared alcoholic beverage tax paid to cities and towns for general local support. The total amount distributed to cities and towns under this program is approximately one-half of state aid to counties for highways. This general support for cities and towns must be seen as partially offsetting any favoritism toward counties and rural areas under the state aid programs for highways.

School Consolidation

A state government's role in school district consolidation is a major aspect of state-local relations in many states, and is generally a good indication of whether a state is playing a leadership role in major areas of joint state-local responsibility. Among the four selected states, the state government of South Dakota has been by far the least active in the field of school consolidation.

As a general rule, farm states tend to have more and smaller school districts than urban states. South Dakota stands out in this respect, having the second largest number of school districts of any state in the nation. (Nebraska has the largest number.) South Dakota had 2,873 school districts in 1964. Of the total, 1,190 (38 per cent) did not operate any schools, thus providing sizable "tax haven" benefits for many residents because of the much lower property taxes in these districts. Furthermore, the inefficiency of this proliferation of small school districts is suggested by the fact that South Dakota had the *lowest* pupil-teacher ratio in the nation in 1963.[39]

State Role in Property Tax Administration

Another important indication of a state's role in state-local relations is property tax administration. In contrast to Maine, the state of South Dakota has been active and has made progress in this field. Under a law enacted in 1955, the Office of County Director of Equalization was established to supervise assessments in every county. Prior to 1955 there were 1,900 county assessors, 17 of whom were full-time. By 1960 this number had been reduced to 230, with 110 full-time.

D. State Government

South Dakota's executive machinery is characterized by a large number of specialized administrative agencies and boards with highly fragmented authority. According to an Advisory Commission on Intergovernmental Relations study of South Dakota:

> The plethora of executive agencies is headed by an assortment of elective and appointive department heads and officers, full- and part-time commissions, and ex-officio boards and committees. Some appointments require

---

[39] South Dakota had 19.5 pupils per classroom teacher in 1963, compared to a national average of 25.5. Although there are advantages to small classroom size, the fact that South Dakota had the lowest classroom-teacher ratio in the nation is also a reflection of the inefficiency of the organization of school districts in the state. If the state had fewer districts, its salary scale for teachers undoubtedly could be improved, a widely shared goal among education groups. South Dakota's estimated average teacher salaries of $4,000 in 1964-65 ranked forty-ninth in the nation. (National Education Association, *Ranking of the States,* Washington, D.C. 1965.)

Senate confirmation while others do not. In some cases the tenure of office is defined, in others it is indefinite.[40]

This unwieldly administrative machinery tends to undermine the power and effectiveness of the Governor. As an illustration, the Governor currently serves as an ex-officio member of 17 boards on which he can be outvoted by other members, many of whom are separately elected "Constitutional Officers."[41] The state has eight Constitutional Officers (including the Superintendent of Public Instruction), each separately elected by the voters and therefore not directly responsible to the Governor. The Governor's role and responsibility are further limited by a two-term limit (two terms of two years each).

In sum, the Governor in South Dakota, as in Maine, is limited in his capacity to make and implement central expenditure and revenue policy decisions. Despite considerable sentiment for constitutional reform to eliminate the "long ballot" and reorganize the state's cumbersome administrative machinery, the state has never revised its 1889 Constitution.

Budget Staff

Another and related aspect of the Governor's position is the availability of qualified professional staff personnel to assist him in the formulation of state expenditure and revenue policies. Until 1963, the Governor of South Dakota did not have an effective central budget-making staff. The new three-man Office of the Budget established in 1963 has made it possible for the Governor to enlarge significantly his role in determining state expenditure priorities and policies. To further this objective, $85,000 was voted in 1965 for a study of state finances and accounting in an effort to

---

[40] Commission on Intergovernmental Relations, *A Survey Report on the Impact of Federal Grants-in-Aid on the Structure and Functions of State and Local Governments,* (Washington, D.C.: U.S. Government Printing Office, 1955), p. 368.

[41] *Ibid,* p. 369.

coordinate and computerize financial systems for purposes of central budgeting by the Governor and the Office of the Budget. This work was completed in March 1967, and as a result the state now has a computerized Central Data Processing system.

The Legislature

The rural and conservative orientation of the South Dakota legislature over the years has been a major factor in state politics. Even with reapportionment voted in 1965, rural areas continue to have a majority in the legislature, since the state's population is over 60 per cent rural as classified by the United States Bureau of the Census.

The rural orientation of the South Dakota legislature raises an important question for an assessment of the impact of general aid from the federal government. Basic to the policy choice between general and categorical aid at the federal level is the question of whether federal aid expenditure decisions should be made by a rural majority in predominantly farm states, such as South Dakota, or by an urban majority in Washington that would determine the way in which federal aid funds could be spent if new and expanded categorical aids were relied upon in the future instead of general aid. Eleven states, including South Dakota, had more than half of their 1960 population classified as rural.

In South Dakota there are a number of issues on which urban groups contend that the cities and larger towns are being shortchanged. Besides the concern of city officials about the distribution of state school and highway aid, other issues cited as illustrations of preferential treatment to rural areas are (1) the role of the state in defining the privileged jurisdiction of non-operating school districts; (2) the fact that state property tax mill levy ceilings are lower for farmland (12 mills) than for nonfarm real property (40 mills); and (3) the fact that gasoline for farm machinery is exempt from the state gasoline tax, while local governments must pay the tax for gasoline consumed by publicly owned vehicles. The effect of these issues cannot be measured with available general data.

Still, the figures cited above on state intergovernmental expenditures for Sioux Falls provide some basis on which to evaluate urban-rural fiscal relationships in South Dakota. Sioux Falls receives high per capita aid for education relative to the major cities in the other states studied and relative to its real property valuation. Although highway aid is limited to counties, cities receive general local support in the form of shared taxes. These factors at least suggest that there is not a marked imbalance in the treatment of cities in the distribution of existing financial aid. Moreover, if all county commissions are reapportioned as a result of the Minnehaha County court case, the issue of the distribution of highway aid is likely to be considerably alleviated as far as the cities and larger towns are concerned.

E. Summary Analysis

Under a general aid plan which distributed 1 per cent of the 1964 federal personal income tax base to the states, South Dakota would receive approximately $9.5 million without either an equalization or tax effort factor in the distribution formula. This is equal to 10 per cent of current state revenues exclusive of existing federal grants-in-aid.

Furthermore, South Dakota would materially benefit from an equalization factor if it is based on United States Office of Business Economics personal income data. This points up an important issue for a general aid plan. The analysis of South Dakota in this report suggests that in the development of a general aid program consideration should be given to whether available United States Department of Commerce per capita income data is a satisfactory index of economic need, or whether a more refined index should be used in the equalization factor for the distribution of general aid. The same reasoning and conclusions apply to any consideration of a tax effort "bonus" factor in a general aid distribution formula.

In South Dakota, as in Maine, it is likely that a major share of general aid from the federal government would go for education. Local schools would make a major claim, and would probably receive a sizable share of the state's general aid allocation. The same is true of the State University, although needs in the field of higher education in South Dakota do not appear to be as large as those of local schools.

Besides education, a second important possibility in South Dakota is that part of the state's general aid allocation would be channeled into local tax relief. (State funds were appropriated in 1966 to reduce local property taxes; further reductions were mentioned, but not spelled out in detail, in the Governor's 1967 message to the legislature.) This possibility points up a key potential problem area for a tax sharing program. While local tax relief may be a highly desirable objective in many states, this is contrary to an essential goal of many general aid plans which is to stimulate the public sector through increased state and local spending.

In South Dakota, it appears unlikely that any appreciable amounts of general aid funds would be allocated either for health or welfare. This is particularly true of public health in light of the strong resistance to spending in this area. In the welfare field the unpopularity of the Aid for Families With Dependent Children program and the fact that South Dakota public assistance benefit levels have tended to roughly equal, but not exceed, federal matching levels probably can be taken as an indication that the state on its own would not allocate any substantial amounts of unconditional aid funds for welfare purposes.

Highway financing in South Dakota is completely outside of the state's General Fund, and is given only "limited, sporadic consideration" by the Governor and the legislature.[42] Since a new form of general aid would in all probability be handled as part of the General Fund, the Department of Highways would not be expected to be a major recipient under present circumstances. The already high level of federal aid for highways is another factor which would mitigate against the use of general federal aid funds in this area.

A final purpose to which a major share of general aid might well be allocated in South Dakota is capital improve-

---

[42]State of South Dakota, *Governor's Budget Report, 1965-67*, p. a.

ments. In conjunction with the 1963 budget reforms, a capital improvements budget system was developed for the state. The principal area of state capital spending under this system is higher education. A 1964 study of State University capital construction needs indicated that an investment of $40 million will be needed for academic facilities to meet projected higher education enrollment needs of the 1970's.[43] (This is exclusive of separately financed dormitory construction.) The already noted high priority assigned to university expenditure needs in South Dakota can be taken as an indication that some part of a new general aid allotment received by South Dakota would be allocated under the state's capital improvements budget for State University academic facilities construction. As for local capital spending, the role of the state in this area has been limited to the general local support provided through tax sharing. State General Fund revenues have not been used for this purpose. Although there are needs in this area, the likelihood of federal general aid funds for the State of South Dakota being allocated for this purpose is not nearly as great as the likelihood of *direct* state capital spending.

In the political sphere, several potential problems of a general aid program have already been discussed. One is the lack of leadership by the state in major areas of intergovernmental relations. South Dakota's traditional fiscal conservatism makes it difficult for even a vigorous Governor to expand the leadership role of the state in this field. State school aid is limited. And the state has lagged in the field of school consolidation, an important area of state responsibility in sparsely populated states. In the health field, the fact that the state has done even as much as it has is largely due to federal aid. The same is true, though to a lesser degree, of public welfare. While it can be argued that this lack of state leadership presents problems from the point of view of a general aid plan, it can be pointed out on the other side that the state has made progress in property tax administration and that the state universities and colleges are well developed and financed.

---

[43]State of South Dakota, *Capital Improvement Budget,* 1965-67, p. ix.

A second potential problem relates to the organization of the state government. The state has not revised its Constitution since it was adopted, despite considerable sentiment for reform of the state's highly complex administrative structure.

3. Georgia - Mississippi

Of the 16 lowest income states, all but five are in the Southern region as classified by the U.S. Bureau of the Census. Moreover, the policy issue raised by a general aid program is particularly important for the South in light of the frequently expressed concern that unconditional general aid funds distributed to Southern states would be used for segregated public facilities and programs. Because of these special considerations, two states in the South were selected for this study.

The two selected Southern states (Georgia and Mississippi) offer an interesting contrast. Georgia ranked eighth in 1963 per capita income among the 16 lower-income states and third among the 11 lower-income Southern states. Mississippi ranked at the very bottom of the 50 states. Georgia with an estimated population of 4.3 million in 1964 is nearly twice as large as Mississippi. In the decade 1952-62, the population of Georgia grew by 14 per cent compared to the 19 per cent for the nation. In the same period the population of Mississippi grew by only 2.8 per cent. Georgia and Mississippi also differ in rural-urban population composition. Forty-six per cent of the population of Georgia lived in Standard Metropolitan Statistical Areas in 1960 as compared to 8.6 per cent for Mississippi. Mississippi has the highest percentage of Negroes of all states — 42 per cent in 1960, compared to 29 per cent in Georgia.

A. Impact of Existing Federal Aids

In 1964 Georgia received $214 million in intergovernmental revenues from the federal government, accounting for 29.4 per cent of total state general expenditures. Mississippi received $123 million, accounting for 28.4 per cent of total general expenditures.

Table 10   **Intergovernmental Revenue from the Federal Government: Georgia and Mississippi, 1964**

	Georgia		Mississippi	
	Dollars (Thousands)	%	Dollars (Thousands)	%
Education	$ 26,416	12.3	$ 13,764	11.2
Highways	88,191	41.2	45,649	37.0
Public welfare	80,246	37.5	47,941	38.9
Health and hospitals	6,863	3.2	5,549	4.5
Natural resources	5,125	2.4	4,258	3.4
Employment Security Administration	6,474	3.0	4,405	3.6
Other	856	.4	1,754	1.4
TOTAL	$214,171	100.0	$123,320	100.0

SOURCE: U.S. Bureau of the Census, *Compendium of State Government Finances in 1964* (Washington, D.C.: U.S. Government Printing Office, 1965).

As in Maine and South Dakota, there is considerable resentment toward federal aid in Georgia and Mississippi. This is especially notable in Georgia in the field of education as discussed below. For Mississippi, a study by a White House task force on federal aid to Mississippi found the state a "paradox." According to a *New York Times* report: "While publicly condeming the Administration and Great Society programs, state political leaders are quietly accepting and seeking federal help."[44]

---

[44]*The New York Times,* April 19, 1966, p. 10.

On an over-all basis, the total amount of federal inter-governmental revenues received by Georgia and Mississippi does not reflect a high degree of income equalization. Per capita intergovernmental revenues from the federal government in 1964 averaged $47.48 for the 50 states. Georgia and Mississippi were above average with $49.88 and $53.29 respectively. However, their share was not nearly as high as South Dakota's ($79.97) and that of other more sparsely populated states.

A major characteristic of the impact of federal grants-in-aid on Georgia and Mississippi is that in key areas the two states have failed to utilize available federal aid by significant amounts. For this reason, undermatching (or under-utilization, as the term applies in the public welfare field) is treated in more detail here than for the preceding two states.

Education

At the state level, Georgia received $26.4 million and Mississippi $13.8 million in aid from the federal government for education in 1964. Federal aid for education had a relatively small fiscal impact, accounting for some 9 per cent of total state educational spending in both states.

Uncertainty about pending school desegregation controversies makes it much more difficult to assess present attitudes toward federal aid for education in Georgia and Mississippi than in Maine and South Dakota.

Despite objections from educators, the Georgia General Assembly in 1965 enacted an amendment to the state appropriations act requiring that if federal aid funds for "new program areas" are accepted by the state Board of Education, "the Budget Bureau shall reduce the (state) appropriation for any item or part thereof which can be financed with federal funds in lieu of state funds."[45] A proviso was added that this substitution of funds is not to go into effect "if it shall in any way reduce the eligibility of the state for federal funds." As a result of this proviso, the amendment has been

---

[45] General Assembly of Georgia, Act No. 37 (H.B. No. 25), Section 18.

found not to apply in the case of aid under the Elementary and Secondary Education Act of 1965. This act contained a requirement that state and local spending for education combined be not less than in fiscal year 1964.[46]

Table 11

State Revenue from the Federal Government for Education by Program: Georgia and Mississippi, 1964 (Thousands of dollars)

	Georgia	Mississippi
School lunch and special milk programs	$ 5,496	$ 4,680
Cooperative vocational education	2,798	2,737
Vocational rehabilitation	5,303[a]	418
Defense Education Activities	2,543	821
Manpower development and training and Area redevelopment training activities	N.A.	336
Amounts received by state universities (not included elsewhere)	9,916	4,306
Other	360	466
TOTAL	$26,416	$13,764

N.A. — Not available

[a] Includes amounts for manpower training and development.

SOURCE: Based on data from worksheets of the U.S. Bureau of the Census, Governments Division.

Until 1965, the largest single federal aid program for elementary and secondary education was financial aid to schools in federally impacted areas. Although these funds are not paid to or through state governments, this program is of special interest for this study because of its negative redistributional effect. Mississippi, for example, receives significantly less on a per capita basis than the national average. In 1964 school districts in Mississippi received $.72 per capita under P.L. 815 and P.L. 874. This was $.97 below the national average of $1.69. Georgia, which has more federal installations than Mississippi, received $1.67 per capita under these two Acts.

---

[46] U.S. Congress, P.L. 89-10, Section 207 (c) (2).

Employment Security

In 1964, Georgia received $6.5 million and Mississippi $4.4 million from the federal government for employment security administration. As in the case of Maine and South Dakota, the administrative impact of this aid was found to be substantial.

Health and Hospitals

In the South a larger proportion of hospitals and health facilities are publicly operated than in other regions. The bulk of these facilities are locally operated hospitals receiving Hill-Burton construction aid. Two aspects of Hill-Burton aid are important for this study. As discussed below, hospitals present some of the most serious problems in terms of compliance with Title VI of the Civil Rights Act of 1964 prohibiting segregation in federally aided facilities. Another important aspect of the Hill-Burton Act for an analysis of the lower-income states is that it involves a very high degree of income equalization. Mississippi in 1964 received an allocation of $2.21 per capita under this program, almost twice the national average of $1.15 per capita. Georgia received an allocation of $1.69 per capita.

In the case of public health services, it is notable that the fiscal impact of federal aid (as a percentage of total state spending) is smaller in Georgia and Mississippi than in Maine or South Dakota. This is partly due to the fact that both Georgia and Mississippi have strong and active state health agencies which receive good support from their respective legislatures. This is in marked contrast to South Dakota, where the legislature in 1965 refused to provide federal aid matching funds. The state health departments of both Georgia and Mississippi are in a position to obtain the necessary financial support to take advantage of all available federal grants-in-aid.

Federal aid accounted for 31 per cent of the expenditures for regular operations (exclusive of state health institutions) by the Georgia Department of Public Health in 1964, and 35 per cent of the expenditures of the Mississippi

State Board of Health for essentially the same purposes. Federal aid, plus the required state matching funds, accounted for between 50 per cent and 60 per cent of total state public health service expenditures in the two states. (This compares to two-thirds for Maine and virtually 100 per cent for South Dakota.)

Georgia and Mississippi also stand out in that under-matching of federal public health service aid programs is limited. Mississippi in 1964 took full advantage of all eight of the formula grant-in-aid programs of the Public Health Service (PHS) for which it is possible to compare figures on formula allotments with the actual expenditures of federal aid funds. It was the only state of the four selected for this study which used its full allotment under all of these programs.

The generally high levels of health spending in Georgia and Mississippi reflect both the stimulus of federal aids and the popularity of public health programs. The degree of expenditure priority attached to health programs in the two states is shown by the fact that in 1964 Mississippi and Georgia ranked first and second respectively among the 50 states in state-local expenditures for health and hospitals per $1,000 of personal income.

Highways

Federal funds for highways accounted for approximately 60 per cent of state highway construction expenditures in Georgia in 1964 and 65 per cent in Mississippi. There was sentiment in some quarters in both Georgia and Mississippi that there has been a tendency to put too much emphasis on highway construction because of the stimulative effect of federal aid. The policy-making impact of this program is not treated here, as the separate status of highway financing in the two selected Southern states results in an effect very similar to that already described above for Maine and South Dakota.

Natural Resources

Natural resources was the smallest major functional category of intergovernmental revenues from the federal government in both Georgia and Mississippi in 1964. Federal aid payments to Georgia in 1964 accounted for 16 per cent of state expenditures for natural resources. Payments to Mississippi accounted for 27 per cent of state expenditures in this category. In both Georgia and Mississippi the bulk of the funds received under the agricultural programs are administered by the State University. Thus, these agricultural grant programs tend not have a major and direct impact on the central administrative and policy-making machinery of the state government.

Public Welfare

Georgia and Mississippi differ in the way in which public welfare programs are administered. In Mississippi (as in Maine and South Dakota) the state administers and finances the federally aided public assistance programs. In Georgia, on the other hand, the state "supervises" the administration of the four major categorical federal aid programs and provides most of the required matching funds, but assistance payments are actually made and administered at the county level.

General relief is financed entirely by the county in Georgia and Mississippi and is a negligible factor in both states compared to public assistance spending under the federally aided categories. Based on the 1962 Census of Governments, cash assistance other than under the four federally aided categories was *less than 1 per cent* of total payments in the aided categories for both states.

The fiscal impact of federal aid for public welfare is very large in both Georgia and Mississippi. The federal government directly financed approximately three-fourths of state public welfare expenditures in both states in 1964.

The impact of public assistance federal aid in Georgia and Mississippi is of considerable interest for this report, thus it is described at some length. We begin by comparing the impact of federal aid for health programs with that for public assistance. As already pointed out, the state health agencies in both Georgia and Mississippi are in a position to take full advantage of all of the various federal grants-in-aid for public health services. In sharp contrast, the legislatures of both states consistently provide *significantly less* than the amount necessary to take full advantage of available federal aid for public assistance. The legislatures of both states make lump sum appropriations to be allocated among the federally aided public assistance categories by state welfare officials. In each of the states, welfare officials indicated that these state funds are not sufficient to finance public assistance benefits up to the need limits set by the state for all beneficiaries qualified under the state's own eligibility standards. State legislators, in turn, contend that the reason for this short-fall is that the total amount of available state funds is limited, a condition which does not apply for the apparently high priority health programs.

In light of this disparity, between the impact of health and welfare federal grants-in-aid, underutilization of federal public assistance aid in Georgia and Mississippi warrants special analysis. Using the limited survey data available on the extent of unmet public assistance need per recipient, estimates of public assistance underutilization by state have been developed by the staff of the United States Senate Subcommittee on Intergovernmental Relations.[47] The amount of underutilization as measured by these data was greatest under Aid for Families with Dependent Children (AFDC). For example, these data indicated that Mississippi in November-December of 1961 could have received an additional $1 million in federal aid under AFDC by putting up state funds of $400,000. This would have doubled the amount of federal aid received by Mississippi under AFDC. Georgia did not underutilize AFDC on this basis, but its relatively strict eligibility requirements tend to have the same effect, as shown below.

---

[47] Data developed by Arnold H. Raphaelson of the Staff of the Senate Subcommittee on Intergovernmental Relations of the Committee on Governmental Operations. (Unpublished.)

Although lump sum state appropriations are made for public assistance in both states, different types of devices have been used by the legislatures of Georgia and Mississippi to hold down spending under the AFDC program. The Mississippi legislature since 1952 has placed a flat ceiling of $3.2 million on the amount of the state lump sum public assistance appropriation which can be used for AFDC. This means that state welfare officials have to spread AFDC funds further than in the other federal public assistance categories. This is reflected in the estimate above of AFDC underutilization in Mississippi. In Georgia, on the other hand, the General Assembly has set various statutory AFDC eligibility requirements which likewise limit total AFDC spending.

In effect, two types of underutilization are involved here: (1) cases in which benefit levels are lower than the state defined levels of need up to which the federal government will provide aid; and (2) cases in which eligibility rules remove people from the roles who would in other states receive federally matched public assistance benefits. Mississippi has wider AFDC coverage and lower benefits than Georgia, reflecting the first of the two types of underutilization. Georgia has higher AFDC benefits but narrower program coverage, reflecting the second. These distinctions are illustrated in the following data on benefits levels and recipient rates.

Average monthly AFDC payments in Mississippi in June 1963 were $9 per recipient, by far the lowest level in the nation.[48] For the same period Mississippi's benefit ceilings were $25 for one child and $90 for a family. In Georgia, with ceilings of $34 for one child and $134 for a family, average AFDC payments were $23 per recipient — 2.5 times as high as in Mississippi.

The difference in AFDC coverage between the two states is shown by the contrast between Georgia and Mississippi in AFDC recipient rates. Mississippi had more than twice the proportion of children under 18 on AFDC in June

---

[48] Advisory Commission on Intergovernmental Relations, *Statutory and Administrative Controls Associated with Federal Grants for Public Assistance,* Washington, D.C., May 1964, p. 25.

of 1963. In Mississippi 67 children per 1,000 under 18 were aided under AFDC, compared to 29 children per 1,000 under 18 in Georgia,[49] indicating that, while Mississippi could receive significant additional AFDC funds from the federal government by raising benefit levels, Georgia probably could achieve the same result by liberalizing its eligibility requirements and putting more people on the roles.

Taking AFDC underutilization as a whole (both types described), the magnitude of underutilization under AFDC by Georgia and Mississippi is suggested in Table 12. This table shows comparative state figures on aid under the four federally aided public assistance categories in 1964 relative to total state population.

Table 12

Per Capita Federal Grant Expenditures for Public Assistance: Georgia, Mississippi, and the National Average, 1964

	OAA	AFDC	AB	APTD	Total
Georgia	$11.50	$ 3.22	$ .44	$ 3.31	$18.47
Mississippi	12.74	3.91	.56	3.21	20.42
50 State Average	$ 7.27	$ 5.35	$ .28	$ 1.49	$14.39

SOURCE: U.S. Bureau of the Census, *Compendium of State Government Finances in 1964* (Washington, D.C.: U.S. Government Printing Office, 1965).

Per capita payments under AFDC for Georgia and Mississippi in 1964 were below the national average by 27 per cent and 40 per cent respectively. Per capita expenditures in both states under the other three programs were well above the national average.

The reasons given for the unpopularity of the AFDC program in Georgia and Mississippi are essentially the same as in Maine and South Dakota. Added to these considerations is a racial factor. Some opposition to AFDC in Georgia and Mississippi undoubtedly arises from the fact that a high

---

[49] *Ibid.,* p. 51

proportion of Negroes are receiving aid under this program. Figures available for Mississippi indicate that 80.6 per cent of the AFDC cases in September 1964 were Negroes.[50] Negroes on the other hand constitute 42 per cent of the total population of Mississippi. The 1955 survey report on Mississippi for the Kestnbaum Commission stressed racial considerations underlying the unpopularity of the AFDC program in the state:

> Many critics in Mississippi contend that under the aid to dependent children program the state has been induced to undertake a governmental program that undermines the social and moral standards of the state's large Negro population. The state legislature has reflected popular opposition by reducing appropriations. Consequently, average monthly payments per recipient are about one-quarter of the national average.[51]

While Georgia and Mississippi differ in the way in which they underutilize AFDC, the two states underutilize the three other federally aided public assistance categories on the same basis. That is, benefit levels are below the state defined levels of need up to which the federal government will provide matching aid. The data developed by the U.S. Senate Subcommittee on Intergovernmental Relations estimate public assistance underutilization for Old Age Assistance (OAA) on a monthly basis for the summer of 1960. Using these data, Georgia could have received an additional $100,000 by putting up $55,000 in state funds. Mississippi could have received an additional $300,000 by putting up $160,000 in state funds. On an annual basis this would have been approximately 3 per cent of federal intergovernmental revenues for OAA in Georgia and 15 per cent in Mississippi. Both states were also found to be underutilizing aid for the disabled and aid for the blind, although the amounts involved were smaller. Interviews with state officials indicate that these data are likely, if

---

[50] Mississippi State Department of Public Welfare, Memorandum No. 1447, Jackson, Mississippi, December 30, 1964.

[51] Commission on Intergovernmental Relations, *Summaries of Survey Reports on the Administrative and Fiscal Impact of Federal Grants-in-Aid* (Washington, D.C.: U.S. Government Printing Office, 1955), p. 60.

anything, to understate the extent of the discrepancy between actual federal aid payments and the states' entitlement to federal aid.

B. Public Finance

State governments of the South characteristically play a more dominant role in public finance than state governments in other regions. Southern state public finance tends to be characterized by: (1) a comparatively high proportion of state-local taxes collected at the state level; (2) heavy reliance on sales and gross receipts taxes; (3) below average effective property tax rates; and (4) relatively high state intergovernmental expenditures, with well above average state support for local schools. These four characteristics for Georgia and Mississippi are shown in Table 13.

In Georgia and Mississippi, tax and intergovernmental expenditure policies have been relatively more constant over the years than in Maine and South Dakota. The state governments of both states already play a dominant role in state-local finances as shown in Table 13. Thus, the most important consideration for the study of Georgia and Mississippi public finance is not so much what is likely to happen in the future, but what these two states are doing now and have done in the past. In addition to a stress on past expenditure and revenue trends in this section, more is done here than for the two other states to relate public finance in the selected states to neighboring states. This has been done because so many of the Southern states are lower-income states.

Tax Effort in the South

Assessment of state-local public finance trends in the South from the point of view of a general aid program involves important questions of tax effort and resource allocation. An underlying assumption of general aid is that, on the whole, states with substantial unmet public needs are making a strong tax effort to satisfy these needs.

Table 13   **Major Characteristics of Public Finances
in Georgia and Mississippi**

1. *State tax revenues as a percentage of total state-local tax revenues (1963-64):*	
Georgia	65.8%
Mississippi	66.0%
U.S. Average	50.7%
2. *Sales and gross receipts taxes as a percentage of total state taxes (1964):*	
Georgia	73.2%
Mississippi	74.9%
U.S. Average	57.7%
3. *Effective 1960 property tax rates (valued at market prices):*	
Georgia	.9%
Mississippi	.7%
U.S. average	1.4%
4. *Estimated percentage of revenues for public elementary and secondary schools from state governments (1964-65):*	
Georgia	65.5%
Mississippi	57.7%
U.S. average	40.0%

SOURCES:
1. U.S. Bureau of the Census, *Governmental Finances in 1963-64.* (Washington, D. C.: U.S. Government Printing Office, 1965.)
2. U.S. Bureau of the Census, *Compendium of State Government Finances in 1964* (Washington, D.C.: U.S. Government Printing Office, 1965).
3. Advisory Commission on Intergovernmental Relations, *Measures of State and Local Fiscal Capacity and Tax Effort* (Washington, D.C., October 1962).
4. National Education Association, *Ranking of the States, 1965,* Washington, D.C., 1965.

There is often a tendency to select one or two Southern states which make a high tax effort and generalize that, while the Southern states may have low per capita expenditure levels, their tax effort to maintain even these levels is very high. Two Southern states stand out as having a high tax effort — Louisiana and Mississippi. A closer analysis indicates that these two states are atypical. Of the 11 states in the Southern region in the lowest third of the states in 1963 per capita income, only two (Louisiana and Mississippi) were above average in tax effort in fiscal 1964, using as the definition of tax effort state and local taxes relative to personal income. Moreover, tax effort in the South has been declining relative to the rest of the nation in recent years. There was a noticeable weakening in the tax effort of the Southern states between the 1957 and 1962 comprehensive Census of Governments. (These are done on a five-year basis.) The tax effort rank of all but three of the 11 lower-income Southern states dropped from 1957 to 1962.

The relative decline in tax effort in Georgia and Mississippi from 1957 to 1962 can be seen by comparison with the nation as a whole. For the nation as a whole, state-local taxes grew 1.7 times the growth in personal income from 1957 to 1962. Georgia and Mississippi had close to the same tax effort levels in 1962 as in 1957, indicating that state and local taxes grew at approximately the same rate as personal income. Georgia state-local taxes rose by 33.4 per cent from 1957 to 1962, and personal income grew by 32.8 per cent, resulting in a ratio of increased taxes to increased income of 1.02:1. In Mississippi state and local taxes grew by 35 per cent and personal income by 35.8 per cent, resulting in a ratio of .98:1.

Only West Virginia and Louisiana of the 11 lower-income Southern states had higher ratios than the national average of 1.7:1.

Table 14	**Percentage Increase in State-Local Taxes and Personal Income: Georgia, Mississippi, and the United States Average, 1957-1962**		
	% Increase Taxes	% Increase Income	Ratio
Georgia	33.5	32.8	1.02:1
Mississippi	35.2	35.8	.98:1
U.S. Average	44.5	26.2	1.7:1

SOURCE: U.S. Bureau of the Census, *Compendium of State Government Finances in 1964* (Washington, D.C.: U.S. Government Printing Office, 1965).

Relationship of Tax Effort to Expenditure Effort

In interpreting tax effort data, it is helpful to compare tax effort with expenditure effort in order to determine whether a given change in tax effort produces a similar change in expenditure effort. (Expenditure effort for purposes of this comparative analysis of Georgia and Mississippi public finance trends is defined as state-local general expenditures, minus federal grants-in-aid, per $1,000 of personal income.)

Table 15

Expenditure Effort: Georgia, Mississippi, and the United States Average, 1957 and 1962
(General expenditures, minus federal grants-in-aid, per $1,000 of personal income)

	1957	1962	Increase
Georgia	$112.80	$117.76	$ 4.46
Mississippi	113.72	137.35	23.64
U.S. Average	$104.76	$119.01	$14.25

SOURCE: U.S. Bureau of the Census, *Historical Statistics on Governmental Finances and Employment: 1962 Census of Governments,* Vol. VI, No. 4 (Washington, D.C.: U.S. Government Printing Office, 1964).

Ordinarily it would be expected that a change in tax effort would be reflected in a change of approximately the same magnitude in expenditure effort. The important point brought out in Table 15 is that, while tax effort for Mississippi declined from 1957 to 1962, Mississippi's expenditure effort rose quite sharply. In fact, it rose almost twice as much as the U.S. average.

The key to this discrepancy is *state-local debt.* Mississippi began the period with a very high tax effort (second highest in the nation). The failure of Mississippi tax effort to rise from 1957 to 1962 may well be a reflection of the widely held view that once a certain point is reached in the relationship between state-local taxes and income it is difficult to increase tax rates any further. Beyond this point, other sources, such as debt, have to be relied upon to finance increases in expenditure levels. The alternative is to defer expenditure increases until such time as personal income rises sufficiently to permit tax rate increases without markedly raising tax effort, or until tax effort in other states catches up and it is then possible to increase taxes relative to income.

In the 1957-62 period Mississippi total state and local debt approximately doubled. Looking at debt per $1,000 of personal income, Mississippi's debt grew by $74.29, compared to $31.68 for the nation. This increase in debt permitted Mississippi's expenditure effort to increase without a corresponding increase in tax effort.

Table 16 **State-Local Debt per $1,000 of Personal Income: Georgia, Mississippi, and the United States Average, 1957 and 1962**

	1957	1962	Increase	% Change
Georgia	$161.01	$183.63	$ 22.62	+14.0
Mississippi	151.64	225.93	74.29	+49.0
U.S. Average	$152.10	$183.78	$ 31.68	+20.0

SOURCE: U.S. Bureau of the Census, *Historical Statistics on Governmental Finances and Employment: 1962 Census of Governments,* Vol. VI, No. 4 (Washington, D.C.: U.S. Government Printing Office, 1964).

The data for Georgia indicates quite a different picture. The decline in Georgia tax effort from 1957 to 1962 relative to the nation carried over into the expenditure area. Excluding federal grants-in-aid, Georgia general expenditures per $1,000 of personal income grew by 5 per cent from 1957 to 1962, approximately one-third of the average for the nation as a whole. The state's debt relative to income also increased more slowly than the average for the nation (14 per cent for Georgia as compared to 20 per cent for the nation). In sum, Georgia differs from Mississippi in two important respects. Georgia did not begin the period with such a high tax effort that there are extenuating circumstances which can explain its failure to raise tax effort as fast as the rest of the nation. Secondly, Georgia did not go nearly as far as Mississippi in offsetting its relative weakening in tax effort by increasing state-local debt.

Expenditure Effort by Major Function

In the preceding state case studies, 1957 and 1962 Census of Governments data were used to compare rates of change in expenditure effort by major function as in Table 17.

Table 17

Changes in Expenditure Effort by Function: Georgia, Mississippi and United States Average, 1957 to 1962 (Expenditures per $1,000 of personal income)

	Georgia % Change	Mississippi % Change	U.S. Average % Change
Education	+ 5.0	+34.2	+24.6
Highways	+26.9	+ 7.7	+ 5.0
Public welfare	− 4.1	+15.7	+ 5.7
Health and hospitals	+21.9	+44.6	+10.4
All other	+ 9.5	+40.5	+34.0

SOURCE: U.S. Bureau of the Census, *Historical Statistics on Governmental Finances and Employment: 1962 Census of Governments,* Vol. IV, No. 4 (Washington, D.C.: U.S. Government Printing Office, 1964).

From 1957 to 1962 Mississippi expenditure effort grew at a faster rate than the U.S. average in every category. Georgia expenditure effort grew by less than the average in all but one category — highways. The most significant relative expenditure effort decline for Georgia as far as the impact of a general aid program is concerned was in education. In 1957 Georgia's state-local expenditure effort for education was 16.5 per cent above the national average. Five years later in 1962 it was 1.7 per cent *below* the national average.

Georgia's relative decline in expenditure effort for education does not appear to be due to any lack of need for increased educational spending. It was estimated in 1965 by Georgia State Department of Education officials that an additional $100 million annually was needed for elementary and secondary education in Georgia simply to make the state's education expenditure levels comparable to the national average. This would have meant an increase of 28 per cent in total expenditures for public elementary and secondary education. Of this $100 million, it was estimated that $40 million was needed for increased teachers' salaries and the remainder for school construction and the development of new programs. This additional $100 million is above and beyond estimated allocations for Georgia under the Elementary and Secondary Education Act of 1965.

In the welfare field Georgia's expenditure effort actually declined by 4.1 per cent from 1957 to 1962, while Mississippi and the U.S. average rose 15.7 per cent and 5.7 per cent respectively. Georgia's decline in this area is made all the more significant by the fact that for every additional dollar the state spends for welfare, the state receives on the average three federal aid dollars.

Set against the large increase in expenditure effort for highways (for which all required state matching funds are provided), the relative lag in Georgia's expenditure effort for education and welfare raises serious questions for a general aid plan. There are bound to be major highway needs in states such as Georgia where recent urban population growth has been significant and transportation is important for further industrial development. But the marked discrepancies in expenditure effort increases for education, welfare, and highways between Georgia and Mississippi, and between Georgia and the national average, suggest that the pattern of spending priorities in Georgia is quite different from those of other states. It also appears to be quite different from that of the federal government as reflected in recent federal domestic spending policies and programs.

At this point several offsetting factors should be noted which could have the effect of making Georgia's spending priorities under a program of general federal aid to the states more closely resemble the national pattern. Since 1962,

Georgia's expenditure effort for education has increased slightly faster than the national average. It is also relevant that in Georgia the state government plays a dominant role in education financing, and the localities have tended to lag in raising their share of school expenditures. With respect to public welfare, the General Assembly is said to have become increasingly more receptive to proposals for expanding programs in this area. As a result, new and well-financed programs were initiated in 1965-66, particularly in the child welfare service areas. Finally, it appears quite likely on the basis of current data that Georgia highway spending relative to income may have been unrepresentative in the 1962 data. In 1964 Georgia highway expenditure effort was above the national average, but by considerably less than in 1962. Taken together, these mitigating factors could result in a different assessment of priorities in the allocation of unconditional general aid than have been characteristic of Georgia's expenditure policies in the 1957-62 period. But, as this is by no means certain, Georgia's historical expenditure pattern, as well as the 1965 state policy on using federal school aid to reduce state spending, must be taken into account in an evaluation of the likely effect of a federal general aid program in Georgia.

C. State-Local Relations

The high proportion of state-local taxes collected at the state level in the South is reflected in a correspondingly high level of state support for major local services. The principal state-aided service in the South, as in the nation as a whole, is education. State governments provided more than one-half of revenue receipts for public elementary and secondary education in all but two of the 11 lower-income Southern states (Arkansas and Oklahoma) in fiscal 1965. State aid for education accounted for 65.5 per cent of local school revenues in Georgia and 57.7 per cent in Mississippi in 1965.[52]

---

[52] National Education Association, *op. cit.,* p. 50.

The principal difference in the level and composition of intergovernmental expenditures between Georgia and Mississippi is that Georgia devotes proportionately more of its intergovernmental expenditures to education. Georgia devoted 82 per cent of state intergovernmental spending to education in 1964, compared to 65 per cent for Mississippi. Approximately 21 per cent of Mississippi's intergovernmental payments in 1964 were for highways as compared to 12 per cent in Georgia. Another 8 per cent of Mississippi's intergovernmental expenditures in 1964 were in the form of reimbursements for state granted homestead exemptions.

The homestead exemption is more prevalent in the South than in other regions, thus warranting special attention in this chapter. The use of the homestead exemption as a state tax device grew up in the Depression. In the 1930's, 14 states adopted homestead exemptions, basically as a means of avoiding tax foreclosures. Seven states still have homestead exemptions of sufficient size and scope to influence local property taxation in a major way. Of these seven states, five are in the South. Both Georgia and Mississippi grant homestead exemptions. However, Mississippi reimburses localities for the exemption, while Georgia does not.

Frederick and Edna Bird, in their study of *The Role of the State in Strengthening the Property Tax* for the Advisory Commission on Intergovernmental Relations criticize the practice of homestead exemptions as discriminatory against "tenant and business classes."[53] The homestead exemption is subject to further criticism in Mississippi because it is very costly to administer (3 per cent of the value of the exemption is required to administer the program) and because it has an unfavorable effect on property tax administration. Above all, the exemption tends to keep assessment ratios at arbitrarily low levels. The lower the assessment ratio, the more valuable is the exemption. According to the ACIR study, "on the basis of a 20 per cent assessment ratio in Mississippi, a $5,000 exemption would

---

[53] Advisory Commission on Intergovernmental Relations, *The Role of the State in Strengthening the Property Tax,* Vol. 1, Washington, D.C., June 1963, p. 79.

actually give tax exemption to a $25,000 dwelling."[54]

The homestead exemption in Georgia is less inclusive than in Mississippi, covering 33.7 per cent of the total assessed value of locally assessed real estate in 1961, compared to 44.5 per cent in Mississippi.[55]

State Role in Property Tax Administration

Despite the effect of the state granted homestead exemption in narrowing the local property tax base, Georgia has been more active in recent years in strengthening the property tax and improving its administration than any of the other three selected states. Mississippi has not been active in this area, which in part reflects the desire of local governments to avoid jeopardizing advantages which they now receive as a result of the state's homestead exemption reimbursement system.

The Georgia Revenue Department's program for strengthening the property tax is based on state interest-free loans and state approved commercial loans for county property tax revaluation and equalization. For a locality to obtain a loan, the state must approve the appraisal firm, and the locality must agree to comply with detailed "minimum standards" prescribed by the state for the conduct of revaluation and equalization programs. Of the state's 159 counties, 50 had completed revaluation and equalization programs and 45 have programs in process in 1965. Completed programs have resulted in major increases in the total amount of local property taxes.

State Aid for Local Schools

In Maine and South Dakota the most controversial current intergovernmental, as well as public finance, issue is the level of state aid for local schools. This subject was not found to be as important a political issue in Georgia and

---

[54] *Ibid.*

[55] U.S. Bureau of the Census, *Property Tax Assessments in the United States: Census of Governments 1962,* Preliminary Report No. 4, Washington, D.C., 1963.

Mississippi, probably because school aid is already at high levels relative to total elementary and secondary public school spending.

Aside from the level of school aid, the distribution of school aid is important to an assessment of the likely effect of a general aid program. The biggest question in this area is whether there is reasonable equity between urban and rural areas in the selected states.

Until January 1964, when the Georgia Minimum Foundation Program was revised, urban areas received a significantly smaller share of state school aid than rural communities. This situation was changed markedly under the new law. Prior to the enactment of the 1964 law, Atlanta's per pupil share of state aid for education was 63.5 per cent of the state average per pupil payment. Under the 1964 law, Atlanta's percentage of aid was increased to approximately 75 per cent of the state average. This is larger than the share received by Portland, Maine (58 per cent), but smaller than that for Sioux Falls, South Dakota (82 per cent).

The main point here is that the increase in the share of state school aid to urban areas in Georgia was largely a result of the changes in the political climate brought about by United States Supreme Court reapportionment decisions. Reapportionment has also resulted in substantial increases in the amounts of state aid received by Georgia cities for highways and health purposes. Further reapportionment has been ordered in Georgia to give additional representation to the urban areas, and it is possible that there will also be further upward revisions in the share of inter-governmental assistance allocated to urban communities.

Under the Mississippi Minimum Foundation Program enacted in 1954, the share of school aid to Jackson, the largest city in the state, is greater than that of Atlanta under the 1964 revisions in the Georgia school aid distribution formula. Using 1963-64 data, the Jackson school district received 81 per cent of the state per pupil average under the Minimum Foundation Program.[56]

---

[56] *Rankings of Mississippi School Districts, 1963-64,* Mississippi State Department of Education, Division of Administration and Finance, June 1965.

School Consolidation

In Maine and South Dakota it was found that a key index of the willingness of the state to assume leadership in the field of state-local relations is its role in school district consolidation. In Maine, under an appointive Education Commissioner, considerable progress has been made in this field; while in South Dakota, which has an elected State School Superintendent, the state has lagged. Both Georgia and Mississippi also have elected chief state school officials, which many contend mitigates against educational leadership at the state level. Nevertheless, both states have done more in the way of school consolidation than South Dakota.

The Mississippi school consolidation program initiated in 1955 is now largely completed. Under Mississippi's program the state used the $6.5 million state capital construction school aid fund as a lever to achieve its school consolidation objectives. These funds are distributed only to school districts which adhere to state standards as to the size and composition of school districts. Georgia is presently in the midst of a major school consolidation program, under which it too is using state capital construction aid to localities as an instrument to obtain compliance.

County Consolidation

Although progress has been made on school district consolidation in Georgia and Mississippi, the consolidation of other local governmental units has not been achieved in either state. The size of local governmental units varies among the states, as does the type of units which are most important. In Maine there is an unusually large number of towns, and town consolidation is strongly favored by those interested in governmental reform. In Georgia, county consolidation has for a number of years been a major objective of those interested in governmental reform. Now that the General Assembly has been reapportioned, it is felt there may be a better prospect for action. While there is some support in Mississippi for county consolidation, no serious county consolidation programs are presently being offered.

D. State Government

As in Maine and South Dakota, the formal powers of the Governor in the two selected Southern states are restricted, although this is more true of Mississippi than of Georgia. In both states the Governor cannot succeed himself (both have four-year terms). Moreover, many key state officials are elected in general election or by the legislature. Thus, the Governor is not in a strong position to develop and implement his own program for the state government as a whole.

Mississippi of the four states selected for this study has the largest number of state elective officials (17), and the largest number of state agencies with elective officials (13).[57] Among the officials responsible for key state programs, both the Superintendent of Education and the Highway Commissioner are elected in Mississippi. Furthermore, the state budget is prepared by the Commission on Budget and Accounting, a five-member joint executive-legislative commission on which the Governor serves but can be outvoted by the other four members, all of whom are members of the Legislature. Besides the Commission on Budget and Accounting, the Governor of Mississippi serves on 20 boards or commissions on which he can be outvoted by other members of the board.

In Georgia the State Superintendent of Schools is also an elective office, although a 1963 study by the Governor's Commission for Efficiency and Improvement in Government recommended that this be made an appointive position.[58]

---

[57] *The Book of the States, 1964-65, op. cit.,* p. 151. Georgia has 15 elective officials, Maine 13, and South Dakota 12. Seven of the elected officials in Maine are members of the Executive Council chosen by the legislature.

[58] The Governor's Commission for Efficiency and Improvement in Government, *Organization and Administration of the Georgia Department of Education,* Report No. 3, December 2, 1963, p. vii.

Two important differences are that in Georgia the state has an executive budget system and the Director of the Highway Department is appointed by the Governor, not elected. Georgia's Bureau of the Budget in the office of the Governor is of recent origin, having been established under a law enacted in 1962. Under this law, the Governor is ex-officio Director of the Budget Bureau which has a wide range of fiscal responsibilities.

Governmental Reorganization and Reform

There is a further important area of difference between Georgia and Mississippi. In Georgia considerable emphasis in recent years has been placed on state governmental reorganization and reform. Measures in this area have materially strengthened the office of the Governor. Both Governor Carl E. Sanders (1962-66) and his predecessor appointed "little Hoover Commissions" on governmental organization. A number of the areas in which these commissions have been active have already been mentioned. In addition to the Budget Act of 1962, examples of governmental reorganization and reform are:

— the Georgia Department of Revenue was strengthened and reorganized resulting in what are considered significant improvements in the efficiency of state revenue collections;

— the Department of Education was reorganized and the General Assembly in 1964 authorized the development of a "Master Plan for Education;"

— other state functions and agencies reorganized recently are: state purchasing, the prison system, the state mental health institutions, and the Department of Family and Children Services.

The governmental systems of many Southern states have been dramatically affected by the 1962 and subsequent reapportionment rulings of the United States Supreme Court. These rulings have had the most marked effect in Georgia among the four states studied. The population of Georgia is almost evenly divided between rural and urban areas.

Until the Supreme Court decision in *Gray v. Sanders* in 1963, the General Assembly had been heavily dominated by representatives from rural areas under the "county unit" system which the Court struck down in *Gray v. Sanders.*[59] As a consequence of reapportionment in compliance with this decision, there has been a large increase in the representation of urban areas in the General Assembly. Fulton County (which contains most of Atlanta) formerly had three members of the House out of a total of approximately 200. Under the reapportionment of the House in 1965, Fulton County was given 24 members. This number is expected to increase again, as the courts have ordered the state to reapportion further.

Reapportionment has already had a major effect on state-local relations in Georgia. Until 1965, for example, the Highway Department provided some $9 million in aid to counties plus approximately an equal amount in county road contracts paid out of state funds. No highway aid funds were given to cities. In 1965 the General Assembly under the leadership of the Governor voted an equal amount in aid to cities for street work and traffic controls, reflecting the enhanced political strength of the urban areas. As noted above, the same type of revision was made in the distribution formula under the foundation school aid program in 1964. The Georgia Department of Public Health also revised the formula under which it shares in county health department costs in 1965. The new formula increases the proportion of aid for public health offices in urban areas which have in the past received relatively smaller amounts of aid than those in rural areas.

In Mississippi the relationship between rural and urban areas is not as important a political factor as it is in Georgia. The state's largest city, Jackson (1960 population: 144,422), has objected to certain state aid policies as being unfair to the city, namely the distribution of gasoline tax receipts and to a lesser extent the economic index for determining need under the foundation education aid program. Even with the

---

[59] Robert B. McKay, *Reapportionment: The Law and Politics of Equal Representation* (New York: The Twentieth Century Fund, 1965), pp. 83-89.

reapportionment of the Mississippi legislature in 1963, rural interests predominate and representatives of the cities in Mississippi are not in as good a position to change state policies in these areas as those in Georgia.

E. Summary Analysis

Without either an equalization or tax effort adjustment, distribution of 1 per cent of the current personal income tax base to the states would mean approximately $56 million annually for Georgia and $30 million for Mississippi. In the summary analysis (Part E) on Maine and South Dakota, an effort was made to identify areas in which these funds would be likely to be used, bearing in mind the obvious difficulties involved in any such analysis. Continuing uncertainty about the effect of the 1964 and 1965 Civil Rights Acts in the South makes it even more difficult to predict the major areas in which general aid funds would be used.

Both of the selected Southern states appear to have high-level local school needs, as indicated by the fact that Georgia ranked forty-second and Mississippi fiftieth in per pupil elementary and secondary public school expenditures in 1964-65 (Georgia $330, Mississippi $273, and the United States average $483).[60] This was also indicated by the estimate cited above of Georgia state educational officials of additional public school needs of $100 million per annum. Despite these indications of need, the position taken by the Georgia General Assembly in 1965 that, in effect, additional federal aid is not needed for elementary and secondary education suggests that in some Southern states general aid funds would not be used for this purpose.

Substantial needs also exist in the field of higher education in Georgia and Mississippi. As in the case of South Dakota, these needs do not appear to be as large as those at the elementary and secondary level. Both states rank

---

[60] National Education Association, *op. cit.,* p. 49.

higher in per capita expenditures for higher education than for elementary and secondary education. This is particularly true for Mississippi. In 1963 Mississippi ranked thirty-third in per capita spending for institutions of higher education, compared to a ranking of fiftieth in per capita expenditures for local schools. Georgia ranked fortieth in per capita state spending for higher education and forty-second in per capita expenditures for local schools. The study of higher education needs by Selma Mushkin and Eugene McLoone confirms the relatively higher degree of elementary-secondary school needs for the two states. Compared to a projected national increase from 1962 to 1970 of 150 per cent to meet student higher education expenditures, Georgia was found to require an increase of 135 per cent and Mississippi 100 per cent.[61]

In the welfare field, the underutilization of existing federal grants-in-aid for public assistance probably can be taken as an indication that unconditional federal aid would not be used for cash assistance payments despite existing low-benefit levels. Underutilization in the welfare field is characteristic of a number of the lower-income Southern states. This poses a difficult question for a general aid plan. If the federal government provides general aid funds, it is quite possible that Georgia, Mississippi, and other states now underutilizing federal public assistance grants-in-aid would decide that other needs take precedence over increased public assistance benefit levels, and would continue to underutilize federal aid in the welfare field. The net result in this situation could in some instances be for the federal government to provide general aid funds to meet needs that are considered of a lower priority than welfare needs, for which the full amount of available federal aid is not being used.

In the fields of health and highways both Georgia and Mississippi have per capita spending levels that are reasonably in line with the national averages. Thus, the need for additional funds would not appear to be as great in these areas as in the case of education and welfare. Both health and highway programs are popular in the two states. This

---

[61] Mushkin and McLoone, *op. cit.,* p. 58

may be an indication that, despite the relatively lower levels of need in these areas, some portion of a general aid allocation to Georgia and Mississippi might be used for highways and/or public health.

Focusing now on the structure and political responsiveness of state government, the comparison between Georgia and Mississippi provides useful insights. In Georgia the state government has been making progress in governmental reorganization and reform and as a result is playing an increasingly more active role in a number of areas of state governmental responsibility. At the same time, both the state and local governments in Georgia have not responded fiscally to rising postwar public needs to the same relative degree as have other states. Tax effort in Georgia is below the national average as measured by the relationship between state-local taxes and personal income. The evidence available (using national and state data and based on interviews with state officials) suggests that Georgia's relatively low level tax effort does not reflect a situation in which basic public needs are already being adequately financed, thus obviating the need for increased tax effort. Significant unmet needs were found to exist for education, welfare, and local capital spending.

Mississippi differs from Georgia in that the state is making a tax effort well above the national average, although its tax effort compared to other states has declined in recent years. While Mississippi's tax effort is greater than Georgia's, the state has not been giving emphasis, as has Georgia, to expanding the leadership role of the state government and reorganizing and modernizing its administrative machinery.

The comparison between Georgia and Mississippi reflects a basic distinction of importance for all of the states. State governments on the whole have responded fiscally to rising postwar needs to a degree unexpected by their critics. In contrast to this fiscal response, state governments in many states have not been nearly so responsive in terms of modernizing and revitalizing the governmental machinery of the state to deal with new problems and complexities. Mississippi fits the general pattern quite closely. Georgia, on the other hand, does not fit the pattern. It would be a mistake to overstate Georgia's progress in the field of governmental reorganization and reform, but the state has moved forward in this area. At the same time it has lagged in its fiscal response to the rising public service needs of state-local government.

As far as general aid plan is concerned, the Southern states present problems connected with the possible use of federal general aid funds for segregated public programs and facilities. Experience with Title VI offers much useful information, particularly concerning school and hospital federal aid programs. Here, the most important questions are: Is Title VI enough, or should some specially devised prohibition be included in a general aid plan? How will general aid dollars be identified? Who will do this and what sanctions will be used for violations? It must be remembered that Title VI will continue to have effect for categorical aids (which now cover almost all areas of state-local spending), even if a general aid plan were to be adopted.

Just as the civil rights argument presents a potential problem for a general aid plan, rural domination of state governments has been frequently used as an argument against general and unconditional aid. The United States Supreme Court reapportionment rulings in *Baker v. Carr* (1962) and subsequent cases have had their greatest impact in Georgia among the four selected states.

Until 1963 the Georgia General Assembly had been heavily weighted in favor of the rural areas. The policies of the Governor and the various departments of the state government likewise tended to reflect the rural composition and orientation of the General Assembly. Formulas for allocating funds to localities gave decided preference to rural areas. The reapportionment of the state Senate in 1963 and the House in 1965 have already brought about dramatic changes in the intergovernmental policies of the state government of Georgia. Reapportionment has resulted in major revisions in the formulas for distributing state aid funds for education, highways, and health, which give greater recognition to the politically strengthened urban areas. This effect of the Supreme Court rulings in curbing the domination of state governments by rural minorities is of basic importance in terms of the likely effect of a general aid program as viewed from the states.

III.

The Outlook for

State and Local Finance

Lawrence R. Kegan
Director of Special Studies

and

George P. Roniger
Research Staff

Committee for Economic Development

Introduction[1]

Since World War II, state and local governments, for the most part, have done a remarkable job in attempting to meet their fiscal responsibilities. Between 1948 and 1965 general revenues from their own sources increased four times, from $15 billion to $63 billion. Population growth, increasing urbanization, and rising prosperity continue to generate a strong demand for improved public services—for more and better schools and hospitals, housing and recreational facilities, as well as for increased efforts to meet traffic, crime, and pollution problems.

This continuing demand for increases in scope and quality of public services has renewed fears of impending crises in state and local government finance. Many politicians and political scientists are predicting that state and local needs will rise much faster than gross national product, while state and local revenue potentials will fall far short. They argue that the heavy reliance of state and local governments on property and sales taxes limits the response of state and local revenues to economic growth. Thus, it would appear irrational to anticipate that state and local governments could meet their foreseeable needs from the revenue sources now available to them.

Therefore, it is most important that we try to appraise the outlook for state and local finance. Our view of the state-local finance picture could strongly influence our fiscal choices and could, in the process, affect the future of our federal system. If, for example, we believe that there will be serious crises in the financing of state and local expen-

[1] The authors wish to acknowledge the contribution of Seong H. Park in the development of the statistical data.

diture needs, then we are more likely to advocate general federal fiscal support to state and local governments. If we find that state and local fiscal crises are not about to occur, such support may not be justified—or it must be justified on other grounds. In short, we ought to know the extent to which state and local governments can secure the funds that they require without substantial changes in governmental revenue systems.

Projecting "Public Needs"

What are the considerations that affect the expenditure outlook for state and local finances? Expenditure projections involve factors which are often difficult to evaluate with great accuracy—economic growth, military risks, social and political sentiment, and action by state legislatures, city officials, and citizen groups. But an informed and intelligent judgment of reasonable orders of magnitude is a desirable guide to future policy. Sensible public policy planning requires assembling and analysing knowledge about the future, and then filling the gaps in our knowledge with reasonable judgments.

One method of determining the outlook for state and local government expenditures involves a consideration of the level of future "public needs" for quality education, quality housing, more police protection, better roads, etc. The costs of fulfilling these "needs" are then summed up to determine public expenditure requirements.

One difficulty with this method is that the concept of "public needs" lacks objectivity. "Public needs" are often equated with "social goals." But in a democratic society there are many different and often conflicting views of social goals. Furthermore, to the extent that goals are not based on an evaluation of real costs and feasible programs, there is a gap between what is desirable and what is practical. Resources are always scarce. And it may be true that the extent of unmet "public needs" necessarily grows with the growing affluence of a democratic society. The quality and scope of services that might be felt necessary by various groups tend to multiply with the opportunities for increased discretionary expenditures. In the public sector as in the private, we must always make choices as to how, when, and where available resources should be put to use.

There is a narrower notion of "public needs" which forms the basis for program proposals by interested community groups and state and local government authorities. On this view, "public needs" are those articulated in active program proposals made by informed people. These people may agree on the need for action to deal with certain public problems, but they may disagree about values or in their interpretations of the available facts, and such disagreement could result in different policy prescriptions. The requirement for developing priorities comes into focus when a price tag is put on the unmet "public needs," even of this narrower sort, because resources are clearly not available to meet all "needs." Moreover, in viewing the obviously great "unmet needs," one should not ignore real limitations on the speed with which *real* resources, as distinct from *fiscal* resources, can be shifted from one activity to another, i.e., manpower from industry to teaching, or from dressmaking to social work.

To improve the basis for studying the fiscal outlook, a number of analysts have considered the legislative progress of individual programs for improving public services. Since the likelihood of enactment of individual public programs depends largely on the ability to finance such programs, this method helps one to estimate the type and level of public programs that presumably can be financed in the future with available funds, and therefore is predetermined not to yield a 'gap' between the projected level of public expenditures and the means to finance such expenditures.

An Alternative Model

Another approach to the projection of public expenditures evaluates, in light of recent developments, plausible changes in the three major determinants of state and local expenditures: population, prices, and the scope and quality of public services.[2] In this paper we propose to study the population and price factors which require state and local governments to alter the level of their outlays in order to maintain on-going programs, and then to consider what additional outlays could be made to improve the scope and quality of government services.

Population and prices are both "objective" factors. Projections of population growth provide the basis for anticipating the change in the level of public expenditures necessary to maintain a constant level of public services per eligible recipient, at constant prices. Projections of price changes for public services, combined with the estimated change in population, will provide an estimate of the change in public expenditures necessary for a constant real level of public services per capita at current prices.

We assume that the residual change in government outlays not accounted for by population or prices can be accounted for by improvement in the scope and quality of government services. We can then determine the level of governmental revenue required to maintain a fixed level of scope and quality, to maintain the historic rate of improvement, or to vary the rate of improvement by any given proportion. By determining the amount of funds required to meet the cost of improvement in the coming period at various rates, we may become more aware of our options.

Our expenditure analysis is based on a model in which changes in government outlay are determined by the multiple of ratios describing changes in

population $\times$ prices $\times$ scope and quality.

Thus, our model does not attempt to answer the question of what "public needs" are. It permits us to present alternatives, showing what would be required to improve public services

---

[2] Variants of this method have been used and discussed by Dick Netzer in "State-Local Finance in the Next Decade" published in the Joint Economic Committee's *Compendium on Revenue Sharing and Its Alternatives,* July 1967, and by Selma J. Mushkin and Gabrielle C. Lupo in "State and Local Finances Projections: Another Dimension?", *The Southern Economic Journal* (January 1967), and "Project '70: Projecting the State-Local Sector," *Review of Economic Statistics* (May 1967).

at different aggregate rates of speed without prejudging the "need" or desirability of attaining given rates of improvement. But conclusions drawn can be used to appraise the costs, and therefore the requirements, of reaching certain public service goals, however the appraiser may wish to define them.

The Revenue Model

Just as the concept of "public needs" is not absolute but depends on a multitude of subjective matters, the "fiscal capability" of state and local governments is an imprecise concept. It may refer to the productivity of the existing state and local government revenue structure; to the ability of individual jurisdictions to raise their tax rates and charges if no such changes are made in neighboring jurisdictions; to the ability of state and local governments to increase their tax rates and charges under conditions in which other state and local governments seek to do the same; or to the productivity of a changed revenue structure.

Furthermore, one should attempt to distinguish between the various types of limitations upon revenue capabilities. There are limits resulting from unwarranted and artificial restraints which prevent the will of the people from being put into effect — such as those due to interjurisdictional tax competition and the "spillover" of public service benefits from one jurisdiction to another. There are also revenue limitations resulting from the desire of the citizens to reserve a certain proportion of their resources for private use, as well as the limited nature of the total level of resources available for distribution between the public and private spheres of the economy. It is in the public interest to overcome unwarranted restraints but it is not in the public interest to overcome restraints arising from the will of the people. Moreover, it is unrealistic to ignore the restraint arising from the over-all scarcity of resources.

We consider the productivity of the present revenue structure and that of a somewhat strengthened revenue structure. Our findings with regard to revenues will be compared with the results of our expenditure analysis. This will permit us to determine how well the state and local revenue structure can function in the future as compared with the past, and to determine the extent to which the revenue structure must be strengthened to achieve certain rates of improvement of public services. These conclusions will show the extent to which added fiscal efforts may be required to accomplish certain public goals.

The Expenditure Model

In this section we consider, first, the problems of estimating the changes in state and local government general expenditures[3] resulting from changes in the three factors of population, price, and scope and quality. After discussing some conceptual and statistical issues, we shall attempt to measure the changes in these factors for the period 1955-65 and from this experience to project expenditures for 1975.

Population-Workload

The grossest method for estimating the effect of a change in population on public service requirements is to assume that such requirements vary directly with population. For example, the total United States resident population increased by 17.9 per cent in the decade 1955-65. The projected increase in the total resident population between 1965-75, is 15.0 per cent based on the Census Bureau's Series

---

[3] As defined by the U.S. Bureau of the Census, "general expenditures" includes total government revenue and expenditure except for some outlays on utilities, liquor store operations, and insurance trust funds. Interest on the general debt which is included in the Census Bureau definition is however omitted from our initial analysis because such expenditures depend, in part, on the size of the debt which is, in part, determined by the level of expenditures itself. The expenditure data used throughout this paper are derived or computed from material in various issues of *Governmental Finances* and also from *Finances and Employment,* Census of Governments 1962, both issued by the U.S. Department of Commerce.

B projection.[4] This might suggest that population factors accounted for an increase of 17.9 per cent in expenditures of state and local governments in 1955-65 and that an increase of 15.0 per cent in such expenditures will be required between 1965-75 in order to maintain a constant level of per capita public services, other things (mainly prices) being equal.

But certain refinements in estimating the effect of population changes upon public service requirements can be made. In particular, the changing age-structure of the population has great relevance for expenditure needs, since different age groups in the population account for different expenditure requirements. For example, a change in the population age group 5 to 17 will have a major effect on expenditure needs for education as well as on welfare support for dependent children. Similarly, the size of the 65-and-over population group has a major effect on welfare outlays for the aged. Since the numbers of persons in those age groups which result in heavy consumption of relatively high-cost public services may change at rates different from that of the total population, it is important to try to give them proper weight in a more refined measure of the public expenditure effect of population change. Table 1 compares the projected annual growth rate of certain age groups in 1965-75 with the growth rates in the decade 1955-65.

Comparison of the projected growth rates with those in the last decade indicates that the population as a whole will grow at a slower rate than before. The most marked declines in the rate of growth will be among the young and the aged, those groups which have the greatest influence on the demands for public education, welfare, and health and hospital expenditures.

For example, expenditures of $21.9 billion in 1965 for local schools amounted to almost 30 per cent of all state

---

[4] Series B Population Projections are used throughout this paper. This is the commonly used medium-high projection among four Census Bureau Projections. The population data used throughout this paper are derived from various issues of the *Current Population Reports* issued by the U. S. Bureau of the Census, except where noted.

and local government expenditures. The rate of growth in the population for the age group (5-17) that most significantly affects enrollment in public elementary and secondary schools will decline from 3.1 per cent per year in 1955-65 to about 0.7 per cent per year in 1965-75. It is evident that the pressure from sheer numbers of additional pupils on local school budgets will be considerably less than in the past. Therefore, the requirements for additional teachers and new classroom facilities necessary to maintain the current level of educational scope and quality will increase at a much slower rate than in the recent past.

Table 1 **United States Resident Population Growth by Age Group: 1955-65 and 1965-75**

Age Group	Annual Growth Rate (Per Cent)	
	Actual 1955-65	Projected 1965-75
0-4	1.0	1.8
5-17	3.1	0.7
18-21	4.0	2.9
22-64	0.8	1.5
65 and over	2.3	1.5
TOTAL POPULATION	1.7	1.4

There is also likely to be a significant decline in the growth rate of young people of college age (18-21), from 4.0 per cent a year in the period 1955-65 to 2.9 per cent in 1965-75. The crisis due to the growth in the numbers of college age persons (a result of the baby boom) is upon us today but will ease in the near future.

There is a more substantial proportionate decline in the growth rate of older citizens, who are relatively important beneficiaries of welfare, health, and hospital expenditures. The rate of growth of the 65-and-over age group will decline from 2.3 per cent in 1955-65 to 1.5 per cent in 1965-75.

Increased growth rates relative to the immediate past will occur in the youngest age group, those under 5, and in the age group from 22 to 64, which makes up a large part of the labor force. But the effect of these rate increases on general expenditures for public services are more than offset by declines in other age groups.

The locational structure of the population is also a factor affecting public service requirements. Urban governments, for example, must provide more water, sewerage facilities, sanitation, lighting, fire and police protection, parks and perhaps greater educational facilities than most rural governments. However, difficult conceptual and statistical issues are raised in accounting for the special nature of urban services. To what extent are these services "necessary" in urban areas and "unnecessary" in rural areas? To what extent are "urban" services provided privately in rural areas? "Urban" services may be defined as newly created "needs" arising when rural-to-urban migration takes place. But should they be considered as new expenditures required to maintain a constant level of scope and quality as rural residents migrate to urban areas? Or since their provision permits persons to move to urban areas to seek a better standard of living, should they be considered as changes in public service scope and quality?

Answers to these difficult questions are not attempted here. For purposes of our model, we assume that certain public services which are basically "urban" in nature are required only in nonfarm areas and must be enlarged in proportion to increases in non-farm population, in order to maintain a constant level of scope and quality of public services.

In our discussion below, we attempt to devise a factor which describes the change in public service "workload" that results from the change in the age and locational structure of the population, as well as its total size. This factor is termed "population-workload." We attempt to estimate changes in population-workload for each of six major general expenditure categories — education, welfare, health and hospitals, "urban" services, highways and "other" general expenditures (excluding interest). For each of these six individual expenditure categories, the change in workload over a given period will be presented in terms of a population-workload *ratio,* the ratio being the size of the relevant population at the end of the period relative to the size at the beginning. A weighted average for the population ratio for all general expenditures (excluding interest) will then be calculated, the weights being the expenditures in the base period in each respective category.[5]

1955-65 Estimates

Public education expenditure requirements are more directly affected by the number of persons in certain age groups than any other broad expenditure category. For example, about 99 per cent of persons aged 6-15 are in school. But complicating factors arise because of the smaller proportions of persons aged 5 and over 15 in local schools and the much smaller proportion of persons of college and graduate school age in institutions of higher education. In 1964, the school population included about 68 per cent of persons aged 5, 88 per cent of persons aged 16-17, and substantially less than half the population of college age.[6] Furthermore, the proportion of persons in school who attend public, as opposed to private, institutions varies among the several educational levels. In 1965, about 83 per cent of elementary school students and about 92 per cent of secondary school students were in public institutions.[7]

Another complicating factor arises from differences in the average per pupil expenditure among the several educational levels. Thus, costs per pupil in higher education are higher than such costs in secondary schools, and these in turn are higher than those in elementary school.

In order to take account of these factors without unduly

---

[5] Our use of the population age-structure and a distinction between farm and non-farm population to estimate the "population-workload" is based on the judgment that these are the most relevant factors which can be taken into account, given the availability of data. Further refinement of the concept of "population-work-load" is no doubt possible but would be at the expense of increased complexity.

[6] U.S. Department of Health, Education, and Welfare, Office of Education, *Digest of Educational Statistics,* OE-10024-65, Washington, D.C., 1965, Table 94.

[7] U.S. Department of Health, Education, and Welfare, Office of Education, *Projections of Educational Statistics to 1975-76,* OE-10030-66, Washington, D.C., 1966, Table 3.

complicating the methodology, we have separated public expenditures for the three major levels — elementary, secondary, and higher education. The population-workload ratio with regard to the total population within the age group most important for the respective educational levels has been estimated. We have taken the group 5-13 as being relevant for elementary school outlays, the group 14-17 for secondary school outlays, and the age group 18-21 as most important for higher education outlays.

Although expenditure data are available for higher education, there is no breakdown of local public school expenditures into expenditures for elementary and secondary schools. But data on the number of teachers in each category are available.[8] It was assumed that the relative proportion of local public school costs at each level is directly related to the proportion of local public school teachers at each level. Since 64 per cent of local public school teachers in 1955 taught in elementary schools, we assume that public expenditure for elementary schools was 64 per cent of total local public school expenditures. Thus, of public expenditures totaling $10.3 billion for local public schools in 1965,[9] we assume that $6.6 billion was spent at the elementary school level and $3.7 billion at the secondary level.

Table 2   **Population-Workload: Education**

Age Group	A Population 1955 (1,000)	1965	B Population Ratio 1955-65	C Expenditure 1955 (Million $)	D Relative Expenditure Weight (%)	E Weighted Ratio [B × D]
5-13	27,797	35,886	1.2910	6.636[a]	55.73	71.95
14-17	9,195	14,109	1.5344	3.701[a]	31.08	47.69
18-21	8,033	11,880	1.4789	1.570	13.19	19.50
TOTAL	45,025	61,875		11.907	100.00	139.14

[a] Estimated. Includes part of expenditures for "other education," as defined by the Census Bureau.

[8] *Ibid.*, Table 22.

[9] Including the Census Bureau categories of "other" education expenditures.

Table 2 shows the changes in the size of the relevant population groups for 1955-65. Column E shows the individual population ratios for the three relevant age groups multiplied by the expenditure weight attributed to each group respectively. The sum of the weighted ratios, shown on the bottom of column E, indicates the weighted population-ratio for all public education. The computation yields an estimate that the population-workload for purposes of education increased by 39.1 per cent between 1955-65.

Expenditures for *health and hospital* facilities are determined in part by the age structure of the population. The expected relatively high use by the young and the elderly is borne out by data compiled by the Department of Health, Education, and Welfare, which provides estimates of the number of visits to hospital clinics by age group. The period closest to 1955 for which data are available are averages for 1957-58.[10]

Table 3 shows the changes in the size of the various population age groups for 1955-65 (Column B). The sum of the weighted population ratios (Column E) yields an estimated increase of 19.7 per cent in the population-workload for public health and hospitals in 1955-65.

Table 3   **Population-Workload: Health and Hospitals**

Age Group	A Population 1955	A Population 1965	B Population Ratio 1955-65	C Estimated Number of Clinic Visits 1957-58	D Relative Expenditure Weight	E Weighted Ratio $[B \times D]$
	(1,000)			(Million)	(%)	
0-4	18,467	20,433	1.1065	11.9	13.40	14.83
5-14	30,248	39,475	1.3050	13.8	15.54	20.28
15-24	21,041	30,269	1.4386	16.5	18.58	26.73
25-44	46,667	46,483	.9961	20.8	23.42	23.33
45-64	33,396	38,981	1.1672	19.1	21.51	25.11
65 & over	14,489	18,154	1.2530	6.7	7.55	9.46
TOTAL	164,308	193,795		88.8	100.00	119.74

---

[10] U.S. Department of Health, Education, and Welfare, Public Health Service, *Health Statistics,* Series B, No. 19, August 1960, Table 4.

Welfare expenditures for the major public programs are designed to aid persons in specific age groups. There are six categories of welfare programs: old age assistance, medical assistance for the aged, aid for dependent children, assistance for the totally and permanently disabled, assistance for the blind, and general assistance. The first five categories are supported in part by federal government funds and the last is the residual category not so supported.

Beneficiaries of the two programs for the aged are limited to persons 65 and over; aid for dependent children is given for the support of persons under 18; the program for the disabled is limited to persons 18 and over. There is no age limit for recipients of aid for the blind. Regulations for general assistance vary under different state and local laws, but eligibility is generally not limited according to age.

Table 4   **Population-Workload: Welfare**

Program and Age Group	A Population 1955-1965 (1,000)		B Population Ratio 1955-65	C Expenditure[a] 1955 (Million $)	D Relative Expenditure Weight (%)	E Weighted Ratio [B × D]
Old Age Assistance and Medical Assistance for the Aged: 65 and over	14,489	18,154	1.2530	1,705	57.17	71.63
Assistance for the Disabled: 18 and over	108,849	123,367	1.1334	175	5.86	6.64
Aid for Dependent Children: 0-17	55,459	70,428	1.2699	699	23.46	29.79
Assistance for the Blind and General Assistance: Total Population	164,308	193,795	1.1795	403	13.51	15.94
Total				2,981	100.00	124.00

[a]Definitions of expenditure categories by the Department of Health, Education and Welfare, which is the original source of this data, and the Census Bureau, which is the source of most of the data used in this study, vary. Thus, welfare expenditures shown in this table, which are used only to estimate the weighted population ratio for welfare, are somewhat at variance with the welfare expenditures shown in other tables. Expenditure data shown here are derived from U. S. Bureau of the Census, *Statistical Abstract of the United States: 1966* (Washington, D.C.: U.S. Government Printing Office, 1966), Table 430.

In Table 4, we have applied the change in the size of the relevant age group in the period 1955-65 to the portion of welfare outlays attributed to each basic public assistance program in 1955[11], in order to develop the total population-workload change for welfare. Our calculations yield an estimated growth of 24 per cent in the population-workload for welfare between 1955-65.

Urban services have been defined to include police protection, local fire protection, sewerage, sanitation other than sewerage, local parks and recreation, housing and urban renewal, airports, water transportation and terminals, and parking facilities. We have defined the urban population as being the nonfarm population.

We have not subdivided the category of urban services into services relevant to particular age groups. We assume that these services are provided for the entire nonfarm population.[12] Thus, the change in the population-workload for these services is equivalent to the change in nonfarm population, which was 24.9 per cent in 1955-65 as indicated in Table 5.

Highways and the residual *"other"* category are the major expenditure categories, for which the total population is considered as most relevant. Therefore, there is no breakdown by population group and the workload change is defined as the change in the total resident population, which was about 18.0 per cent in 1955-65 as indicated in Table 5.

The 1955-65 population-workload changes for the several categories of state and local government general expenditures which we have distinguished can be combined by weighting the change within each category by the proportion of general expenditures which the respective category en-

---

[11] Based on data from U.S. Bureau of the Census, *Statistical Abstract of the United States: 1966* (Washington, D.C.: U.S. Government Printing Office, 1966), Table 430.

[12] The nonfarm population is estimated as the total resident population less farm population. Source: U.S. Bureau of the Census, *Current Population Reports,* Series P-27, No. 37; and U.S. Department of Agriculture, *Farm Population Estimates for 1910-1962,* ERS-130.

tailed in the base period 1955. On this basis, the population-workload for general expenditures (excluding interest) grew by about 27.3 per cent, as shown in Table 6.

Table 5   **Population-Workload: Urban Services, Highways and "Other" Services**

Program	Population Group	Population 1955 (1,000)	1965	Population Ratio 1955-65
Urban services	Nonfarm population	145,230	181,432	1.2493
Highways and "other"	Resident population	164,308	193,795	1.1795

Table 6   **Total Population-Workload: 1955-65**

Program	Population Ratio 1955-65	Expenditures 1955 (Million $)	Relative Expenditure Weight (%)	Weighted Ratio
Education	1.3914	11,907	36.21	50.38
Health & hospitals	1.1974	2,524	7.67	9.18
Welfare	1.2400	3,168	9.63	11.94
Urban services	1.2493	4,341	13.20	16.49
Highways	1.1795	6,452	19.62	23.14
"Other" services	1.1795	4,494	13.67	16.12
TOTAL		32,886	100.00	127.25

1965-75 Projections

The method for projecting the future change in population-workload parallels the method of estimating past changes.

Population projections, as noted previously, are based on the Series B Projection of the Bureau of the Census. This set of projections is shown in Table 7. For purposes of estimating changes in the urban nonfarm population, it is assumed that the proportion of the total population on farms will continue to decline at the 1960-64 rate.

Table 7   **Population Ratios: 1965-75**

Program	Population Group	Population 1965	1975[a]	Population Ratio 1965-75
		(1,000)		
Education				
Elementary	5-13	35,886	36,599	1.0199
Secondary	14-17	14,109	16,886	1.1968
Higher	18-21	11,880	15,763	1.3269
Health & hospitals				
	0-4	20,433	24,350	1.1917
	5-14	39,475	40,925	1.0367
	15-24	30,269	39,528	1.3059
	25-44	46,483	53,514	1.1513
	45-64	39,981	43,329	1.0837
	65 & over	18,154	21,159	1.1655
Welfare				
Old Age Assistance and Medical Assistance for the Aged	65 & over	18,154	21,159	1.1655
Aid to the Disabled	18 & over	123,367	144,970	1.1751
Aid to Families with Dependent Children	0-17	70,428	77,835	1.1052
Aid to the Blind and General assistance	Total population	193,795	222,805	1.1497
Urban	Nonfarm population	182,432	215,007	1.1786
Other expenditures	Total population	193,795	222,805	1.1497

[a]Projected on the basis of the Census Bureau Projections of total population including armed forces, less the number of armed forces abroad in the relevant male age group as of July, 1966 (except for nonfarm population, which is projected as noted in text).

Table 8   **Expenditure Weights: 1965**

Program	Expenditures	Relative Expenditure Weight %
Education[a]	28,563	(39.65)
Elementary	12,803	17.77
Secondary	9,897	13.74
Higher	5,863	8.14
Health & Hospitals[b]	5,361	(7.44)
Age Groups 0-4	886	1.23
5-14	710	.99
15-24	940	1.30
25-44	1,303	1.81
45-64	1,009	1.40
65 & over	513	.71
Welfare[c]	6,315	(8.76)
Old Age Assistance and Medical Assistance for the Aged	2,913	4.04
Aid for the Disabled	652	.91
Aid for Families with Dependent Children	2,173	3.01
Aid for the Blind and General assistance	577	.80
Urban	9,368	13.00
Highways	12,221	16.96
Other	10,228	14.19
TOTAL	72,056	100.00

[a] Breakdown is estimated on basis of relative numbers of teachers. Source: U.S. Dept. of Health, Education, and Welfare. Office of Education, *Projections of Educational Statistics to 1975-76*. OE-10030-66, Table 22. Includes estimated expenditures for "other education."
[b] Breakdown is estimated on the basis of the number of visits to hospital clinics during the period from June, 1963 to June, 1964. Source: U.S. Dept. of Health, Education, and Welfare, Public Health Service, *Vital & Health Statistics,* Series 10, No. 18, Table 11.
[c] Breakdown is estimated on the basis of data from the *Statistical Abstract of the United States, 1966, op. cit.,* Table 430.

The weights utilized to estimate the change in population workload for 1965-75 are based on the proportion of 1965 general expenditures accounted for by the relevant expenditure category. The methods used to develop the expenditure estimates parallel those used to develop the equivalent estimates for 1955-65. In this section, instead of combining the subcategories into major categories (for example, elementary, secondary and higher education into total public education) for purposes of calculating the total change in population-workload, one series of calculations combining the subcategories into the weighted whole is made. Table 8 develops the relative expenditure weights.

Table 9 develops the weighted population ratios, whose sum is our estimate for the growth in population-workload in 1965-75. Thus, given the population ratios and the weights by program, we project the population-workload for state and local government general expenditures to increase by about 15.2 per cent in the decade 1965-75.

The Price Factor

There is no official index showing changes in the over-all price level of the goods and services relevant for state and local government general expenditures. But these expenditures can be divided into two categories, to which existing price indexes and deflators can be applied.

The Department of Commerce provides a price deflator to measure the relation between outlays of state and local governments for purchases of goods and services in current and in constant dollars.[13] This deflator may be used as a measure of changes in the prices of goods and services purchased by these governments. The total coverage of such purchases is, in fact, somewhat broader than the purchases included under "general expenditures," for the latter do not include outlays for utilities or liquor stores. But recognizing this imperfection, we use the deflator

---

[13] See U.S. Department of Commerce, Office of Business Economics, *The National Income and Product Accounts of the United States, 1929-1965: Statistical Tables,* Washington, D.C., August 1966.

Table 9   **Population-Workload: 1965-75**

Program	Population Ratio 1965-75	Relative Expenditure Weight 1965 %	Weighted Ratio
Education			
Elementary	1.0199	17.77	18.12
Secondary	1.1968	13.74	16.44
Higher	1.3269	8.14	10.80
Health & Hospitals			
Age Groups 0-4	1.1917	1.23	1.47
5-14	1.0367	.99	1.03
15-24	1.3059	1.30	1.70
25-44	1.1513	1.81	2.08
45-64	1.0837	1.40	1.52
65 & over	1.1655	.71	.83
Welfare			
Old Age Assistance Medical Assistance for the Aged	1.1655	4.04	4.71
Disabled	1.1751	.91	1.07
Aid for Dependent Children	1.1052	3.01	3.33
Blind General assistance	1.1497	.80	.92
Urban	1.1786	13.00	15.32
Highways	1.1497	16.96	19.50
Other	1.1497	14.19	16.31
TOTAL		100.00	115.15

as an estimate of the change in prices paid for government goods and services included in general expenditures. The deflator rose by 40.8 per cent in the decade 1955-65.[14]

Changes in prices paid by governments for goods and services by major program for the period 1955-65 have been developed recently by Joseph Wakefield of the Bureau of Labor Statistics.[15] Some of this data is shown in Table 10.

---

[14] Calendar years, which is the basis for all the price data in this paper.

[15] The data was developed by Joseph C. Wakefield in conjunction with his article "Expanding Functions of State and Local Governments, 1965-70," in *Monthly Labor Review* (July 1967).

Table 10   **Changes in the Deflator of State and Local
Government Purchases of Goods and Services,
by Program: 1955-1965**

Program	Deflator 1955 (1958 = 100)	1965	Percentage Change 1955-65
Education	85.5	127.8	149.5
Public schools	86.1	127.4	148.0
Higher education	80.9	129.9	160.6
Health and hospitals	90.5	125.6	138.8
Highways	87.7	111.6	127.3
Urban services and other[a]	89.1	123.6	138.7
TOTAL GOVERNMENT PURCHASES	87.5	123.2	140.8

[a] Residual, computed from original data by authors.

In addition to government purchases of goods and services, general expenditures include transfer payments for welfare purposes. A more relevant index of price changes for welfare transfers than the deflator discussed above is the Consumer Price Index (CPI),[16] since welfare transfer funds are spent by consumers.

Between 1955 and 1965, the Consumer Price Index rose by 17.8 per cent. In the base period (1955), welfare transfer expenditures accounted for about 8.9 per cent of state and local government general expenditures.[17] We have calculated an over-all price index for the period 1955-65 for state and local government general expenditures by weighting the rise in the CPI by 8.9 per cent and the rise in the deflator by the remainder, or 91.1 per cent, as shown in Table 11.

---

[16] Published by U.S. Department of Labor, *Monthly Labor Review*.

[17] Computed from the Department of Health, Education and Welfare data for the total public assistance payment and the public assistance expenditures, including expenditures for administration. Source: U.S. Bureau of the Census, *Statistical Abstract of the United States, 1966, op. cit.*, Tables No. 428 and 430.

Table 11   **Price Index for State and Local Government General Expenditures: 1955-1965**

Category	Index: 1965 (1955 = 100)	Weight	Weighted Index
Purchases	140.8	91.1	128.3
Welfare transfers	117.8	8.9	10.5
TOTAL		100.0	138.8

The rise in the over-all price index for state and local government general expenditures over the decade 1955-1965 is estimated at 38.8 per cent.

The projection of price changes is an imperfect art at best. But we believe that there is some merit in basing our assumptions on the experience of the recent past. It is generally agreed that price stability basically existed in the first half of the decade of the 1960's. During this period, the price deflator for the economy as a whole, defined as the gross national product [GNP], rose at an average rate of 1.4 per cent per annum. It is likely that this index somewhat overstates the true rise in prices because its calculation neglects improvements in efficiency of government workers, and many students believe that it may not take full account of improvements in the quality of goods and services in general. The price experience of the late 1950's (which is the first half of the 1955-65 decade being studied) was somewhat less favorable, with the GNP deflator rising at an average annual rate of 2.6 per cent.

Thus, the experience of the decade of 1955-65, although not ideal, might be considered to have been fairly good. We believe it reasonable to project a continuation of this price performance through the decade 1965-75.

There have been consistent differences between changes in the price levels of goods and services purchased by state and local governments and in the Consumer Price Index on the one hand, and the GNP deflator on the other hand. In particular, there was a great difference between changes in the deflator for state and local governments and in the

GNP deflator. The state and local government deflator rose at an annual average of 3.5 per cent in 1955-65, compared with a rise in the GNP deflator of 2.0 per cent per annum. The differential is believed to result from three factors: (1) The lesser increase in productivity in the services as compared with the goods producing sector of the economy and the relatively heavy use of services by state and local governments; (2) the upward bias of the government deflator because the deflator takes no account of increases in productivity of government employees; and (3) an over-all shortage of certain government employees, particularly public school teachers, which required a relatively rapidly rising salary level.

The major factors which led to this differential are expected to continue to exert influence. It has been argued that the proportionately greater than average wage increases in certain governmental sectors will not continue in the coming period because of some previous catch-up and because of an anticipated easing in the need for additional local public school teachers. The peak postwar birth rates will supply an influx of new entrants to the teaching profession in the public schools in the late sixties, yet the children who will be enrolling for the first time will be those born in the early sixties, when birth rates had already fallen sharply. But, the growing militancy of government workers and the increased demand for teachers arising from new federally supported educational programs may result in the continuation of relatively great wage increases.

We assume that the over-all price level in the coming decade will reflect the experience of the past decade, and we assume that the differentials in the rate of change among the over-all economy, the government, and the consumer sectors will continue. Thus, we project the deflator for state and local government purchases of goods and services to rise by 40.8 per cent in the decade 1965-75, and the Consumer Price Index to rise by 17.8 per cent, repeating the experience of the 1955-65 decade.

Weighting these projected rates of change of the two indexes by the proportion of general expenditures accounted for in 1965 by purchase of goods and services on the one hand, and by welfare transfer payments on the other hand, we project the change in prices for the total of state and local government general expenditures over the decade 1965-75 to be 39.0 per cent,[18] as shown in Table 12.

Table 12   **Projected Change in Prices for State and Local Government General Expenditures: 1965-75**

Category	Index: 1975 (1965 = 100)	Weight	Weighted Index
Purchases	140.8	92.1	129.7
Transfers	117.8	7.9	9.3
TOTAL		100.0	139.0

Changes in Scope and Quality

We have assumed that the residual change in public expenditures not due to population-workload and price changes, is due to the change in scope and quality of public services. But due to its residual nature, errors and omissions will also fall into this category. Thus, biases in the price data will have equivalent but opposite effects on the residual factor,[19] as will imperfections in the calculation of population-workload. Also to the extent to which changes in capital outlay affect the scope and quality of government services only after a capital project is completed, our simplifying assumption that changes in residual expenditures yield immediate scope and quality benefits results in imperfections.

[18] Although we project the changes in the state and local government deflator and in the Consumer Price Index to repeat the past performance, the weighted average of these changes is somewhat different than in the past because the relative importance, and therefore weights, of welfare transfers and government purchases have changed between the two base periods of 1955 and 1965.

[19] To the extent that this bias overstates the change in prices paid for government services, our price index for general expenditures is overstated and our estimates of changes in public service scope and quality, which is the residual expenditure item, is understated to an equivalent extent. But since our projections of expenditures are based on past experience both of price change and changes in scope and quality, the mutually neutralizing overstatement of price change and understatement of scope and quality changes create no bias in terms of total expenditures.

The residual change in state and local government expenditures may be calculated in dollar terms by subtracting the effects of workload and price from the total change in government outlays. For comparative purposes, however, it is convenient to state the residual factor in ratio terms, indicating the proportionate improvement in scope and quality implicit in the residual term over the relevant time period. Thus, the total change in state and local government expenditures over a period may be derived from the following equation:

Expenditures × Population-Workload × Price × Scope & = Expenditures
    Period A   Ratio   Ratio   Quality   Period B
                                                    Ratio

The above relationship indicates that the ratio of expenditures in one period relative to another is equal to the multiple of the population-workload ratio, the price ratio, and the scope and quality ratio. Thus:

Population-Workload × Price × Scope & Quality = Expenditure
    Ratio   Ratio   Ratio   Ratio

In 1965, state and local government general expenditures (excluding interest) were 2.191 as great as in 1955. The population-workload ratio for this period was estimated to be 1.273 and the price ratio as 1.388. Thus, for 1955-65, the scope and quality ratio is 1.240. We may say that the scope and quality factor of local public services improved by 24 per cent in the period 1955-65. These relations are shown below.

Population-Workload × Price × Scope & Quality = Expenditure
    Ratio   Ratio   Ratio   Ratio
    1.273   × 1.388 ×   1.240   =   2.191

For projection purposes, we may be aided by a knowledge of the historical change in scope and quality by major state and local government public service programs. These rates may be determined by calculating the residual expansion in outlays by program, after taking account of the effects of population and price changes, also by program.

We have used the data developed by Wakefield and

shown on page 252 for estimates of price changes for goods and services purchased by state and local governments for public schools, higher education, health and hospitals, highways and "other" expenditures. In the case of public welfare, however, we have developed our own price index by applying the Consumer Price Index to such transfers and the index for government purchases of goods and services for welfare purposes to the remainder of welfare expenditures.

For population-workload changes, we have utilized data shown on page 247 for higher education, public welfare, health and hospitals, and highways. The available price data are not subdivided into elementary and secondary public schools. Therefore, we have combined our population-workload for the two subcategories. For "other" expenditures, the population-workload ratio is a weighted average of the total population ratio and the nonfarm population ratio. The weights were determined by the relative importance of "urban" expenditures and the other expenditures subsumed in this category.

Table 13 shows the extent to which changes in expenditures over the period 1955-65 by program are accounted for by changes in workload, prices, and the residual scope and quality. The rate of improvement of scope and quality ranged from 8 per cent for public schools to 57 per cent for higher education. Higher education showed the greatest rate of increases in workload and prices in addition to the greatest rate of increase for scope and quality. The major public service programs other than education all showed improvements of scope and quality in the area of 30 per cent.

There is no question that there will continue to be effective demands for increasing the scope and quality of public services. Although public services do not automatically respond to economic growth, there is an observable tendency for increased demands for more and better services of all kinds to occur together with increases in the standard of living. Just as the consumer with a rising income shifts his private consumption pattern toward more and better goods purchased through the market process, so the voter with rising income tends to demand more and better public services through the political process. In a growing economy and an increasingly interdependent society, the business community, too, tends to demand better trained labor and better community facilities for the labor force. For these and other reasons, state and local governments are expected to do more things and to do them better, as the standard of living increases.

Table 13   **Analysis of Change in Expenditures, by Program: 1955-65**

| Program | Expenditures 1955 (Million $) | Percentage Change 1955-65 | | | Expenditures 1965 (Million $) |
		Workload	Price	Scope & Quality	
Education	(11,907)	(1.391)	(1.495)	(1.154)	(28,563)
Public schools	10,337	1.378	1.480	1.077	22,700
Higher education	1,570	1.479	1.606	1.572	5,863
Health & hospitals	2,524	1.197	1.388	1.278	5,361
Public welfare	3,168	1.240	1.195	1.345	6,315
Highways	6,452	1.180	1.273	1.261	12,221
Urban services & other	8,835	1.214	1.387	1.317	19,596
TOTAL	32,886	1.273	1.388	1.240	72,056

Unlike changes in population-workload, and to a greater extent than changes in prices, the improvement in scope and quality is subject to policy determination. The extent of the expansion in scope and quality of public services depends on political decisions made by the people acting in their role as voters and government officials. Our model will not, therefore, attempt to project a single rate of change in scope and quality. Instead, it will indicate the cost of changes of scope and quality of different magnitudes, in order to enable us to relate these magnitudes, and costs to the experience of the past.

In order to develop alternative plausible rates of growth in scope and quality, we consider the historical growth rates for each program for each half of the decade 1955-65. Such rates of improvement experienced over a recent period and over a number of successive years may suggest feasible rates for the future because they are a realistic measure of the speed with which resources can be drawn to public programs. The extent to which changes in program expenditures in each five-year period, 1955-1960 and 1960-65, are accounted for by changes in workload, prices, and the residual scope and quality, are shown in Tables 14 and 15.

Table 14   **Analysis of Change in Expenditures, by Program: 1955-60**

| Program | Expenditures 1955 (Million $) | Percentage Change 1955-60 | | | Expenditures 1960 (Million $) |
		Workload	Price	Scope & Quality	
Education	(11,907)	(1.193)	(1.265)	(1.042)	(18,719)
Public schools	10,339	1.198	1.260	.994	15,517
Higher education	1,570	1.161	1.313	1.338	3,202
Health & hospitals	2,524	1.102	1.191	1.145	3,794
Public welfare	3,168	1.140	1.113	1.096	4,404
Highways	6,452	1.095	1.123	1.188	9,428
Urban services & other	8,835	1.114	1.204	1.170	13,861
TOTAL	32,886	1.141	1.200	1.115	50,206

Table 15   **Analysis of Change in Expenditures, by Program: 1960-65**

| Program | Expenditures 1960 (Million $) | Percentage Change 1960-65 | | | Expenditures 1965 (Million $) |
		Workload	Price	Scope & Quality	
Education	(18,719)	(1.175)	(1.181)	(1.100)	(28,563)
Public schools	15,517	1.155	1.174	1.079	22,700
Higher education	3,202	1.274	1.223	1.175	5,863
Health & hospitals	3,794	1.075	1.165	1.128	5,361
Public welfare	4,404	1.087	1.074	1.228	6,315
Highways	9,428	1.077	1.133	1.062	12,221
Urban services & other	13,861	1.090	1.152	1.126	19,596
TOTAL	50,206	1.118	1.155	1.112	72,056

Although aggregate scope and quality showed substantially equal rates of improvement of about 11 per cent over each five-year period, the rates by programs showed significant changes. The rates of improvement shown for the five-year period 1960-65 increased above those shown for the period 1955-60, in the categories of public schools and public welfare, and fell for the categories of higher education, health and hospitals, highways, urban services and "other." The rates range from a decline of 1 per cent for public schools to an improvement of 34 per cent for higher education, both for the period 1955-60.

1965-75 Estimates of State-Local Government General Expenditures

For the decade 1965-75, we have projected an increase in the population-workload for state and local government general services of 15.2 per cent and in the price paid by state and local governments of 39.0 per cent. This suggests that an increase in general expenditures of 60.1 per cent would be required in 1965-75 in order to maintain a constant level of real per capita public service (by weighted public service recipient). Workload and price changes accounted for an increase of 76.7 per cent of general expenditures in the decade 1955-65. The difference between the 1955-65 and 1965-75 change in requirements for constant per capita public expenditure levels is due in major part to a sharp decline in the rate of increase in the population-workload, from 27.3 per cent in 1955-65 to 15.2 per cent in 1965-75. Thus, the fiscal pressure on state and local governments may ease somewhat in the coming period.

We have estimated that aggregate scope and quality increased by 24.0 per cent in the decade 1955-65. If the voters, through their representatives, choose to continue to improve aggregate scope and quality at an unchanged rate, state and local government expenditures would, under our workload and price assumptions, increase by a total of 98.5 per cent in the period 1965-75, as shown below.

Population-Workload Ratio	×	Price Ratio	×	Scope & Quality Ratio	=	Expenditure Ratio
1.152	×	1.390	×	1.240	=	1.985

This compares with an actual increase of 119.1 per cent in 1955-65. Alternatively, if general expenditures were to increase in 1965-75 at the 1955-65 rate, the expansion in scope and quality allowed for would be 36.9 per cent.

We may also project the state and local government expenditures which would be required in 1975 if the rate of improvement in scope and quality indicated in 1955-65 for each major program were to continue. Table 16 shows expenditures in 1975, based on such projections. It utilizes our workload projections and the assumption of a continuation of past price trends by program, which parallels our earlier assumption of a constant aggregate rate of change of prices paid by state and local governments. These assumptions yield a projection of state and local government general expenditures of $146 billion in 1975, an increase of 102.9 per cent over 1965.[20]

Table 16   **State and Local Government Expenditures: 1975 Maintenance of Rates of Improvement by Program**

Program	Expenditures 1965 (Million $)	Percentage Change 1965-75 Workload	Price	Scope & Quality	Expenditures 1975 (Million $)
Education	(28,563)	(1.144)	(1.506)	(1.205)	(59,335)
Public schools	22,700	1.097	1.480	1.077	39,693
Higher education	5,863	1.327	1.606	1.572	19,642
Health & hospitals	5,361	1.160	1.388	1.278	11,031
Public welfare	6,315	1.145	1.200	1.345	11,670
Highways	12,221	1.150	1.273	1.261	22,560
Urban services & other	19,596	1.163	1.387	1.317	41,630
TOTAL	72,056	1.152	1.390	1.267	146,226

Another experiment may be undertaken by assuming that the improvement in scope and quality by program in the 1965-75 period will proceed at rates equivalent to those experienced in the five year periods 1955-60 or 1960-65 — whichever is higher for each respective program. By projecting a change in scope and quality at a rate experienced during the more rapid five-year period of change, we use a model which will project an over-all improvement in scope and

---

[20] The assumption of a continuation of the past rates of change by program yields a higher level of expenditures in 1975 than the level projected on the assumption of a continuation of past aggregate rates of change because the relative importance (and therefore the implicit weights) of the individual program categories in 1955 and 1965 respectively were different.

quality at a rate significantly above that experienced in the decade 1955-65. But since the projected rates have actually been experienced in each public service program over a period of five years, such rates of improvement in the future may be plausible, although limited by the speed with which real resources may be drawn to specific public programs. The projections shown in Table 17 indicate expenditures of about $155 billion in 1975, an increase of 114.4 per cent over 1965, with an over-all improvement in scope and quality of 33.9 per cent.

Table 17 **State and Local Government Expenditures: 1975**
High Rate of Improvement by Program

Program	Expenditures 1965 (Million $)	Percentage Change 1965-75			Expenditures 1975 (Million $)
		Workload	Price	Scope & Quality	
Education	(28,563)	(1.144)	(1.506)	(1.326)	(65,269)
Public schools	22,700	1.097	1.480	1.164	42,903
Higher education	5,863	1.327	1.606	1.790	22,366
Public welfare	6,315	1.145	1.200	1.508	13,085
Health & hospitals	5,361	1.160	1.388	1.311	11,315
Highways	12,221	1.150	1.273	1.411	25,250
Other	19,596	1.163	1.387	1.369	39,600
TOTAL	72,056	1.152	1.390	1.339	154,519

Other Requirements for State-Local Government Outlays

We have not yet included interest on the general debt in our calculations because of the distinctive nature of its determinants. Nor have we yet considered other claimants upon state and local government resources which are not included under the Census Bureau's definition of general expenditures, such as additions to working capital and sinking funds, certain contributions to government employee retirement funds,[21] and the net expenditure from operation

---

[21] "General expenditures" as defined by the U.S. Bureau of the Census, excludes retirement fund payments made from state governments to state controlled funds and from local governments to local government controlled funds, although it includes payments from one governmental level to funds controlled by the other governmental level.

of government-owned utilities and liquor stores.[22] These items are projected below.

The level of interest expenditures depends upon the size of the debt and upon interest rates, the latter being the price of maintaining outstanding debt. Interest rates cannot rise indefinitely, as do other prices; rather, they tend to fluctuate. Thus, they are likely to exhibit a relative stability in the long-run superimposed on short-run variations. The long-run stability of the unit cost of outstanding government debt is enhanced by the fact that various parts of the debt are financed at different times with different rates of interest. Thus, the total interest outlay of state and local governments at a given time reflects an average of interest rates existing over a period of previous years.

In the period 1955-65, during which the major portion of state and local government debt outstanding in 1965 was issued, the average yield for state and local government bonds was 3.3 per cent, which was also the average yield for the year 1965.[23] The 1965 yield appears to have been a long-term average rate also. We, therefore, assume that the average cost of credit for state and local governments will be the same in 1975 as in 1965. Since we assume no change in interest rates on state and local government debt, our projection of the change in interest outlays will depend directly on the projected change in the size of the debt. Our model projects the size of the debt to bear a fixed relation to the level of revenues from state and local government sources, which is detailed on page 276. Under two different assumptions concerning the level of general revenue, we project the debt to rise by 84.7 per cent or 103.9 per cent. The lower figure is consistent with our assumptions of the revenue required to maintain a rate of improvement in scope and quality of general government services in 1965-75 equal to the aggregate rate in 1955-65. The higher debt figure is more

---

[22] That is, the excess of expenditures over revenues from operations of these government-owned enterprises. The net gain from liquor store operations is exceeded by the net subsidization of government-owned utilities.

[23] Yields are for total state and local government bonds, as published in the *Federal Reserve Bulletin*.

consistent with the revenue requirements to finance an increased aggregate rate of improvement in scope and quality, as in our other two expenditure models. Thus, we project interest payments on the general debt to rise from $2.5 billion in 1965 to $4.6 billion or $5.0 billion in 1975, depending on the improvement in scope and quality of government services.

In order to project requirements for employee retirement funds and government-owned enterprises not included in general expenditures, we shall assume that such requirements grow as rapidly as state and local government general expenditures. The retirement fund contributions included above were $1.8 billion in 1965, and net expenditures due to government enterprises were $700 million. We will also project the level of requirements for working capital and sinking funds (excluding insurance trust funds) to remain in constant relation to state and local government general expenditures. This means that the extent of necessary additions to liquid assets is determined by the rate of change of state and local government expenditures. These funds totaled $43.8 billion in 1965, or 58.8 per cent of general expenditures including interest costs.

Total Requirements

In Table 18, we total the actual outlays of state and local funds in 1965, and also the projected requirements consistent with our assumptions concerning their determinants for 1975, showing three different examples of rates of improvement in scope and quality of general government services over the period 1965-75: 1) an improvement at the 1955-65 aggregate rate,[24] 2) an improvement of each major program at the 1955-65 rate,[25] and 3) an improvement of each major program equivalent to the rate in either the five-year period 1955-60 or 1960-65, depending on which was greater.[25] As outlined above, we assume that interest costs are not directly affected by the rate of improvement in scope and quality but

---

[24] Assuming that aggregate prices continue to rise at the 1955-65 rate.

[25] Assuming that prices by program continue to rise at the 1955-65 rate.

are affected by the size of the debt; that increases in retirement fund contributions and outlays for net expenditures of government enterprises parallel increases in general expenditures; and that requirements for additions to liquid assets are affected by the rate of change of general expenditures.

Table 18

Projections of State and Local Government Outlays: 1975 at Alternative Rates of Improvement of Scope & Quality (Million $)

Type of Expenditure	Outlays 1965	Rate of Improvement of Scope & Quality: 1965-75		
		Aggregate 1955-65 Rate (Million $)	1955-65 Rate by Program (Millions $)	High 5 Year Rate, 1955-60 or 1960-65 by Program (Millions $)
General expenditures (excluding interest)	72,056	143,031[a]	146,226[b]	154,519[b]
Interest on the general debt	2,490	4,599[c]	5,077	5,077[d]
Additional retirement fund expenditures	1,794	3,561	3,640	3,846
Net expenditures of enterprises	703	1,395	1,427	1,507
Additions to working capital & sinking funds	4,549	5,767	6,030	6,862
TOTAL	81,592	158,353	162,400	171,811

[a] Assuming continuation of 1955-65 aggregate price trends.
[b] Assuming continuation of 1955-65 price trends by program.
[c] Assuming that the size of the debt is consistent with the fixed revenue structure model.
[d] Assuming that the size of the debt is consistent with the minimum strengthened revenue model.

The calculations indicate that the total outlays considered would grow by 94.1 per cent between 1965-75 if the aggregate improvement of scope and quality estimated for 1955-65 were to continue through 1975; by 99.0 per cent if the rate of improvement by program were to continue; and by 110.6 per cent if plausible but rapid rates of improvement by program were to take place. This compares with an increase in such outlays of 124.4 per cent between 1955-65.

The Revenue Model

State and local governments secure general revenue from taxes, charges and miscellaneous general revenue, and from intergovernmental revenue from the federal government, mainly grants-in-aid. Tax revenues respond automatically to changes in income, production and wealth, and charges respond automatically to increases in the services provided at a charge. The level of collections can be changed by legislation affecting the rate of taxes or level of charges, by changes in the items or transactions covered, and by changes in the administrative efficiency of the tax collection process. The level of federal grants-in-aid depends, in the case of open-ended grants, upon state and local government action. But changes in the level of other grants depend to a major extent on federal legislation. The discussion below considers the potential for changes in state and local government general revenue in the decade 1965-75, based on the factors noted above.

Automatic Increases in Tax Revenues

Many studies of the response of the various state and local taxes to economic growth have been made in recent years. Table 19 shows the range of estimates of the responsiveness of individual taxes in 11 independent studies published between 1956 and 1961, as compiled by the Advisory Commission on Intergovernmental Relations.[26]

The results of three additional recent studies are shown in Table 20. One was specially prepared for the Committee for Economic Development by Dick Netzer.[27] The other two are by The Tax Foundation[28] and by Project '70, a study prepared for the Interagency Study of Economic Growth

---

[26] Advisory Commission on Intergovernmental Relations, *Federal State Coordination of Personal Income Taxes,* Report A-27, Washington, D.C., 1965, p. 42.

[27] Dick Netzer, *op. cit.*

[28] Tax Foundation, Inc., *Fiscal Outlook for State and Local Government to 1975,* Government Finance Brief No. 7, New York, 1966.

and Employment Opportunities.[29] Based on these studies, we shall assume the responsiveness of state and local government taxes to economic growth to be as shown in the last column of Table 20.

Table 19   **Per Cent Increase in Tax Revenue per One Per Cent Economic Growth: Advisory Commission Compilation**

Tax	Range of Responsiveness
Property	0.7 - 1.1
General sales & gross receipts	0.9 - 1.05
Selective sales & gross receipts[a]	0.5 - 0.7[a]
Personal income	1.5 - 1.8
Corporate income	1.1 - 1.3
Other[a]	0.5 - 0.6[a]

[a] Computed by the authors based on greater breakdown of individual taxes published in the independent studies and weighted by 1965 revenues.

Table 20   **Percentage Increase in Tax Revenue per One Per Cent Economic Growth: Recent Studies and CED Staff Assumptions**

Tax	Netzer	Tax Foundation	Project '70	CED
Property	1.0	0.9	1.0[a]	1.0
General sales & gross receipts	1.0	1.1	1.0	1.0
Selective sales & gross receipts	[b]	0.7[c]	0.7	0.7
Personal income	1.75	1.7	1.7	1.7
Corporate income	1.15	1.2	1.3	1.2
Other	[d]	0.7[c]	0.7[c]	0.7

[a] Assuming continuation of the lag in reassessment observable between 1956 and 1961. The growth of the market value of property was projected as 1.2 times the growth in gross national product.

[b] Alcoholic beverage tax, including excess of revenue over expenditure of liquor monopoly systems, 0.6; tobacco products, 0.75; other selective sales and gross receipts, excluding motor fuel taxes, 1.4.

[c] Computed from greater breakdown of individual taxes developed by the authors of the studies shown and weighted by 1965 revenues.

[d] Death and gift taxes, 1.8; other, excluding motor vehicle and operators licenses, 1.1.

---

[29] For a report on this study see: Selma J. Mushkin & Gabrielle C. Lupo, *op. cit.*

The annual rate of growth of real gross national product averaged 3.5 per cent between 1955-65. But the labor force is expected to grow more rapidly during 1965-75 than during 1955-65. It grew by about 13.4 per cent in 1955-65 but is expected to grow by 19.4 per cent during the 1965-75 period according to projections made in the Department of Labor.[30] This suggests that an increased rate of growth of real national product is possible. A study prepared for the Joint Economic Committee of Congress concludes that the economy can grow at a rate of 4 per cent per annum in the 1965-75 period, under reasonable assumptions of an unemployment rate of 4 per cent in 1975, a 3 per cent per annum increase in productivity and a slight decline in hours worked per week.[31] The projection for the Joint Economic Committee is consistent with projections made by the Tax Foundation,[32] by the National Planning Association based on its "more realistic" model for the period 1967-73,[33] and by the Interagency Growth Study Project of the United States government for the period 1965-70.[34] In light of the above projections, we assume that real gross national product will increase at an annual rate of 4 per cent, or by 48 per cent over the decade 1965-75.

As indicated in the previous section, we project an increase in the over-all price level (as represented by the GNP deflator) equivalent to the experience of the period 1955-65, resulting in a rise of 22 per cent in the period 1965-75. Thus, the increase in gross national product in current dollars is projected as 80.6 per cent.

Table 21 shows 1975 tax revenue based on the assump-

[30] Sophia Cooper and Denis F. Johnston, "Labor Force Projections for 1970-80," *Monthly Labor Review,* Vol. 88, No. 2 (February 1965), p. 180.

[31] U.S. Congress, Joint Economic Committee, *U.S. Economic Growth to 1975: Potentials and Problems,* Washington, D.C., 1966, p. 8 ff.

[32] Tax Foundation, Inc., *op. cit.,* p. 11.

[33] Gerhard Colm and Peter Wagner, *Federal Budget Projects* (Washington, D.C.: The Brookings Institution, 1966), pp. 6-7.

[34] U.S. Department of Labor, *Projections 1970,* Bulletin No. 1956, Washington, D.C., 1966, p. 8.

tions of tax responsiveness as indicated in Table 20, an increase in current dollar GNP of 80.6 per cent, and no change in the tax structure as it existed in 1965. It suggests that an increase in gross national product of 80.6 per cent would result in an increase of tax revenue to state and local governments of about $40.4 billion, or 78.8 per cent, with no change in the state and local government tax structure. These calculations suggest that the 1965 state and local government tax structure was such that tax revenues respond approximately proportionately to changes in national product.

By the end of fiscal year 1965, five states had legislated new general sales taxes not yet put into effect.[35] Personal income in these states was 28.7 per cent of personal income in the 37 states taxing personal sales by the end of that calendar year 1964. The 37 states collected 84.1 per cent of general sales taxes in 1965, the remainder having been collected at the local level. Thus, it is estimated that the addition of the five states to those collecting general sales taxes would increase such revenue by about 24.1 per cent (.287 x .841), or about $3.5 billion over the original projection in 1975, and we have made this addition in our projections.

Charges and Miscellaneous General Revenue

State and local governments also secure revenue from their own sources through "charges and miscellaneous general revenue." Interest revenue is excluded from our calculations at this stage. "Charges" accounted for about 80 per cent of the remainder of this category in 1965. Of the 20 per cent accounted for by miscellaneous general revenue, the most important is "special assessments," which may be considered to be a special form of charge.

In some cases, charges are meant to cover the full costs of the relevant public services provided to the payer; in other cases the charges are designed to cover a portion of the cost. Paralleling our assumption that tax rates remain unchanged, we shall define a fixed system of charges and miscellaneous general revenue as one in which the charges for relevant

---

[35] Idaho, Massachusetts, New Jersey, New York, and Virginia.

services are provided in a fixed relation to the cost of the service to the government. Since we assume that the cost of state and local government goods and services will rise by 40.8 per cent over the period 1965-75, we assume that the rate of charges will also rise by 40.8 per cent.

Table 21   **State and Local Tax Revenue, Fixed Tax Structure: 1975**

Tax	Revenue 1965 (Million $)	Respon- siveness	Percentage Growth in Revenue 1965-75[a]	Increase in Revenue 1965-75 (Million $)	Revenue 1975 (Million $)
Property	22,583	1.0	80.6	18,202	40,785
General sales & gross receipts	7,981	1.0	80.6	6,433	14,414
Selected sales & gross receipts	9,136	0.7	56.4	5,153	14,289
Personal income	4,090	1.7	137.0	5,603	9,693
Corporate income	1,929	1.2	96.7	1,865	3,794
Other	5,521	0.7	56.4	3,114	8,635
TOTAL	51,243			40,367	91,610

Note: Because of rounding, detail may not add to totals.

[a] Responsiveness ratio (elasticity) times projected 80.6 per cent increase in current dollar GNP.

We also assume that a constant proportion of the relevant population groups will make use of the public services provided at a charge. Education, hospitals, and "urban" services are the most important subcategories within the category of charges and miscellaneous general revenue and accounted for 61.2 per cent of such revenue in 1965. We have applied the services provided by these programs to the same population groupings as we have in the expenditure section, i.e., the population in the 18-21 age group for higher education; the 5-17 group for "other education"; the weighted population change based on use of hospital clinics for hospitals; the nonfarm population for urban services; and the total resident population for "other." Thus, we calculate a 16.7 per cent increase in the population-workload for the services provided at a charge between 1965-75, as shown in Table 22.

Table 22   **Workload Change for Charges and Miscellaneous General Revenue[a] : 1965-75**

Program	Revenue 1965 (Million $)	Relative Expenditure Weight (%)	Population Ratio 1965-75	Weighted Ratio
Higher education	1,834	17.31	1.3269	22.97
Other education	1,358	12.82	1.0698	12.70
Hospitals	1,372	12.95	1.1599	15.02
Urban services	1,921	18.13	1.1786	21.37
Other	4,109	38.78	1.1497	44.59
TOTAL	10,594	100.00		116.65

[a] Excluding interest receipts.

Assuming that the revenue available to state and local governments in 1965-75 from charges and the provision of miscellaneous services (excluding interest receipts) rises in proportion to the rise in the relevant population-workload and the increase in the cost of state and local government goods and services, such revenue would increase by about 64.3 per cent, or from $10.6 billion in 1965 to $17.4 billion in 1975. This increase excludes further additions to revenue from charges which would accrue to state and local governments if the scope and quality of the services for which charges are made were to increase but if the charges were to continue to be levied at rates such as to maintain a fixed relation to the cost of the services provided.

In 1965, interest earnings classified under "miscellaneous general revenue," at $1.1 billion, were equal to 2.6 per cent of the cash and security holdings (other than insurance trust systems) of state and local governments. Assuming this relationship to hold through 1975, such interest earnings would total about $2.3 billion in 1975, if cash and security holdings rise to the level projected earlier.[36] Thus,

[36] Estimated on the basis of the average of the three levels of cash and security holdings implied by the additions to working capital and sinking funds shown in Table 18.

total charges and miscellaneous general income would increase from $11.7 billion in 1965 to $19.8 billion in 1975. The increase would be larger if there is improved scope and quality of public services for which a charge is made and if the level and extent of charges rise proportionately.

Federal Grants-in-Aid

In addition to general revenue from their own sources, comprising taxes and charges and miscellaneous general revenue, state and local governments receive grants-in-aid from the national government. The proportional increase of such grants in recent years has been dramatic. They rose from $3.1 billion in 1955 to $11.0 billion in 1965 and about $14.8 billion in 1967. The increase between 1960 and 1967 has averaged over 11 per cent per annum. A continuation of this rate of increase would yield a level of grants of $34.7 billion in 1975.

A number of projections of national government grants-in-aid have been made, with the assumption that the programs already legislated are carried out. Project '70 projects a level of grants-in-aid under this assumption of $22 billion in 1970.[37] The Tax Foundation projects a level of $20.3 billion in 1970 and $30.0 billion in 1975.[38] Gerhard Colm and Peter Wagner of the National Planning Association project a level of between $23.5 billion and $33.5 billion for 1973, depending on the assumptions.[39] Based on these studies, it would appear reasonable to assume that a level of grants-in-aid of about $30 billion would be reached in 1975, if programs already legislated are carried out. However, our price projections are somewhat higher than the projections of increases in the GNP deflator of 1.5 per cent used in these studies. We, therefore, use a projection of grants-in-aid of $31.5 billion in current prices for 1975.

---

[37] Selma J. Mushkin and Robert F. Adams, "Emerging Pattern of Federalism," in *National Tax Journal* (September 1966), p. 238.

[38] Tax Foundation, Inc., *op. cit.,* p. 10.

[39] Colm & Wagner, *op. cit.,* p. 80.

Strengthened Revenue Structure

There are many possibilities for changing and improving the revenue-raising structure of state and local governments so as to increase revenue beyond the amounts indicated above.

Through time, the ratio of the assessed value of property for tax purposes to the actual market value of taxable property has fallen. It has been estimated that the lag in reassessment between 1956 and 1961 resulted in an increase of assessed valuations which was almost 20 per cent below the actual increase in the market value of taxable property.[40] A reassessment lag of this proportion between 1965-75 could cost local governments about $3.5 billion in 1975. Additionally, the value of partial exemptions from property taxation for special interest groups, such as veterans and the aged, has been growing due to declines in the ratio of assessed value to market value of property. Between 1956 and 1961, the value of partial exemptions of locally assessed real property increased from 3.3 per cent to 3.7 per cent of total assessments.[41] At this rate of increase, about 5 per cent of potential property tax revenues would be lost in 1975 due to partial exemptions, or about $2.0 billion. Recognizing the difficulties in eliminating the reassessment lag and partial exemptions completely, we estimate that about $2 billion additional revenue could accrue to local governments if they were to make a determined effort to improve and strengthen their property tax systems without raising rates.

In 1965, 37 states had general sales taxes, through which they raised $6.7 billion, equivalent to 1.9 per cent of their personal incomes. The range of collections relative to personal income was from 0.8 per cent in Wisconsin to 4.3 per

---

[40]Mushkin and Lupo, *op. cit.*

[41]U.S. Department of Commerce, *Taxable Property Values in the United States: 1957 Census of Governments,* Vol. V, Washington, D.C., 1959, Table 2; and U.S. Department of Commerce, *Taxable Property Values: 1962 Census of Governments,* Vol. II, Washington, D.C., 1963, Table 2.

cent in Hawaii.[42] The broad differences resulted from differences in coverage as well as in tax rates. We may be able to approximate a level of potential revenue from realistically higher state general sales taxes by estimating the revenue yielded if every state without the tax or with a lower than average general sales tax burden (tax revenue relative to personal income) adopted the tax or raised its rates and coverage to the average of the taxing states.

States with lower than average state general sales tax burdens collected $3.1 billion in general sales tax revenue in 1965. These states plus those not having general sales taxes in effect nor legislated in 1965 would have collected $4.4 billion had their sales tax burdens been 1.9 per cent. The difference of $1.3 billion would grow to $2.4 billion by 1975. Thus, if those states which had not passed general sales taxes by 1965 were to institute such taxes at average rates and coverage, and if those states with relatively low general sales tax burdens in 1965 were to bring themselves up to the 1965 average, about $2.4 billion in additional general sales tax revenue would be available in 1975.

The possibilities for increases in state personal income tax yields are considerable because many large industrial states do not use this tax and other states do not use it effectively. Seventeen states did not have broad-based taxes on personal incomes in 1965.[43] These states accounted for 41.7 per cent of personal income in 1964 (excluding that earned by residents of the District of Columbia). Although the burden of state personal income taxation averaged 1.3 per cent of personal income in the taxing states, states such as Mississippi and Louisiana taxed personal incomes at rates which yielded only 0.3 per cent and 0.4 per cent of personal incomes respectively.

---

[42]U.S. Dept. of Commerce, *Compendium of State Government Finances in 1965,* Washington, D.C., 1966, Table 6.

[43]Michigan and Nebraska legislated state personal income taxes after 1965. Neither tax was yet in effect in 1967. Three states which had personal income taxes of a very narrow type are included among the states without broad-based personal income taxes. These are New Hampshire and Tennessee, which taxed only dividends and interest, and New Jersey, which taxed only income earned in New Jersey by residents of New York.

If the states without broad-based personal income taxes or with burdens below the average had taxed at the average burden level, an additional $3.2 billion of state-local personal income taxes would have been collected in 1965, or an increase of 77.8 per cent. By 1975, this difference could amount to about $7.5 billion.

The above discussion of possible increases in tax rates is limited to the two taxes which are generally considered to be the most equitable and the most responsive to economic growth. Improvements in the equity and efficiency of the property tax, whose yield could be increased without increasing rates, have also been considered. The various alternatives indicate what is possible if the people are willing to pay the price for improvements in their public services.

There should be no presumption that the limits to sales or income taxes have been reached, even in the high tax states. To be sure, tax competition and benefit spillovers may provide constraints to state and local government taxation and expenditures. These constraints may limit the extent to which individual jurisdictions operate in a manner significantly different than others. But such constraints do not prevent the average level and coverage of state and local taxation from rising rapidly, as recent history has proven. The increased revenues shown above as the potential of strengthened tax systems are to be taken, therefore, only as an indication of the minimum possibilities for more state and local tax revenue within an improved tax system.

In sum, the potential for increased state and local general revenue under the assumptions given above is $158.3 billion, as shown in Table 23.

In addition to general revenues, state and local governments supplement their fiscal resources by net increases in their debt. At the end of fiscal 1965, total state and local government debt outstanding was $99.5 billion, which includes an increase of $7.3 billion during that year. The debt was 1.6 times general revenue from own sources, a relationship which remained stable over the 1955-65 decade. If this relationship were to continue through 1975, the total debt in 1975 would be $183.8 billion with the fixed revenue structure and $202.9 billion with the minimum strengthened revenue structure. In order to reach these levels the average annual rates of growth of the debt between 1965-75 would be 6.3 per cent and 7.4 per cent respectively, implying net increases in debt of $10.9 billion and $14.0 billion in 1975. Thus, resources available for the state and local expenditures in 1975 would total $157.2 billion under our fixed structure assumptions and $172.3 billion under our minimum strengthened structure, as shown in Table 24.

Table 23

Potential Increases in State and Local General Revenue: 1965-75

Revenue Source	Revenue 1965 (Million $)	Revenue 1975 Fixed Structure (Million $)	Revenue 1975 Minimum Strengthened Structure (Million $)	Percentage Change 1965-75 Fixed Structure	Percentage Change 1965-75 Minimum Strengthened Structure
Own Sources	62,971	114,847	126,815	82.4	101.4
Taxes	51,243	95,084[a]	107,052	85.6	108.9
Charges & misc. general revenue	11,729	19,763	19,763	68.5	68.5
Grants-in-Aid	11,029	31,500	31,500	185.6	185.6
TOTAL	74,000	146,347	158,315	97.8	113.9

[a] Includes sales taxes in 5 states legislated but not yet put into effect by 1965.

Table 24

State and Local Government General Revenue and Net Debt: 1975

Type of Receipt	Fixed Structure (Million $)	Minimum Strengthened Structure (Million $)
General revenue	146,347	158,315
Net debt	10,867	14,002
TOTAL RECEIPTS	157,214	172,317

Conclusions

Based on the assumptions noted above, receipts from a fixed structure of taxes, charges and miscellaneous general revenue, and net additions to debt are projected to rise from $70.3 billion in 1965 to $125.7 billion in 1975, an increase of 78.9 per cent. If the level of federal grants-in-aid were to remain unchanged at their 1965 level, total state and local government receipts could rise from $81.3[44] billion to $136.7 billion. Our assumptions concerning the increase in population-workload and prices imply a requirement of $127.3 billion in state and local government outlays for general expenditures and for certain liquid assets, additional retirement fund contributions and net expenditures for public enterprises in 1975, simply to maintain a constant 1965 level of state and local government public services per recipient. Thus, $9.4 billion would be available in 1975 from increases in revenue raised from own sources in that year for improved scope and quality of services over those existing in 1965. This suggests that the increase in receipts from a fixed structure of own sources, including net debt, could finance an improvement of 7.3 per cent in scope and quality of general state and local government services in 1975 compared with 1965, as shown in Table 25. This compares with an estimated increase of 24.0 per cent between 1955 and 1965.

It has been estimated that an increase of $20.5 billion in grants-in-aid funds between 1965-75 is built into present federal legislation. These funds, in addition to the funds from a fixed structure of receipts from own sources, would permit outlays of $157.2 billion in 1975. This would be consistent with an improvement in scope and quality of general state and local government public services of 23.1 per cent between 1965 and 1975 as shown in Table 26.

---

[44]Expenditures in the categories discussed in this paper were $81.6 billion, as shown in Table 18.

Table 25   **Projected Factor Distribution of Increased Funds from Fixed Own Receipts Structure**

Item	1965 Expend-itures (Billion $)	Population-×Workload× Factor	Price Factor	Scope & × Quality Factor	1975 = Expend-itures (Billion $)
General expenditures (excl. interest)	72.1	× 1.152	× 1.390	× 1.073	= 123.8
Interest on the general debt	2.5				4.6
Additional retirement fund contributions	1.8				3.1
Net expenditures for public enterprises	0.7				1.2
Additions to liquid assets	4.5				4.0
TOTAL	81.6				136.7

Table 26   **Projected Factor Distribution of Increased Funds from Fixed Own Receipts Structure and Grants-in-Aid**

Item	1965 Expend-itures (Billion $)	Population-×Workload× Factor	Price Factor	Scope & × Quality Factor	1975 = Expend-itures (Billion $)
General expenditures (excl. interest)	72.1	× 1.152	× 1.390	× 1.231	= 142.0
Interest on the general debt	2.5				4.6
Additional retirement fund contributions	1.8				3.5
Net expenditures for public enterprises	0.7				1.4
Additions to liquid assets	4.5				5.6
TOTAL	81.6				157.2

It is likely, however, that state and local government tax rates will be increased in coming years. The minimum potential for a strengthened state and local revenue system, as outlined earlier, would add $12.0 billion to state and local government revenues. This would permit an additional $3.1 billion of net increase in debt in 1975, consistent with our assumptions concerning the level of debt, giving a total of $15.1 billion for state and local government outlays. This would permit an improvement in scope and quality of general government services of 34.3 per cent, as shown in Table 27.

Table 27

Projected Factor Distribution of Increased Funds from Strengthened Own Receipts Structure and Grants-in-Aid (Billions $)

Item	1965 Expenditures (Billion $)	Population- ×Workload× Factor	Price Factor	Scope & × Quality Factor	1975 Expenditures = itures (Billion $)
General expenditures (excl. interest)	72.1	× 1.152	× 1.390	× 1.343	= 155.0
Interest on the general debt	2.5				5.0
Additional retirement fund contributions	1.8				3.9
Net expenditures for public enterprises	0.7				1.5
Additions to liquid assets	4.5				6.9
TOTAL	81.6				172.3

As noted earlier, to the extent that an improvement in scope and quality affects services which are partially financed by charges, the assumed maintenance of a fixed relation between the charge and the cost of the service would dictate an increase in the number of charges paid where scope is affected, or an increase in the level of the charge where quality is affected. Thus, a greater amount of funds could be made available to state and local governments without reducing the extent of the public subsidy to the users of the government services partially financed through charges. For example, if an expansion in scope and quality of 34 per cent is consistent with a proportional expansion in revenue from charges, a further $7 billion would be made available to state and local governments and could be used to improve over-all scope and quality by about an additional 4 per cent.

Our estimates indicate that an improvement in over-all scope and quality between 1965 and 1975 of about 24 per cent is consistent with our assumption of a fixed own revenue structure responsive to economic growth, plus projected increases in grants-in-aid. But increases in tax rates and coverage, if desired, appear to be well within the capabilities of state and local government. Some rate increases and new taxes have already been legislated since 1965. Our strengthened revenue system projects a level of revenue sufficiently high to permit a significant advance beyond the 1955-65 rate of improvement of scope and quality. A continuation of the rate of improvement in scope and quality of each major public program at the rate indicated for 1955-65 is consistent with an increase in tax rates and coverage only about one-third as great as in a minimum strengthened revenue system.

Alternatively, the full revenue from our minimum strengthened system could provide the resources for a substantial increase in the average rate of improvement in scope and quality for the period 1965-75 over that of 1955-65. The revenue from a minimum strengthened system is consistent with our expenditure estimates for improvement in each program at the rate indicated for 1955-60 or 1960-65, whichever is greater.

Different assumptions than ours concerning the over-all trend of prices throughout the economy would have a limited effect on conclusions reached relating the revenue effort necessary to support any given improvement in public services. For example, projections in 1965 prices would give an over-all price level 22 per cent lower than our original projections for 1975. The following would happen, based upon our conclusions and analysis:

1) The level of expenditures necessary to provide a

given level of public services would be 22 per cent lower.

2) The amount of revenue received by state and local government from own sources would also be about 22 per cent lower. This is because state and local government tax revenue responds approximately in proportion to changes in GNP, of which the change in over-all prices is a part, and because we assume that the level of charges placed by governments is determined, in part, by price levels.

3) Expenditures for grant-in-aid programs designed to accomplish fixed and limited purposes would likewise respond approximately proportionately to our changed price assumptions. And since state and local government expenditures respond to price changes, federal grant-in-aid programs which depend on the level of state and local government expenditures are also likely to be affected by price changes.

Table 28 indicates projected 1975 state and local government outlays in 1965 prices for the over-all economy assuming a continuation of the 1955-65 aggregate rate of change in scope and quality of general services and consistent with our assumptions concerning their other determinant. These data reflect a deflation of 22 per cent from the data in the second column of Table 18, except for interest payments and additions to liquid assets, which reflect slower rates of growth of debt outstanding and requirements for liquid assets, respectively.

Table 28   **State and Local Government Outlays, Constant Rate of Improvement in Scope and Quality: 1975 in 1965 Prices**

Outlay	Amount (Billion $)¹
General expenditures (excl. interest)	117.2
Interest	3.8
Additional retirement fund contributions	2.9
Net expenditures for enterprises	1.1
Addition to liquid assets	3.4
TOTAL	128.5

Table 29 indicates projected state and local government receipts in 1965 prices, assuming a fixed structure of receipts from own sources and built-in grant-in-aid increases. Tax revenue is computed on the basis of its responsiveness to an increase of 48 per cent in real GNP, and charges and miscellaneous general revenue reflect changes in workload. The estimate of current dollar 1975 grants-in-aid is deflated by 22 per cent for our estimate in 1965 prices. These data indicate the potential of an improvement in scope and quality in 1965-75 of almost the same rate as in 1955-65 if no changes in over-all prices occur, with a fixed own revenue structure and the grants-in-aid implied in 1965 legislation. The conclusions reached from the data in constant prices are substantially consistent with the conclusions based on the relationships between revenue and expenditure in current prices, as shown in Tables 18 and 24.

Table 29 **State and Local Government Receipts, Fixed Own Revenue Structure and Grants-in-Aid: 1975 in 1965 Prices**

Receipts	Amount (Billion $)
Taxes	77.9
Charges & miscellaneous general revenue	16.2
Grants-in-aid	25.8
Net increase in debt	6.1
TOTAL	126.0

The data provided in this study in no manner indicate the rate of improvement of state and local services which may be proper. They are not predictions of things to come or of revenue requirements necessary to meet future expenditures by state and local governments. Nor has this study addressed itself to the allegations that state and local governments are restrained in their fiscal efforts by inter-area tax competition and the existence of benefit spillovers, and that these restraints call for counteractions. Such allegations are consistent with any findings concerning the fiscal outlook for state and local governments.

The study suggests that state and local governments can secure the funds necessary to improve and expand their services at rates as rapid or more rapid than in the past decade, given a reasonable effort on their part and the national government aid already implicit in present legislation. The data establish the fact that the taxing and spending choices of state and local officials are wide. State and local governments can, in the aggregate, speed the rate of improvement in the scope and quality of public services if they are willing to pay the price in attainable higher taxes.

OTHER SUPPLEMENTARY PAPERS PUBLISHED BY CED

To order CED publications please indicate number in column entitled "# Copies Desired." Then mail this order form and check for total amount in envelope to Distribution Division, CED, 477 Madison Ave., New York 10022.

)rder Number   **Copies Desired**

1S .. THE ECONOMICS OF A FREE SOCIETY
William Benton
October, 1944, 20 pages. (20¢)   _____

6S .. THE CHANGING ECONOMIC FUNCTION
OF THE CENTRAL CITY
Raymond Vernon
January, 1959, 92 pages, 14 tables, 8 charts. ($1.25)   _____

7S .. METROPOLIS AGAINST ITSELF
Robert C. Wood
March, 1959, 56 pages. ($1.00)   _____

8S .. TRENDS IN PUBLIC EXPENDITURES
IN THE NEXT DECADE
Otto Eckstein
April, 1959, 56 pages, 28 tables, 2 charts. ($1.00)   _____

10S .. DEVELOPING THE "LITTLE" ECONOMIES
Donald R. Gilmore
April, 1960, 160 pages, 20 tables. ($2.00)   _____

11S .. THE EDUCATION OF BUSINESSMEN
Leonard S. Silk
December, 1960, 48 pages, 9 tables. (75¢)   _____

13S .. THE SOURCES OF ECONOMIC GROWTH
IN THE UNITED STATES AND THE ALTERNATIVES BEFORE US
Edward F. Denison
January, 1962, 308 pages, 4 charts, 33 tables. ($4.00)   _____

14S .. COMPARATIVE TARIFFS AND TRADE—
THE U.S. AND THE EUROPEAN COMMON MARKET
Prepared by Frances K. Topping
March, 1963, over 1,000 pages. ($37.50)   _____

15S .. FARMING, FARMERS, AND MARKETS
FOR FARM GOODS
Karl A. Fox, Vernon W. Ruttan, Lawrence W. Witt
November, 1962, 190 pages, 16 charts, 46 tables. ($3.00)   _____

SEE OTHER SIDE⟶

☐ Please bill me. (Remittance requested for orders under $3.00)
☐ Please send me CED's current publications list.
☐ I should like to know how I might receive all of CED's future publications
by becoming a Participant in the CED Reader-Forum.

* Hard cover edition available. Prices on request.